Administrative Decision-Making

in Australian Migration Law

Administrative Decision-Making

in Australian Migration Law

Alan Freckelton

Edited by Marianne Dickie

Australian
National
University

eTEXT

ANU
eTEXT

Published by ANU eText
The Australian National University
Acton ACT 2601, Australia
Email: etext@anu.edu.au
This title is also available online at http://press.anu.edu.au/anuetext/

National Library of Australia Cataloguing-in-Publication entry

Title: Administrative decision-making in Australian migration law / Alan
                  Freckelton, author ; Marianne Dickie, editor.

ISBN: 9781925022568 (paperback) 9781925022575 (ebook)

Subjects: Australia. Migration Act 1958.
                  Emigration and immigration law--Australia--Textbooks.
                  Law--Study and teaching (Higher)--Australia.
                  Australia--Government policy--Emigration and immigration.

Other Creators/Contributors:
                  Dickie, Marianne, editor.
                  Australian National University. Faculty of Law. Migration Law Program.

Dewey Number: 342.94082

Cover design and layout by ANU eText

Contents

Chapter 1. Legal Frameworks of Australia's Administrative Migration Law

What is administrative law?

Administrative law is one of the three fields of law that deal with the relationship between the individual and the State. These three areas of law are as follows:

1. **Constitutional law** deals with the ability of the State to pass and enforce laws, and the judicial interpretation of constitutional documents, and not directly with any particular decision made by the Department of Immigration and Border Protection (DIBP). For example, *Singh v Commonwealth*[1] ('*Tania Singh*') considered the interpretation of s 51(xix) of the Australian constitution, and in particular the meaning of the word 'alien'.

    Constitutional law also deals with what rights and freedoms individuals can have against the government. In other words, constitutional law sets boundaries on the legislative, executive and judicial power of the state in relation to the individuals. For example, s 116 of the Constitution states:

    > The Commonwealth shall not make any law for establishing any religion, or for imposing any religious observance, or for prohibiting the free exercise of any religion, and no religious test shall be required as a qualification for any office or public trust under the Commonwealth.

2. **Criminal law** deals with the prosecution of an individual or a corporation by the State after allegations of behaviour that is deemed to be criminal either by statute or common law. Criminal offences are regarded as injurious not just to another party, but to society as a whole, and action against a person accused of a criminal offence is therefore undertaken by the State, and not just a victim of crime, or their relatives.

3. **Administrative law** deals with decisions made by the executive arm of government in relation to individuals or corporations, usually acting under the authority of a particular Act of Parliament. For example, immigration law is one kind of administrative law, because it deals with decisions made by a Minister, usually through his or her delegates, or independent

---

1   (2004) 222 CLR 322. See also *Koroitamana v Commonwealth* (2006) 227 CLR 31.

tribunals created by an Act of Parliament (in this case the *Migration Act 1958*). Administrative law classically tends to focus on judicial review of administrative decisions – that is, review of decisions made by the executive by the courts – but merits review is an equally important concept.

The three arms of government

The **legislature** is responsible for enacting laws, and for supervision of secondary legislation (regulations). In Australia, the Federal legislature consists of the House of Representatives and the Senate. To become law, a bill must pass both Houses, and also obtain the consent of the Governor-General, who is a member of the Executive Government. Regulations are made by the executive, for example the Minister for Immigration, but can be disallowed by either House of Parliament (in practice, always the Senate).

Like other countries with a Westminster system of government, such as the UK, New Zealand and Canada, in Australia the government of the day is the party that controls the House of Representatives, either by having an absolute majority in that House (as at present), or by obtaining the confidence of a number of non-government party members (as happened during the Gillard government). Further, Ministers including the Prime Minister, who are members of the executive, are appointed from amongst Members of the House of Representatives or Senators, meaning that there is a considerable overlap between the legislature and the executive. Compare this situation with, say, the United States, where the President and the Secretaries of State (the equivalent of Ministers) may *not* sit in Congress.

The **executive** consists of the Governor-General, Ministers (including, by convention, the Prime Minister), government departments and independent tribunals created by statute. The executive is responsible for enforcing and applying the law, by means such as making regulations (which can only be done under a power provided for by an Act of Parliament), or determining the application of a particular law to an individual or corporation (e.g. by deciding an application for a visa). As noted above, the Governor-General's assent is also required before an Act of Parliament can come into effect, but this assent, known as Royal assent, has never been withheld in Australia.

The **judiciary** consists of all courts, whether created by the Constitution, such as the High Court and the State Supreme Courts, or by an Act of Parliament, such as the Federal Court, Federal Circuit Court and the Family Court. While there is an overlap between the legislature and the executive, the judiciary is always completely independent of both in Australia and other Westminster system countries. The judiciary is responsible for determining the meaning of the law and applying it to individual cases. In a common law jurisdiction like Australia, a decision of a court has what is known as precedential value. Precedent, to put it in simple words, means an earlier decision of a court that may be either binding or persuasive in solving similar legal issues in later situations. A decision of a higher court binds all lower courts within the same jurisdiction. For example, a decision of the High Court binds all other courts in Australia, and a decision of the Full Federal Court binds all other federal courts (other than the High Court). Other decisions may have persuasive value even though they are not binding. For example, a decision of the US Supreme Court or the Supreme Court of Victoria is not binding on but may have persuasive value to the High Court of Australia.

The 'administrative state'

The 'administrative state' is a concept that is frequently referred to but curiously rarely defined in the literature, at least by lawyers. Indeed, Alan Cairns tells us that 'the modern administrative state defies simple description', and that 'the attempt to pin down the contemporary administrative state is doomed to failure'.[2] Nevertheless, Seymour Wilson and Onkar Dwivedi make the following attempt:[3]

> The administrative state denotes the phenomenon by which state institutions influence many aspects of the lives of citizens, especially those aspects which relate to the economic and social dimensions. It describes a system of governance through which public policies and programs, affecting all aspects of public life, are influenced by the actions of public officials.

It is now nearly impossible for citizens to avoid interaction with the state, and in many cases they simply could not survive without it. This is not to argue that such regulation is always and everywhere a bad thing, but there can be no denying the increasing pervasiveness of the state into the everyday life of the individual. The following passage from Cory J, writing for the Supreme Court of Canada in *Newfoundland Telephone Company v Newfoundland (Board of Commissioners of Public Utilities)*, captures the theme well:[4]

> Administrative Boards play an increasingly important role in our society. They regulate many aspects of our life, from beginning to end. Hospital and medical boards regulate the methods and practice of the doctors that bring us into this world. Boards regulate the licensing and

---

2   Alan Cairns, 'The Past and Future of the Canadian Administrative State', (1990) 40 *University of Toronto Law Journal* 319 at 322.

3   Onkar Dwivedi and Seymour Wilson, 'Introduction', in Onkar Dwivedi (ed.), *The Administrative State in Canada: Essays in Honour of JE Hodgetts*, University of Toronto Press, 1982 at 5.

4   (1992) 1 SCR 623 at 637.

the operation of morticians who are concerned with our mortal remains. Marketing boards regulate the farm products we eat; transport boards regulate the means and flow of our travel; energy boards control the price and distribution of the forms of energy we use; planning boards and city councils regulate the location and types of buildings in which we live and work. In Canada, boards are a way of life. Boards and the functions they fulfill are legion.

The dependence by individuals on the state is another reason why it is now impossible to dispense with review of administrative decisions altogether – the consequences to an individual of an unreasonable or even simply incorrect decision can be disastrous. The courts and review tribunals therefore have a crucial role to play in ensuring that individuals can obtain government services that are no longer a privilege for most people, but necessary for survival. However, the courts face competing public policy objectives in that the government, the elected representatives of the people, have decided to give the power to make the decision in question to an administrative decision maker, and, more pragmatically, that government decision makers need to be able to do their work without being under constant close judicial scrutiny.

It should be noted that judicial review has real impacts on administrative agencies. Some of this impact is beneficial. For example, the emphasis on the review of administrative *reasons* has required agencies to provide detailed reasons for the decisions they make. On the other hand, the same processes have probably helped lead to the use of bland 'boilerplate' or 'standard' paragraphs, that are now common features of the reasons of administrative decision makers. While courts have generally rejected the proposition that the use of standard paragraphs is either unreasonable or an error of law in itself,[5] it may be an unfortunate trend in administrative decision-making. Courts also rarely seem to have much appreciation of the financial impacts of their decisions.

Another distinctive feature of the modern administrative state is, of course, the administrative tribunal. A tribunal is not a court, and is indeed often required by legislation not to act like one. For example, s 420(1) of the *Migration Act 1958* requires the Refugee Review Tribunal (RRT) to conduct itself in a manner that is 'just, fair, economical, informal and quick',[6] and s 420(2) provides that it 'is not bound by technicalities, legal forms or rules of evidence' and 'must act according

---

5   In *Minister for Immigration and Citizenship v SZQHH* (2012) FCAFC 45, the Full Federal Court of Australia rejected the argument that the use of standard paragraphs in a decision record refusing an applicant refugee status amounted to a reasonable apprehension of bias. By way of contrast, see *LVR (WA) Pty Ltd v Administrative Appeals Tribunal* (2012) FCAFC 90.

6   Many of these goals are obviously contradictory – see *Minister for Immigration and Multicultural Affairs v Eshetu* (1999) 197 CLR 611.

to substantial justice and the merits of the case'.[7] It is important to note that tribunals are creatures of the *executive*, not the *judiciary*, despite the fact that their procedures may mimic those of courts to a greater or lesser extent.[8]

As Australia has a Federal system of government, each of the Australian States and mainland Territories has its own legislature, and can pass its own Acts of Parliament. There are many State and Territory Acts that require Ministers or their delegates to make decisions on the basis of applications made to their departments. There are also many State and Territory administrative tribunals, the Victorian Civil and Administrative Tribunal (VCAT) probably being the best known. However, as immigration is a federal jurisdiction, the focus of this book is on federal administrative law.

The Constitutional basis of migration law in Australia

The main provision of the Australian Constitution that grants the Parliament to make laws is found in s 51. Section 51 does not provide for a grant of power to the Commonwealth Parliament to the *exclusion* of the States – powers that can only be exercised by the Commonwealth Parliament are found in s 52 of the Constitution, and immigration is not amongst those powers. This leaves open the theoretical possibility of a State concurrently enacting its own immigration legislation, as the Canadian province of Quebec has done.[9] However, any State or Territory legislature that attempted to pass immigration laws inconsistent with the *Migration Act 1958* would very likely be found invalid under s 109 of the Constitution, which provides that '[w]hen a law of a State is inconsistent with a law of the Commonwealth, the latter shall prevail, and the former shall, to the extent of the inconsistency, be invalid'. It is therefore best to regard immigration as a solely federal area of law.

Section 51 of the Constitution provides three powers that give the Parliament power over matters relating to immigration. The section relevantly provides as follows:

---

7   *Eshetu* (supra) found that this was merely an exhortatory provision and did not impose legal duties on the RRT. However, the Full Federal Court has since found in *Minister for Immigration and Citizenship v Li* (2012) FCAFC 74 that a failure to grant an adjournment in a Migration Review Tribunal (MRT) hearing was a breach of s 353 of the *Migration Act 1958* (which is in similar terms to s 420) in the facts of that case, and amounted to a jurisdictional error.

8   See for example on this point *Ocean Port Hotel Ltd v British Columbia (General Manager, Liquor Control and Licensing Branch)* (2001) 2 SCR 781 and *Minister for Immigration and Multicultural Affairs v Jia* (2001) 205 CLR 507.

9   Quebec's immigration Act is entitled, in the French civil law style, 'An Act Respecting Immigration to Quebec' (*Loi sur l'immigration au Québec*).

The Parliament shall, subject to this Constitution, have power to make laws for the peace, order, and good government of the Commonwealth with respect to: …

(xix) Naturalization and aliens …

(xxvii) Immigration and emigration

(xxviii) The influx of criminals

Immigration laws passed by the Australian Parliament were based on s 51(xxvii) from 1901 to 1984, and s 51(xix) thereafter. Paragraph 51(xxviii) has been relied on very rarely, and more frequently in extradition matters than immigration cases.[10]

Early history of Australian migration laws

A useful early history of Australian immigration legislation can be found in the Full Federal Court case of *NAAV v Minister for Immigration and Multicultural and Indigenous Affairs*,[11] in which the Court, in a unanimous judgment, stated as follows:

[387] One of the first statutes enacted by the Commonwealth Parliament after federation was the *Immigration Restriction Act 1901* (Cth). It was described in its long title as:

'*An Act to place certain restrictions on Immigration and to provide for the removal from the Commonwealth of prohibited Immigrants.*'

[388] It prohibited the immigration into the Commonwealth of 'any person who when asked to do so by an officer fails to write out at dictation and sign in the presence of the officer a passage of fifty words in length in a European language directed by the officer' (s 3(a)). Persons excepted were, inter alia, those possessed of a Certificate of Exemption signed by the Minister or an officer (s 3(h)). The Act was of modest length by contemporary standards comprising in all some nineteen sections. It was subjected to various amendments in the years that followed its enactment but by 1935 still only comprised some nineteen sections, albeit it was to be read with the *Pacific Island Labourers Act 1901* (Cth) and the *Contract Immigrants Act 1905* (Cth). By 1950, it had undergone further amendments and expanded to sixty-four sections. The 'dictation' test provision was still in force as was the system of entry

---

10   See for example *Truong v R* (2004) 223 CLR 122.
11   (2002) FCAFC 228.

under Certificate of Exemption. That system was the precursor of the entry permit and visa regimes which were successive features of later migration legislation.

[389] The *Migration Act 1958* repealed the *Immigration Act 1901*, the *Pacific Island Labourers Acts* of 1901 and 1906 and the *Aliens Deportation Act 1949* (Cth). It was described briefly in its long title as *'An Act relating to Immigration, Deportation and Emigration'*.

The Act established a completely new statutory scheme for migration. Entry into Australia was regulated by entry permits, the grant of which was within the power of officers of the Department of Immigration (s 6(2)). An immigrant entering Australia without an entry permit was a prohibited immigrant (s 6(1)). The Act provided for the issue of temporary entry permits (s 6(6)) and for their cancellation by the Minister 'in his absolute discretion' (s 7(1)). It also provided for the deportation of aliens and immigrants under various conditions (ss 12, 22)). It created powers of examination, search and detention in relation to suspected prohibited immigrants and persons subject to deportation orders (ss 32–45). It set up a system for the registration of immigration agents (ss 46–53). Somewhat more complex than its immediate predecessor, the Act comprised some sixty-seven sections. ...

[391] [In 1989] the *Migration Legislation Amendment Act 1989* (Cth) was enacted. The amendments were comprehensive including new provisions for the control of entry into Australia involving entry permits and visas. A new Part III related to review of decisions. This Part created the Immigration Review Tribunal and provided for a process of internal review. The Federal Court was given jurisdiction to entertain appeals on questions of law from decisions of the Tribunal (new ss 64V and 64X). The general jurisdiction of the Court to review administrative decisions made under the Act, conferred by the *Administrative Decisions (Judicial Review) Act 1977* (Cth) and the *Judiciary Act,* remained intact ...

[392] The next major amendment to the Act was effected by the *Migration Reform Act 1992* (Cth) ('Migration Reform Act') which was passed in November 1992 ... The amending Act introduced an objects clause into the *Migration Act* and made the visa the single authority under which, for the most part, a non-citizen could be permitted to enter into or remain in Australia. It also established what was described in the Second Reading Speech as '... a uniform regime for detention and removal of persons illegally in Australia' (Parliamentary Debates, House of Representatives, 4 November 1992, p 2621). The 1992 Act established a statutory mechanism for merits review of decisions relating to the grant

of protection visas to persons claiming to be refugees. For this purpose it created the Refugee Review Tribunal. The provisions relating to the Tribunal commenced on 1 July 1993. The rest were to come into effect on 1 November 1993 but their operational date was deferred by subsequent amendment to 1 September 1994 – *Migration Laws Amendment Act 1993* (Cth) (No 59 of 1993).

An important matter not considered in *NAAV* was amendments to the *Migration Act 1958* made in 1984 that shifted the constitutional basis of the Act from s 51(xxvii) to s 51(xix) of the Constitution. This change was made by way of the *Migration Amendment Act 1983*, which came into effect on 2 April 1984. The reason for this change was the decisions of the High Court in *Salemi v Mackellar (no 2)*[12] and *Pochi v MacPhee*,[13] which found that an 'immigrant' can be 'absorbed' into the Australian community over time and thereby cease to be an immigrant.[14] The change has been vindicated by later High Court decisions, such as *Shaw v Minister for Immigration and Multicultural Affairs*[15] and *Tania Singh*,[16] which have found that an alien can only cease to be an alien by becoming an Australian citizen – an interesting example of the High Court allowing the Parliament to define words in the Constitution.

Current structure of migration legislation

The current migration legislation consists of the *Migration Act 1958* and the *Migration Regulations 1994*. Some key features of the current legislation are as follows:

1. All non-citizens entering Australia require a visa (s 29 of the Act).

2. Any non-citizen in the 'migration zone' (roughly the Australian territorial landmass) without a visa is an 'unlawful non-citizen' (ss 13, 14 of the Act) and must be detained (s 189).

3. Criteria for the grant of visas are set out primarily in the Regulations, but in some cases in the Act itself. If an applicant for a visa meets all legislative criteria for the visa applied for, the Minister must grant that visa; if not, it must be refused (s 65).

---

12   (1977) 137 CLR 396.
13   (1982) 151 CLR 101. See also *Nolan v Minister for Immigration and Ethnic Affairs* (1988) 165 CLR 178, which reached a similar conclusion. The reasoning behind these decisions can be traced back at least as far as *Ex parte Walsh and Johnson* (1925) 37 CLR 36.
14   See also Michelle Foster, 'An "Alien" by the Barest of Threads: The Legality of the Deportation of Long-Term Residents from Australia', (2009) 33 *Melbourne University Law Review* 483.
15   (2003) 218 CLR 28.
16   Supra n1.

4. All onshore refusals and cancellations, and refusal decisions where the applicant is sponsored by an Australian resident, are subject to merits review by the Migration Review Tribunal (MRT), Refugee Review Tribunal (RRT) or the Administrative Appeals Tribunal (AAT), depending on the kind of visa in question (Parts 5 and 7, and s 501 of the Act respectively).

5. The scope of judicial review of migration decisions is limited (or intended to be limited) by the privative clause in s 474 of the Act.

6. The Act and Regulations distinguish between criteria going to the *validity* of an application and those going to *grant*. The requirements for making a valid application are mostly set out in s 45 of the Act and Schedule 1 of the Regulations. Failure to meet validity requirements means that the application is a legal nullity and cannot be considered by the Minister (s 47 of the Act).

7. Criteria for grant are generally further divided into criteria to be met at the time of application, and those that must be met at the time of decision. Some newer visa subclasses have done away with this distinction (see for example Parts 186 and 187 of Schedule 2 of the Regulations).

8. Criteria for grant of a visa are primarily set out in Schedule 2 of the Regulations.

9. Visas are grouped into classes and subclasses. The validity criteria for each class of visa are set out in Schedule 1 of the Regulations, while grant criteria are set out by subclass in Schedule 2.

Who is an 'alien'?

The definition of the term 'alien' can best be seen by examining three High Court decisions from the 2000s: *Re Patterson Ex parte Taylor,*[17] *Shaw v Minister for Immigration and Multicultural Affairs*[18] and *Tania Singh.*[19]

Taylor

Graham Taylor was a British citizen who had been resident in Australia since the 1960s. In 1996, he pleaded guilty to a number of sexual offences against children and was sentenced to three-and-a-half years imprisonment. Whilst he was in prison, Senator Patterson, the Parliamentary Secretary to the Minister, cancelled his visa under s 501 of the Act. On release from prison, Taylor was taken into immigration detention pending his removal from Australia, and he sought

---

17   (2001) 207 CLR 391.
18   Supra n15.
19   Supra n1.

judicial review of Senator Patterson's decision. Taylor argued several grounds, including that Senator Patterson was not 'the Minister' for the purposes of the Act (an argument that failed), but only one is relevant here.

A bare majority of the High Court (Gaudron, McHugh, Kirby and Callinan JJ) accepted Taylor's argument that he was not an 'alien' for the purpose of the Commonwealth's power to make laws with respect to aliens (s 51(xix) of the Constitution) and that the visa and deportation provisions of the *Migration Act* were therefore not valid in their application to him. In doing so, they overruled the High Court's decision in *Nolan*.[20]

Although non-citizen British subjects who migrate to Australia today would be within the aliens power, the effect of the four majority judgments is that the deportation and removal provisions of the *Migration Act* could not apply to a person such as the applicant as a British subject who migrated to Australia before, at the earliest, 1973 (when the *Royal Style and Titles Act 1973* (Cth), referring to the Queen of Australia, was passed) and, in the view of three of the majority, 1987 (when changes to the *Australian Citizenship Act 1949*, which removed any special status for British citizens, came into effect), at least where the person has been 'absorbed' into the Australian community (remembering that prior to 1984 the Act was based on s 51(xxvii) of the Constitution). Prior to 1973, there was no 'Queen of Great Britain' or 'Queen of Australia', and instead a person in Taylor's position was simply a 'British subject'. The majority viewpoint is well encapsulated by the following comments from Kirby J:

> [306] For the respondent it was conceded, correctly in my view, that there were limits on the power of the Parliament to determine who is to be an alien. That must be so. For example, it would not, in my view, be competent to the Parliament to enact a law declaring that all Aboriginal persons were aliens; or that all persons of Chinese descent in Australia were aliens – although necessarily all such latter persons came to Australia, or were descended from those who came, from outside Australia. If, as this Court has held, the legislative power over immigrants does not, for the purposes of deportation, extend once such persons are absorbed into the Australian community, I see no reason of principle why a less protective rule should be applied to persons in the class of British subject migrating to Australia prior to 1987 ...
>
> [307] If when that person arrived, he or she was a British subject when that status was accorded constitutional and statutory equivalence to Australian nationality, that person was likewise beyond the operation of the naturalisation and aliens power. If such application could be

---

20   Supra n13.

revived in such a person's case, and applied retrospectively, it could (in terms of principle) be revived and applied to other persons and groups within Australia who themselves, or whose families, were made up of immigrants and those descended from, or adopted by, them. A line must be drawn, as it was in *Ex parte Walsh and Johnson*.[21] In my view, that line excludes a person such as the prosecutor. He never was an 'alien' for the purposes of the Constitution. At least in his case, when the attempt was made to treat him as an 'alien' (if that was the purpose of the *Migration Act*) he had been absorbed into the people of the Commonwealth. Once so absorbed, he could not *ex post facto* be deprived of his nationality status as a non-alien. In particular, he was not subject to legislative or executive power to order his deportation, any more than this could be done in the case of another Australian whose nationality status is now that of a citizen. Only after due process of law and a judicial order (as in extradition) may a citizen be involuntarily removed from Australia.

Gleeson CJ, Gummow and Hayne JJ dissented on this point and upheld *Nolan*.

Shaw

The High Court reversed itself only two years later in *Shaw*. That case also concerned a British citizen who was a long-term permanent resident of Australia, and whose visa had also been cancelled under s 501 of the Act. A significant feature of the High Court bench was that Gaudron J, who was a member of the majority in *Taylor*, had retired and been replaced by Heydon J.

In the end, Heydon J adopted the position of the *Patterson* dissenters. The new majority (Gleeson CJ, Gummow and Hayne JJ in a joint judgment, with whom Heydon J agreed) held that Mr Shaw entered Australia as an alien in the constitutional sense, and remained an alien because he did not become an Australian citizen (a status created purely by statute). Accordingly, his visa could be cancelled, and he could be removed in accordance with the provisions of the *Migration Act*.

In *Shaw*, Gleeson CJ, Gummow and Hayne JJ stated, '[t]his case should be taken as determining that the aliens power has reached all those persons who entered this country after the commencement of the Citizenship Act on 26 January 1949 and who were born out of Australia of parents who were not Australian citizens and who had not been naturalised'.[22] That is, the constitutional term 'alien' was to be interpreted in the light of the statutory term 'citizen'. Whether one agrees with the outcome in *Shaw* or not, this is a peculiar form of reasoning. Will the High Court also allow the Parliament to define words like 'taxation' or

---

21   Ibid.
22   Supra n15 at paragraph 151.

'trade and commerce' as it has allowed the Parliament to define the term 'alien'? The High Court made a similar finding in *Commonwealth v Australian Capital Territory* (the 'same-sex marriage case'),[23] in which the High Court struck down the ACT's same-sex marriage legislation under s 109 of the Constitution, finding it to be inconsistent with the Commonwealth *Marriage Act 1961*, but also stated that the Commonwealth Parliament had the power to define the term 'marriage'.

McHugh, Kirby and Callinan JJ all dissented (writing separate judgments), holding that Mr Shaw was not an 'alien'. McHugh J stated that he remained of the view that *Patterson* was correctly decided, despite having no clear ratio.[24] Furthermore, all three judges pointed out that the majority in *Patterson* had clearly overruled *Nolan* on the meaning of 'alien'. In affirming the correctness of the majority position in *Patterson*, Kirby J made an appeal to judicial restraint, and criticised the 'spectacle of deliberate persistence in attempts to overrule recent constitutional decisions on identical questions on the basis of nothing more intellectually persuasive than the retirement of a member of a past majority and the replacement of that Justice by a new appointee who may hold a different view'.[25] The spectacle of Kirby J criticising 'judicial activism' was rather amusing in itself.

It should be noted that the High Court, *Re Minister for Immigration and Multicultural Affairs; Ex parte Te*,[26] also rejected the proposition that a person who is accorded refugee status is not an 'alien' in the country that grants him or her that status. The definition of 'alien' was clearly narrowing before the crucial decision in *Tania Singh*.

Tania Singh

Tania Singh concerned a then five-year-old girl born in Australia to Indian parents, who held temporary visas at the time of her birth. The Singh family argued that Tania, having been born in Australia, was not an alien, and the provisions of the *Australian Citizenship Act 1949* that prevented her from obtaining Australian citizenship were simply irrelevant to her.

The High Court rejected this argument, finding that as Tania was not an Australian citizen, she was an alien. The High Court seemed at pains to point out that the Australian Parliament could not simply define the word 'alien' as it wished, but gave no real indication of where the boundaries of that power might be. For example, Gleeson CJ stated as follows early in his judgment:

---

23   (2013) HCA 55.
24   Supra n15 at paragraph 155.
25   Ibid at 161–62.
26   (2003) 212 CLR 48.

[4] I have previously stated my view that, subject to a qualification, Parliament, under pars (xix) and (xxvii) of s 51, has the power to determine the legal basis by reference to which Australia deals with matters of nationality and immigration, to create and define the concept of Australian citizenship, to prescribe the conditions on which such citizenship may be acquired and lost, and to link citizenship with the right of abode. In that regard, Brennan, Deane and Dawson JJ said in *Chu Kheng Lim v Minister for Immigration*,[27] that the effect of Australia's emergence as a fully independent sovereign nation with its own distinct citizenship was that alien in s 51(xix) of the Constitution had become synonymous with non-citizen. The qualification is that Parliament cannot, simply by giving its own definition of 'alien', expand the power under s 51(xix) to include persons who could not possibly answer the description of 'aliens' in the Constitution. Within the class of persons who could answer that description, Parliament can determine to whom it will be applied, and with what consequences. Alienage is a status, and, subject to the qualification just mentioned, Parliament can decide who will be treated as having that status for the purposes of Australian law and, subject to any other relevant constitutional constraints, what that status will entail.

[5] Everyone agrees that the term 'aliens' does not mean whatever Parliament wants it to mean. Equally clearly, it does not mean whatever a court, or a judge, wants it to mean.

The key judgment, however, was probably the joint judgment of Gummow, Hayne and Heydon JJ. Their Honours took the view that Tania was an Indian citizen and therefore owed an allegiance to India. This in and of itself made her an alien, unless she was also an Australian citizen (which she was not). Their Honours stated as follows at paragraph 195:

Whatever may be the outcome of debate about the validity of laws alleged to depend upon other powers given to the federal Parliament, it is central to the plaintiff's argument that the constitutional word 'aliens' has a meaning which cannot include a person born within Australia. If that is the proper construction of 'aliens' the result would be that, through the exercise of the naturalization aspect of the power conferred by s 51(xix), the class of persons born outside Australia who otherwise would be aliens can be altered or reduced by valid federal legislation, but the class of non-aliens contains an irreducible core. Understood in that way, the naturalization and aliens power would provide a one-way

---

27   (1992) 176 CLR 1. This was the case that upheld the Constitutional validity of Australia's first mandatory immigration detention laws.

street: empowering legislation permitting persons to become non-aliens but not empowering legislation that would affect the status of a person born in Australia, regardless of that person's ties to other sovereign powers.

Their Honours summed up by stating as follows at paragraph 205:

It was common ground that the plaintiff is a citizen of India. She is, therefore, a citizen of a foreign state. She is a person within the naturalisation and aliens power.

Kirby J, seemingly shifting from his reliance on historical interpretation of the word 'alien' that was on display in *Taylor* and *Shaw*, argued that the meaning of the word 'alien' had to be interpreted in the light of changes in law and society since 1901. His Honour stated that the legislative power with respect to aliens is 'capable of application to a larger, contemporary condition of things beyond what might have been the generally accepted meaning of the word at the time of Federation'[28] and that Parliament's ability to make laws relating to citizenship could not be 'forever to be limited to the approach of birthright'.[29]

McHugh and Callinan JJ, in separate judgments, dissented and took a diametrically opposite approach to that of Kirby J, by focusing on what they believed to be the intention of the drafters of the Constitution. They each took the view that in 1901 the concept of alienage was, with few and irrelevant exceptions, limited to birth outside a particular country. In their view, Tania Singh was therefore not an alien.

The remaining issue is, if Parliament cannot simply define the term 'alien' however it sees fit, what are the limits on its power? As the joint judgment seemed to be most concerned with the fact that Tania Singh was already a citizen of a foreign country, it may be the case that a future court could, consistently with *Tania Singh*, find that a stateless child born in Australia is not an alien. Presumably a law depriving people of Australian citizenship simply because of their membership of a class (say, persons of Aboriginal descent) would also be unconstitutional. However, this issue will have to be determined at a later date.[30]

---

28   Supra n1 at paragraph 249.
29   Ibid at paragraph 251.
30   For a further discussion on this issue, see Michelle Foster, 'Membership in the Australian Community: *Singh v The Commonwealth* and its Consequences for Australian Citizenship Law', (2006) 34(1) Federal Law Review 161.

Other issues relating to the scope of the immigration and aliens powers

The High Court has considered on a number of occasions what the scope of the immigration and aliens powers might be. Immigration cases came early to the High Court. The 1908 decision of *Potter v Minahan*[31] concerned an applicant who had been born in Australia to a Chinese father and European mother, and who had accompanied his father back to China. Minahan attempted to return to Australia after the death of his father, and was detained as a 'prohibited immigrant' under the *Immigration Restriction Act 1901*. By majority, the High Court found that the applicant was not an immigrant, and O'Connor J stated as follows at 305:

> A person born in Australia, and by reason of that fact a British subject owing allegiance to the Empire, becomes by reason of the same fact a member of the Australian community under obligation to obey its laws, and correlatively entitled to all the rights and benefits which membership of the community involves, amongst which is a right to depart from and re-enter Australia as he pleases without let or hindrance unless some law of the Australian community has in that respect decreed the contrary.

Two cases from the 1990s and a series of related cases in the early 2000s demonstrate that the High Court has taken quite a wide view of the immigration and aliens powers, especially when considered alongside the 'incidental power' in s 51(xxxix) of the Constitution.

Cunliffe v Commonwealth

Cunliffe v Commonwealth[32] considered the constitutional validity of Part 2A (now Part 3) of the *Migration Act 1958*, which is the part of the Act regulating the practice of migration agents. At paragraph 19 of his judgment, Mason CJ set out the constitutional arguments of the applicants as follows:

(a) it [Part 2A] is beyond the legislative powers of the Parliament;

(b) it is contrary to the implied freedom of communication of information and opinions relating to the government of the Commonwealth; and

(c) it contravenes the freedom of intercourse guaranteed by s 92 of the Constitution.

In (a) Mr Cunliffe argued that ss 51(xix) and 51(xxvii) of the Constitution only empowered the Parliament to make laws that directly affected aliens or

31   (1908) 7 CLR 277.

32   (1994) 182 CLR 272.

immigrants, not Australian citizens who were providing services to such persons. The High Court unanimously rejected this argument. Mason CJ stated as follows at paragraphs 24 and 25 of his judgment:

> [24] [T]hose provisions in Pt 2A which regulate the conduct of persons who provide immigration assistance to aliens by prohibiting them from providing that assistance otherwise than in accordance with the requirements of Pt 2A are not laws which stand outside the core or heart of the subject-matter of the power. The provision of immigration assistance to aliens, especially by persons who act on their behalf and for them by representing them and giving them advice, is, in my view, at the core of both the aliens power and the immigration power. It can make no difference that the law operates by way of creating rights, duties and privileges on non-aliens in terms of the services they wish to provide to aliens rather than by way of creating rights, duties and privileges on aliens in terms of the services they wish to receive from non-aliens. The point is that Pt 2A seeks to regulate the provision of immigration assistance to aliens and to no one else.

> [25] It matters not that one can also describe Pt 2A as containing provisions which are laws with respect to the conduct which they proscribe. It is well established that a law may bear several characters (*Actors and Announcers Equity Association* (1982) 150 CLR at 192 per Stephen J; *Tasmanian Dam Case* (1983) 158 CLR at 151 per Mason J). And as the conduct proscribed here is that of persons acting as migration agents for aliens who seek to enter Australia, the conduct is within the subject-matter of the aliens power. To the extent to which those aliens are also immigrants, the proscribed conduct is also within the immigration power. But, an alien who has been absorbed into the Australian community ceases to be an immigrant, though remaining an alien. Because some entrance applicants are not immigrants, Pt 2A cannot completely be supported as an exercise of the immigration power. However, the immigration power can be put to one side because the aliens power provides a more expansive source of power.

None of the other judges gave any greater analysis to this argument. For example, Brennan J stated at paragraph 17 of his judgment as follows:

> By regulating the provision of services to entrance applicants, Pt 2A both operates selectively upon aliens and does so in respect of activities peculiarly significant to aliens. That is enough to establish the character of Pt 2A as a law with respect to aliens.

Gaudron and Deane JJ took a slightly different approach, and would have struck down Part 2A to the extent that it applied to lawyers and providers of pro bono immigration assistance, but would have done so under the 'implied freedoms' principle, not because the laws did not fall under ss 51(xix) or (xxvii) of the Constitution.

Immigration detention cases

A number of High Court cases have considered challenges to the legality of immigration detention. Only one has succeeded to date, and that was the first case of all, *Park v Minister for Immigration and Ethnic Affairs.*[33] In *Park*, departmental compliance officers conducted a series of 'raids' on construction sites in the Sydney area, and found a large number of Koreans working illegally. Many were taken into immigration detention. Departmental officers formed the view that there was an organised 'racket' involving deliberate importation of illegal Korean labour in existence, and instead of immediately deporting the illegal workers, kept them in detention to attempt to discover the names of the organisers. This was held to be an impermissible purpose of immigration detention, and the detention of the illegal workers was found to be unlawful.

Lim v Minister for Immigration, Local Government and Ethnic Affairs[34]

Lim[35] concerned the constitutional validity of Division 4B of Part 2 of the *Migration Act* (now Division 6 of Part 2). These were the first mandatory immigration detention laws in Australia, and provided for the mandatory detention of 'designated persons'. The term 'designated persons' was defined in s 54K as follows:

'designated person' means a non-citizen who:

(a) has been on a boat in the territorial sea of Australia after 19 November 1989 and before 1 December 1992; and

(b) has not presented a visa; and

(c) is in Australia; and

(d) has not been granted an entry permit; and

---

33   (1989) 167 CLR 637.
34   For further discussion on *Lim* and later High Court challenges to the legality of immigration detention, see Alan Freckelton, 'Canada's Implementation of Australian Immigration Detention Legislation', (2013) 1 *Frontiers of Legal Research* 58.
35   Supra n27.

(e) is a person to whom the Department has given a designation by:

    (i) determining and recording which boat he or she was on; and

    (ii) giving him or her an identifier that is not the same as an identifier given to another non-citizen who was on that boat;

and includes a non-citizen born in Australia whose mother is a designated person.

It can be seen that all designated persons were unauthorised *boat* arrivals, meaning that Division 4B was the first legislative example of Australia's continuing paranoia about such arrivals.

Section 54L then provided that a designated person must be 'kept in custody' until either removed from Australia or granted an entry permit. Section 54N permitted an officer to detain a designated person not already in detention, without a warrant, and recapture any escapee. Removal of designated persons from Australia was dealt with by s 54P, which provided for removal on written request of the person, when no application for an entry permit was made within two months of being detained, or when an application for an entry permit had been refused and all avenues of review had been exhausted.

The most confusing section was s 54Q, which purported to provide that a designated person could be detained for a maximum of 273 days (nine months). However, the 273-day 'clock' could be 'stopped' in the circumstances described in ss 54Q(3)(c)–(f), which provided as follows:

    (c) the Department is waiting for information relating to the application to be given by a person who is not under the control of the Department;

    (d) the dealing with the application is at a stage whose duration is under the control of the person or of an adviser or representative of the person;

    (e) court or tribunal proceedings relating to the application have been begun and not finalised;

    (f) continued dealing with the application is otherwise beyond the control of the Department.

In other words, the 273-day period only ran when the applicant had provided all relevant information to the Department. Paragraphs (d) and (f) in particular were very vaguely worded, and indeed could mean nearly anything. It was extraordinarily difficult, therefore, to determine whether a particular detainee's 273-day period of detention had expired or not.

Finally, the most controversial provision of Division 4B was s 54R, which provided that 'a court is not to order the release from custody of a designated person'. This was ultimately the only provision of Division 4B found to be unconstitutional.

The applicant in *Lim* argued that the division was unconstitutional on a number of grounds, including that orders for detention were inherently punitive in nature, and therefore amounted to an exercise of the judicial power of the Commonwealth by the legislature and/or the executive. The High Court unanimously found that ss 54L and 54N were valid, as they were powers exercised in accordance with s 51(xix) of the Constitution, and were not an exercise of judicial power. They could therefore be exercised by administrative decision-makers.

The leading judgment was given by Brennan, Deane and Dawson JJ. At paragraph 27 of their judgment, their Honours quoted from a Canadian case that proceeded on appeal to the Privy Council, *Attorney-General for Canada v Cain*, in which Lord Atkinson stated as follows:[36]

> One of the rights possessed by the supreme power in every State is the right to refuse to permit an alien to enter that State, to annex what conditions it pleases to the permission to enter it, and to expel or deport from the State, at pleasure, even a friendly alien, especially if it considers his presence in the State opposed to its peace, order, and good government, or to its social or material interests.

Brennan, Deane and Dawson JJ explained this decision as follows:[37]

> The question for decision in *Attorney-General for Canada v Cain* was whether the Canadian statute 60 and 61 Vict c11 had validly clothed the Dominion Government with the power to expel an alien and to confine him in custody for the purpose of delivering him to the country whence he had entered the Dominion. The Judicial Committee concluded that it had, as the emphasised words in the above passage indicate, the power to expel or deport a particular alien, and the associated power to confine under restraint to the extent necessary to make expulsion or deportation effective, were seen as *prima facie* executive in character.

---

36   (1906) AC 542 at 546.
37   *Lim*, supra n27 at paragraph 28 of the judgment of Brennan, Deane and Dawson JJ.

At paragraph 29, their Honours noted that previous Australian cases, dating back to *Koon Wing Lau v Calwell*[38] in 1949, had upheld the Constitutional validity of legislation providing for discretionary immigration detention, and that s 51(xix) permitted the Parliament to make laws that 'extend to authorising the Executive to restrain an alien in custody to the extent necessary to make the deportation effective' – in other words, to ensure that the non-citizen cannot evade removal from Australia. Probably the key part of the judgment is set out in paragraph 30:

> It can therefore be said that the legislative power conferred by s 51(xix) of the Constitution encompasses the conferral upon the Executive of authority to detain (or to direct the detention of) an alien in custody for the purposes of expulsion or deportation. Such authority to detain an alien in custody, when conferred upon the Executive in the context and for the purposes of an executive power of deportation or expulsion, constitutes an incident of that executive power. By analogy, authority to detain an alien in custody, when conferred in the context and for the purposes of executive powers to receive, investigate and determine an application by that alien for an entry permit and (after determination) to admit or deport, constitutes an incident of those executive powers.

Brennan, Deane and Dawson JJ also regarded the fact that the detainee could bring their detention to an end by requesting their own removal as important. Their Honours stated at paragraph 34 of their judgment as follows:

> Section 54P(1) ... provides that an officer must remove a designated person from Australia as soon as practicable if the designated person asks the Minister, in writing, to be removed. It follows that, under Div 4B, it always lies within the power of a designated person to bring his or her detention in custody to an end by requesting to be removed from Australia. Once such a request has been made, further detention in custody is authorized by Div 4B only for the limited period involved, in the circumstances of a particular case, in complying with the statutory requirement of removal 'as soon as practicable' ... In the context of that power of a designated person to bring his or her detention in custody under Div 4B to an end at any time, the time limitations imposed by other provisions of the Division suffice, in our view, to preclude a conclusion that the powers of detention which are conferred upon the Executive exceed what is reasonably capable of being seen as necessary for the purposes of deportation or for the making and consideration of an entry application. It follows that the powers of detention in custody

---

38   (1949) 80 CLR 533.

conferred by ss 54L and 54N are an incident of the executive powers of exclusion, admission and deportation of aliens and are not, of their nature, part of the judicial power of the Commonwealth.

The result of this reasoning was that ss 54L and 54N of the Act were found to be valid. Section 54R, on the other hand, was struck down by Brennan, Deane and Dawson JJ because it could prevent a court from releasing a designated person who, by the terms of the Act itself, should have been released. Their Honours stated as follows at paragraph 37:

> In fact, of course, it is manifest that circumstances could exist in which a 'designated person' was unlawfully held in custody by a person purportedly acting in pursuance of Div 4B. The reason why that is so is that the status of a person as a 'designated person' does not automatically cease when detention in custody is no longer authorized by Div 4B.

Brennan, Deane and Dawson JJ cited as examples of unlawful detention of designated persons situations where a designated person remained in detention despite making a written request to be removed from Australia, the 273-day limit had expired, or the person had not made an application for an entry permit within two months of the commencement of their detention. Their Honours summed up by stating that '[o]nce it appears that a designated person may be unlawfully held in custody in purported pursuance of Div 4B, it necessarily follows that the provision of s 54R is invalid'.[39]

Gaudron J agreed that s 54R was invalid,[40] and her Honour would have read ss 54L and 54N somewhat more narrowly than the other judges,[41] but her reasoning did not prevent the application of these sections to the applicants. Mason CJ, and Toohey and McHugh JJ, who each wrote separate judgments, upheld the validity of s 54R by reading it down to cover only those designated persons who were being lawfully detained under Division 4B.[42]

As a concluding point, Division 4B, as were many other provisions of the *Migration Act*, was renumbered by the *Migration Reform Act 1992*, which came into effect on 1 September 1994, and is now Division 6 of Part 2 of the Act. This is despite the fact that since the introduction of s 189 of the Act, which provides for mandatory detention of *all* unlawful non-citizens, with effect from the same date, Division 6 of Part 2 is redundant and has never been used since that date. Even more strangely, s 54R, now renumbered as s 183, remains in the Act despite it being found to be invalid.

---

39   *Lim*, supra n27, at paragraph 37 of the judgment of Brennan, Deane and Dawson JJ.
40   Ibid at paragraph 18 of the judgment of Gaudron J.
41   Ibid at paragraphs 15–17.
42   Ibid at paragraph 12 of the judgment of Mason CJ; paragraph 34 of the judgment of Toohey J; paragraph 35 of the judgment of McHugh J.

The *Al Masri/Al Kateb* litigation

The Australian immigration detention system has survived a number of domestic legal challenges, the best-known being the *Al Masri/Al Kateb* litigation. In *Al Masri v Minister for Immigration and Multicultural and Indigenous Affairs*,[43] the applicant was a stateless Palestinian who had been refused a Protection Visa. He requested removal from Australia in accordance with s 198(1). However, no country could be found to which he could be removed, meaning that he had to remain in immigration detention. Al Masri challenged his continuing detention, arguing that *Lim* had found that immigration detention was justified for the purpose of ensuring the availability of an unlawful non-citizen for removal. If removal was impossible, detention was unlawful.

Both the Federal Court[44] and the Full Federal Court accepted these arguments. Black CJ, Sundberg and Weinberg JJ, writing a combined judgment in the Full Court, found as follows at paragraphs 120 and 121:[45]

> [120] In our view, the language of s 196, either taken alone or in the context of the scheme as a whole, does not suggest that the Parliament did turn its attention to the curtailment of the right to liberty in circumstances where detention may be for a period of potentially unlimited duration and possibly even permanent. On the contrary, the textual framework of the scheme suggests an assumption by the Parliament that the detention authorised by s 196 will necessarily come to an end. Section 196 contemplates a 'period of detention', and that is how the section is headed. Whilst one purpose of the section is indisputably to authorise the detention of unlawful non-citizens, another purpose is to specify the circumstances in which the period of detention is to come to an end. The latter purpose assumes that the detention will have an end. The assumption is that the detention of unlawful non-citizens will come to an end by the actual occurrence of one of three events: removal, deportation or the grant of a visa.

> [121] The language of s 198(1) supports the conclusion that Parliament proceeded on an assumption that detention would, in fact, end rather than upon an understanding that detention might possibly be of unlimited duration ... Indeed, as we have noted, the assumption made by members of the High Court about the scheme considered in *Lim* was that it had an element, the equivalent of the present s 198(1), that gave a person what was effectively a power to bring detention to an end.

---

43   (2003) FCAFC 70.

44   *Al Masri v Minister for Immigration and Multicultural and Indigenous Affairs* [2002] FCA 1009.

45   Referring to *Lim*, supra n27, at paragraph 34 of the judgment of Brennan, Deane and Dawson JJ.

The Court therefore ordered Mr Al Masri's release from detention. Somewhat ironically, he was successfully removed from Australia within a matter of weeks after the decision, which rendered the Minister's application for special leave to appeal to the High Court moot. However, another stateless Palestinian, Mr Al Kateb, ended up in the High Court. Before the Full Federal Court decision in *Al Masri*, Mr Al Kateb had been refused release from immigration detention by the Federal Court,[46] in which von Doussa J had found that the Federal Court's decision in *Al Masri*[47] was wrongly decided. Mr Al Kateb's appeal was removed directly to the High Court.

The High Court,[48] in a 4-3 judgment, overturned *Al Masri* and found that laws that may have the effect of imposing indefinite detention on unlawful non-citizens were constitutionally valid. A key passage can be found in the judgment of Hayne J at paragraph 268:

> It is essential to confront the contention that, because the time at which detention will end cannot be predicted, its indefinite duration (even, so it is said, for the life of the detainee) is or will become punitive. The answer to that is simple but must be made. If that is the result, it comes about because the non-citizen came to or remained in this country without permission. The removal of an unlawful non-citizen from Australia then depends upon the willingness of some other country to receive that person. If the unlawful non-citizen is stateless, as is Mr Al Kateb, there is no nation state which Australia may ask to receive its citizen. And if Australia is unwilling to extend refuge to those who have no country of nationality to which they may look both for protection and a home, the continued exclusion of such persons from the Australian community in accordance with the regime established by the *Migration Act* does not impinge upon the separation of powers required by the Constitution.

There was a split in the minority judgments. Gleeson CJ and Gummow J found that a law providing for indefinite immigration detention would be constitutionally valid, but that because s 196 did not expressly provide for this possibility, it had to be interpreted in such a way as to not permit it. Only Kirby J found that no legislation providing for indefinite immigration detention, no matter how clearly expressed, would be constitutionally valid.

---

46   *SHFB v Goodwin and Ors* (2003) FCA 294. 'Goodwin' is a typographical error – Mr Al Kateb brought an action against Philippa Godwin, the then Deputy Secretary of the Detention Services Division of the Department of Immigration.

47   Supra n61.

48   *Al Kateb v Godwin* (2004) 219 CLR 562.

Other litigation prior to 2014

The High Court has, since *Lim*, considered a number of other cases in which the legality of immigration detention has been challenged. All have been unsuccessful.

B v Minister for Immigration and Multicultural and Indigenous Affairs[49]

The High Court overturned a decision of the Full Bench of the Family Court,[50] in which that court had found that s 67ZC of the *Family Law Act 1975* allowed the Family Court to make any orders it wished for the benefit of children. Having made this finding, it ordered a number of children from one family released from immigration detention. The High Court found on appeal that s 67ZC could only be invoked in the case of a 'matrimonial cause', such as a divorce, and as no matrimonial cause existed in this case, s 67ZC did not apply and the Family Court had no jurisdiction.

Behrooz v Secretary, Department of Immigration and Multicultural and Indigenous Affairs[51]

Mr Behrooz, a detainee in the particularly infamous Woomera IDC, was charged with escaping from that IDC under s 197A of the *Migration Act*. He sought to defend the charge by arguing that the conditions inside the Woomera IDC were so poor as to be punitive, and not purely for the purpose of ensuring his availability for removal, and therefore not an exercise of the power to detain unlawful non-citizens. The High Court disagreed, finding that he had been legally detained, and that his allegations of ill-treatment in detention could be resolved by an action in tort against the Commonwealth and the private contractors managing the centre on behalf of the government.

Re Woolley, Ex parte M276/2003[52]

Mr Woolley was the Manager of the Baxter IDC in South Australia. The applicants were a number of children detained in the centre who argued that they could not be detained because they lacked the legal capacity to request removal from Australia under s 198(1), and the inherent *parens patriae* jurisdiction of the court should be regarded as a constitutional principle that invalidated s 189 as far as it applied to children, or alternatively gave the court the power to release children from detention regardless of s 189. The High Court found that a minor child can be released from detention if their parent(s) request

---

49   (2004) 219 CLR 365.
50   *B v Minister for Immigration and Multicultural and Indigenous Affairs* (2003) 199 ALR 604.
51   (2004) 219 CLR 486.
52   (2004) 225 CLR 1.

removal. Further, it found that the *parens patriae* role of the court was not a constitutional principle, and could therefore be overruled by statute. McHugh J summed up the decision at paragraph 106 by stating that '[a]lthough it may be accepted that children who are unlawful non-citizens do not pose a flight risk and are not a danger to the community, the Parliament, acting constitutionally, is entitled to prevent any unlawful non-citizen, including a child, from entering the Australian community while that person continues to have that status'. The applicants were unsuccessful once again.

S4/2014 v Minister for Immigration and Border Protection[53]

The High Court's decision in *S4/2014 v Minister for Immigration and Border Protection*[54] was handed down on the propitious date of 11 September 2014, and could potentially have a significant impact on the law relating to immigration detention in Australia. For the first time since *Lim*,[55] the High Court has clearly imposed limits on the purpose, if not the duration, of immigration detention, and there seems little doubt that *S4/2014* will be used as a means for individuals to challenge the legality of their detention.

Facts

S4/2014 was primarily concerned with the Minister's attempts to prevent unauthorised boat arrivals from being granted permanent residence in Australia. The applicant, who was stateless, arrived in Australia by boat at Christmas Island in December 2011. This made him an 'offshore entry person' as defined by s 5 of the Act, and therefore unable to make a valid application for a visa, unless permitted to do so by the Minister – see s 46A of the Act.

Although s 46A is a non-compellable power, the Minister decided to consider exercising this power, and the plaintiff's claims for refugee status were assessed through an administrative process. Two years later, the Department found that the applicant was a refugee and recommended that the Minister permit him to make an application for a visa. However, the Minister did not make a decision under s 46A. Instead, he granted the applicant two visas under s 195A of the Act, which permits the Minister to grant a visa to a detainee. These were a seven-day Temporary Safe Haven (TSH) visa and a three-year Temporary Humanitarian Concern (THC) visa. The effect of the grant of these visas was that the applicant was prevented, by s 91K of the Act, from making any further onshore application other than for another TSH visa.

---

53   See on this case Alan Freckelton, 'The High Court's Decision in *S4/2014 v Minister for Immigration* and its Likely Impact', (2014) 61 *Immigration Review Bulletin* 1.

54   (2014) HCA 34.

55   Supra n27.

It is important to note that the applicant did not challenge the legality of his immigration detention. Indeed, he conceded that if he was successful he would once again become an unlawful non-citizen and be re-detained.[56] However, the applicant was obviously more concerned that he be considered for permanent residence in Australia.

Validity of the grant of the temporary visas

The applicant argued that the grant of the TSH and THC visas were invalid. The High Court agreed, finding that the Minister, having decided to consider exercising his s 46A power, had to make a decision to exercise or not exercise that power, and could not instead grant a visa under s 195A as the granting of the TSH visa (which specifically prevents the applicant from being able to apply for another visa) had the effect of negating the possible outcome of a decision under s 46A to allow the applicant to apply for a protection visa. This meant that the grant of the visas was invalid, and the applicant became once more an unlawful non-citizen. The High Court, in a rare joint judgment, stated as follows at paragraph 46:

> Reading s 195A as empowering the grant of a visa of the kind described wrongly assumes that the powers given by ss 46A and 195A are to be understood as wholly independent of each other. They are not. The Minister may not circumvent the provisions of s 46A by resort to s 195A. Not least is that so when, as in this case, the grant of a visa of the kind just described would deprive the prolongation of the plaintiff's detention of its purpose.

In other words, once the Minister decides, under s 46A, to consider the grant of a visa to an offshore entry person, he or she must proceed to actually make a decision under that section. A person who applies for refugee status as an offshore entry person effectively gets permanent residence or nothing, as the *Migration Regulations 1994* do not currently provide for temporary protection visas.[57]

---

56   Supra n54 at paragraph 9.
57   An amendment to the Regulations to reinstate temporary protection visas was disallowed by the Senate on 2 December 2013. See http://www.abc.net.au/news/2013-12-02/labor-votes-with-greens-to-block-temporary-protection-visa/5130188, extracted 15 September 2014. However, the *Migration and Maritime Powers Legislation Amendment (Resolving the Asylum Legacy Caseload) Bill 2014*, introduced into the House of Representatives on 25 September 2014, would restore these visas, as well as create a new species of temporary humanitarian visa, the Safe Haven Enterprise Visa (SHEV). A SHEV would allow people found to be refugees to live and work in Australia for five years, with a possibility of renewal, if they lived and worked in regional Australia.

Immigration detention

The High Court also made some significant comments on the applicant's detention. Making frequent reference to *Lim*,[58] the High Court pointed out that detention is only lawful when it is carried out for the purposes of the Act. In particular, the court noted as follows at paragraph 24:

> An alien within Australia, whether lawfully or not, cannot be detained except under and in accordance with law. The detention which the Act authorises in respect of an alien who is an unlawful non-citizen can be described most generally as detention under and for the purposes of the Act. Detention under the Act is not an end in itself. It is not detention in execution of any conviction. Detention under the Act is in aid of the objects stated in s 4(1) of the Act.

Further, the Court stated at paragraph 26 as follows:

> Importantly, the Court further held [in *Lim*] that the provisions of the Act which then authorised mandatory detention of certain aliens were valid laws if the detention which those laws required and authorised was limited to what was reasonably capable of being seen as necessary for the purposes of deportation or to enable an application for permission to enter and remain in Australia to be made and considered. It follows that detention under and for the purposes of the Act is limited by the purposes for which the detention is being effected. And it further follows that, when describing and justifying detention as being under and for the purposes of the Act, it will always be necessary to identify the purpose for the detention. Lawfully, that purpose can only be one of three purposes: the purpose of removal from Australia; the purpose of receiving, investigating and determining an application for a visa permitting the alien to enter and remain in Australia; or, in a case such as the present, the purpose of determining whether to permit a valid application for a visa.

The Court added at paragraph 28 that these purposes 'must be pursued and carried into effect as soon as reasonably practicable'. This is the first time that an Australian court has held that not only must a detainee be removed from Australia as 'soon as reasonably practicable' after one of the events described in s 198 of the Act has occurred, but that processes leading up to that stage must *also* be carried out as expeditiously as reasonably practicable.

In other words, the Department must be able to justify the detention of an unlawful non-citizen, at any time, by reference to one of the three purposes

---

58   Supra n2.

stated by the High Court. Deterrence of unlawful arrival is not a valid purpose. The High Court therefore found that the Minister needed to make an s 46A decision as soon as reasonably practicable in order for the applicant's continued detention to be lawful.[59]

Implications of the decision

The High Court did not expressly state that *Al Kateb* was wrongly decided, but it has clearly left the door open for any immigration detainee to challenge the legality of their detention by arguing that their detention is not for one of the purposes listed in *S4/2014*. For example, someone in Mr Al Kateb's position – a stateless person who had been refused refugee status, and who could not be removed from Australia in the foreseeable future – would appear to be in a good position to argue that his or her detention is no longer for the purpose of removal, considering a visa application, or determining whether to permit an application to be made.

Media reporting of the decision varied. In Australia, the *Sydney Morning Herald* made little mention of the decision's impact on immigration detention, instead focusing on the High Court's findings on ss 46A and 195A.[60] On the other hand, the UK *Guardian* newspaper ran an article entitled 'High court verdict spells the end for Australian immigration detention as we know it'.[61] The true impact of the decision will probably not be known until the first individual detainee attempts to challenge the legality of his or her detention by reference to *S4/2014*.

---

59   Supra n54 at paragraph 35.
60   'High Court Defeat for Scott Morrison over Temporary Visa for Refugee', *Sydney Morning Herald* 12 September 2014. Available at: http://www.smh.com.au/federal-politics/political-news/high-court-defeat-for-scott-morrison-over-temporary-visa-for-refugee-20140911-10fgel.html, extracted 12 September 2014.
61   'High court verdict spells the end for Australian immigration detention as we know it', *The Guardian* 11 September 2014. Available at: http://www.theguardian.com/commentisfree/2014/sep/11/high-court-verdict-spells-the-end-for-australian-immigration-detention-as-we-know-it, extracted 12 September 2014.

Chapter 2. Administrative Decision-Making Under the *Migration Act 1958*

Structure of the *Migration Act 1958*

Prior to 1989

The *Migration Act* originally provided a very broad discretion for the Minister (through his or her delegates) to grant a visa or entry permit,[1] and the grounds on which visas and entry permits were granted were set out in policy. For example, in 1973 (a version of the Act that was considered by two High Court cases) ss 6(1)–(3) provided as follows:

1. An immigrant who, not being the holder of an entry permit that is in force, enters Australia thereupon becomes a prohibited immigrant.

2. An officer may, in accordance with this section and at the request or with the consent of an immigrant, grant to the immigrant an entry permit.

3. An entry permit shall be in a form approved by the Minister and shall be expressed to permit the person to whom it is granted to enter Australia or to remain in Australia or both.

It is interesting to note how little instruction or guidance was given to officials in the legislation itself. These provisions would make very little sense to decision makers without detailed policy manuals to guide the exercise of these wide discretionary powers.

The workings of the *Migration Act* and the decision-making processes of the Department were quite opaque until 1989. It is also notable that, prior to 1985, even the High Court had taken the view that immigrants and aliens, or at least some immigrants and aliens, had no right to be in Australia, and therefore had no expectation of procedural fairness in determining their status. Gibbs J (as he

---

1   Prior to 1 September 1994, a visa permitted *travel* to Australia, while an entry permit did what its name suggests, i.e. permit *entry* to Australia. Entry permits were abolished with the coming into effect of the *Migration Reform Act 1992* on 1 September 1994, and the visa became the sole authority for travel and entry to Australia.

then was) in *Salemi v Mackellar (No. 2)* made it clear that, in his view, 'prohibited immigrants' (the equivalent of an unlawful non-citizen) had no expectation of natural justice in their dealings with the department, stating as follows:[2]

> [27] The relevant status of the plaintiff is that of a prohibited immigrant. Aliens, including aliens who are immigrants, are, whilst in Australia, entitled to the protection of our laws, and the common law would not deny to them, in appropriate cases, the application of the principles of natural justice. However the plaintiff is a prohibited immigrant, and as Barwick CJ said in *R v Forbes; Ex parte Kwok Kwan Lee* (1971) 124 CLR 168, at p 173: 'By the very description he is not a person having any title to remain in the country' ... s 18 gives the Minister an unconditional right to order the deportation of a prohibited immigrant. The section does not limit the circumstances or occasions on which the Minister may exercise the power; he is not required to determine any question, or to form any satisfaction or opinion, before making the order – the matter is left entirely to his discretion ... This is a field in which it is unwise to generalise, but the fact that the power is conferred quite unconditionally is a circumstance that suggests – not necessarily conclusively – that the principles of natural justice are not intended to apply. These two matters together quite strongly support the view that the power of the Minister under s 18 is one which he may exercise free from any duty to observe the principles of natural justice ...

> [28] In my opinion the circumstances as a whole lead to the conclusion that the Minister is not bound to afford a hearing to a prohibited immigrant before ordering his deportation under s 18. The very security of the nation may require that the executive should have the power to decide what aliens shall be permitted to enter and remain in Australia, and to expel those who have no right to be in the country. Reasons of security may make it impossible to disclose the grounds on which the executive proposes to act ... At the least, however, it may be said that the earlier authorities warranted the belief, when s 18 was enacted, that a prohibited immigrant would have no right to be heard before an order was made under that section.

A similar conclusion was reached in another 1977 case, *R v Mackellar; Ex parte Ratu*.[3] Again, Gibbs J took a very strict line, noting in particular at paragraph 7 of his judgment that the applicants had clearly been granted only temporary entry permits, and they therefore had no expectation of procedural fairness when they were ordered to be deported after overstaying.

---

2   (1977) 137 CLR 396 at paragraphs 27 and 28 of the judgment of Gibbs J.
3   (1977) 137 CLR 461.

Effect of the *Administrative Decisions (Judicial Review) Act 1977*

A very significant piece of legislation in the history of Australian administrative law, the *Administrative Decisions (Judicial Review) Act 1977* ('the ADJR Act'), came into effect on 1 October 1980. Until 1980, applications for judicial review were made to the High Court in its original jurisdiction under s 75 of the Constitution, but only a handful of immigration cases were decided by the High Court prior to 1985. The ADJR Act did not (and could not) *prevent* an applicant from making use of s 75 of the Constitution, but there was little incentive to do so, as the Federal Court was less expensive and had the same jurisdiction in relation to judicial review of administrative decisions under the ADJR Act as the High Court. Between 1980 and 1994, judicial review of migration decisions was generally undertaken under the ADJR Act.

The ADJR Act has been amended a number of times in its history, but there have been no significant amendments made to ss 3 or 5 of the ADJR Act since 1977 (except to make reference to the Federal Magistrates Court or the Federal Circuit Court). Section 3 is the definitions section, and defines the term 'decision to which this Act applies' as follows:

> **'decision to which this Act applies'** means a decision of an administrative character made, proposed to be made, or required to be made (whether in the exercise of a discretion or not and whether before or after the commencement of this definition):
>
> (a)   under an enactment referred to in paragraph (a), (b), (c) or (d) of the definition of *enactment*; or
>
> (b)   by a Commonwealth authority or an officer of the Commonwealth under an enactment referred to in paragraph (ca) or (cb) of the definition of *enactment*;
>
> (c)   other than:
>
>>   (i)   a decision by the Governor-General; or
>>
>>   (ii)   a decision included in any of the classes of decisions set out in Schedule 1.

'Enactment' is defined by s 3 as follows:

> 'enactment' means:
>
> (a)   an Act, other than:

    (i)   the *Commonwealth Places (Application of Laws) Act 1970*; or

    (ii)   the *Northern Territory (Self-Government) Act 1978*; or

    (iii) an Act or part of an Act that is not an enactment because of section 3A (certain legislation relating to the ACT); or

(b)   an Ordinance of a Territory other than the Australian Capital Territory or the Northern Territory; or

(c)   an instrument (including rules, regulations or by-laws) made under such an Act or under such an Ordinance, other than any such instrument that is not an enactment because of section 3A; or

(ca) an Act of a State, the Australian Capital Territory or the Northern Territory, or a part of such an Act, described in Schedule 3; or

(cb) an instrument (including rules, regulations or by-laws) made under an Act or part of an Act covered by paragraph (ca); or

(d)   any other law, or a part of a law, of the Northern Territory declared by the regulations, in accordance with section 19A, to be an enactment for the purposes of this Act;

and, for the purposes of paragraph (a), (b), (c), (ca) or (cb), includes a part of an enactment.

This is a complex definition, but for our purposes it is sufficient to note that nothing in the ADJR Act, in its original form, could be taken to have excluded the *Migration Act* from its operation. A decision made under the *Migration Act* (or Regulations) is certainly a decision under an enactment, and the term 'decision of an administrative character' has generally been given a wide meaning. As early as 1985, counsel for the Minister in *Minister for Immigration and Ethnic Affairs v Mayer*[4] conceded that a decision under the Act was a 'decision of an administrative character', and no one ever tried to argue the contrary afterwards.

The grounds of judicial review under the ADJR Act are set out in s 5. Subsection 5(1) currently provides as follows:

(a)   that a breach of the rules of natural justice occurred in connection with the making of the decision;

(b)   that procedures that were required by law to be observed in connection with the making of the decision were not observed;

---

4   (1985) 157 CLR 290.

(c)   that the person who purported to make the decision did not have jurisdiction to make the decision;

(d)   that the decision was not authorised by the enactment in pursuance of which it was purported to be made;

(e)   that the making of the decision was an improper exercise of the power conferred by the enactment in pursuance of which it was purported to be made;

(f)   that the decision involved an error of law, whether or not the error appears on the record of the decision;

(g)   that the decision was induced or affected by fraud;

(h)   that there was no evidence or other material to justify the making of the decision;

(i)   that the decision was otherwise contrary to law.

The meaning of s 5(1)(e) is elaborated on by s 5(2) as follows:

(a)   The reference in paragraph (1)(e) to an improper exercise of a power shall be construed as including a reference to:

(b)   taking an irrelevant consideration into account in the exercise of a power;

(c)   failing to take a relevant consideration into account in the exercise of a power;

(d)   an exercise of a power for a purpose other than a purpose for which the power is conferred;

(e)   an exercise of a discretionary power in bad faith;

(f)   an exercise of a personal discretionary power at the direction or behest of another person;

(g)   an exercise of a discretionary power in accordance with a rule or policy without regard to the merits of the particular case;

(h)   an exercise of a power that is so unreasonable that no reasonable person could have so exercised the power;

(i)   an exercise of a power in such a way that the result of the exercise of the power is uncertain; and (j)　any other exercise of a power in a way that constitutes abuse of the power.

Most of the particularly significant migration cases that came to the High Court in the 1980s came by way of appeal from the Full Federal Court under the ADJR Act. These included the crucial decisions of *Kioa v West*,[5] which applied the principles of natural justice to immigration decisions for the first time; *Chan v Minister for Immigration and Ethnic Affairs*,[6] which was the first case to apply ADJR principles to the refugee decision-making process (and found that a decision to refuse refugee status was Wednesbury unreasonable); and *Haoucher v Minister for Immigration and Ethnic Affairs*,[7] which applied the principles of procedural legitimate expectations to a deportation case. Most significantly, these cases did not treat immigration as a privilege that could be conferred at the whim of the Minister, but as an administrative decision capable of judicial review in the same way as any other.

Kioa v West

The key High Court decision of the 1980s concerning the applicability of the ADJR Act to immigration decisions was *Kioa v West*.[8] Mr Kioa was a Tongan national who arrived in Australia in September 1981 as the holder of a visitor's entry permit, granted prior to arriving in Australia. He lodged an application to extend this permit in December 1981, but then left the address he had provided to the Department without informing it and began to work illegally, thus becoming a prohibited non-citizen. His wife, who was also in Australia, also became a prohibited non-citizen, but their daughter, who was born in Australia in 1982, was, under the law at that time, an Australian citizen.

Mr Kioa was detected by compliance officers in July 1983 and detained. He claimed that he had remained in Australia after the expiry of his permit because Cyclone Isaac had devastated parts of Tonga in March 1982 and, as a consequence, his extended family had advised him to remain in Australia so that he might earn money and send it home for their support.

Mr Kioa's extension application, which had been dormant since 1981 because the Department could not contact him, was now reactivated. Mr Kioa argued that he should be permitted to remain in Australia, basically on the basis of a reference from the pastor of a local church in which Mr Kioa had been active. This application was refused on 12 September 1983, but Mr Kioa still made no attempt to depart Australia. In October 1983, a departmental officer drafted a

---

5　(1985) 159 CLR 550.
6　(1989) 169 CLR 379.
7　(1990) 169 CLR 648.
8　Supra n5.

submission to a delegate recommending that a deportation order under s 18 of the Act be issued against Mr and Mrs Kioa, crucially stating that 'Mr Kioa's alleged concern for other Tongan illegal immigrants in Australia and his active involvement with other persons who are seeking to circumvent Australia's immigration laws must be a source of concern'.[9] This allegation had never been put to Mr Kioa. The deportation order was duly issued by the delegate in October 1983.

Mr Kioa's next move was to apply for a written statement of reasons for the deportation order, as permitted by s 13 of the ADJR Act. This was supplied on 11 November 1983. The reasons, prepared by the delegate and not the junior officer who drafted the submission, made no mention of the allegation that Mr Kioa had been 'involved' with other people 'seeking to circumvent Australia's immigration laws', and instead relied on his lengthy history as a prohibited non-citizen and his illegal work.

Mr Kioa sought judicial review of the deportation decision under the ADJR Act, and the junior officer's recommendation was provided to him before the hearing. His arguments were summed up by Gibbs CJ at paragraph 6 of his judgment as follows:

> First, it was submitted that the delegate was required to observe the rules of natural justice and that he failed to do so, in that he did not give the appellants a fair opportunity to answer prejudicial statements affecting them. Secondly, it was submitted that the delegate wrongly failed to take into account the detrimental effect which the order would have on the privileges and benefits which Elvina, as an Australian citizen, was entitled to enjoy, and the provisions of arts 23 and 24 of the International Convenant on Civil and Political Rights and Principles 1–7 of the Declaration of the Rights of the Child, which appear in schs 1 and 2 respectively to the *Human Rights Commission Act 1981* (Cth), and which it was said required the delegate to take into account the possibility that the family of which Elvina was a member would be broken up by the deportation order.

By majority, the High Court rejected Mr Kioa's second argument[10] but upheld the first. The Court in particular noted that, since the decisions in *Salemi (No. 2)* and *Ratu*, the Act had been amended, but more importantly, the ADJR Act had come into effect. Mason J, as he then was, stated as follows at paragraph 19 of his judgment:

---

9   Ibid at paragraph 4 of the judgment of Gibbs CJ.
10   An argument that was accepted 10 years later in *Minister for Immigration and Ethnic Affairs v Teoh* (1995) 183 CLR 273.

The legislative amendments which have been made since *Salemi (No. 2)* and *Ratu* were decided in 1977 are of such significance that we should not regard those decisions as foreclosing the answers to the questions that the appellant's argument now raises. The most important change is that brought about by s 13 of the ADJR Act. The making of a deportation order and the other decisions now complained of are decisions to which the section applies with the consequence that there is an obligation under s 13(2) upon the person making a decision, following receipt of a notice under sub-s (1), to furnish a statement in writing setting out the findings on material questions of fact, referring to the evidence or other material on which those findings were based and giving the reasons for the decision. The existence of this obligation is to be seen in association with the right conferred by s 5(1) of the ADJR Act on a person affected by a decision to apply to the Federal Court for an order of review. The absence of any obligation to give reasons was a factor relevant to the conclusion which I reached in *Ratu* ...

Wilson J agreed with Mason J about the impact of the ADJR Act, and also noted as follows at paragraphs 16 and 17 of his judgment:

[16] Mr Merkel [for the Kioas] draws attention also to the insertion of ss 6A and 66E in the Act. The first of these sections was inserted by amending Act No.175 of 1980 with the object of restricting by law the categories of immigrants eligible to be granted permanent residence subsequent to their arrival in Australia ... The second was inserted by amending Act No.61 of 1981. It enables decisions of the Minister to order the deportation of a person under s 12 or s 13 of the Act to be reviewed on their merits by the Administrative Appeals Tribunal constituted under the *Administrative Appeals Tribunal Act 1975* (Cth) provided that the applicant is either an Australian citizen or a person whose continued presence in Australia is not subject to any limitation as to time imposed by law (s 66E(2)). Section 12 empowers the Minister to order the deportation of any alien convicted in Australia of certain crimes, while s 13 applies to the deportation of immigrants in respect of matters occurring within five years of entry. In each case, after reviewing the decision, the Tribunal shall either affirm the decision or remit the matter for reconsideration in accordance with any recommendations of the Tribunal (s 66E(3)).

[17] I have reviewed in detail the legislative changes to the Migration Act since the decisions in *Salemi* and *Ratu* upon which the appellants rely to establish a statutory framework so significantly different as to render those decisions no longer applicable.

That is, the existence of a right of merits review provided by the Act itself was an important factor in deciding that principles of procedural fairness should apply to migration decisions.

Brennan J, as then was, took a slightly different approach. His Honour found that, absent any clear statutory indication to the contrary, '[i]f a power is apt to affect the interests of an individual in a way that is substantially different from the way in which it is apt to affect the interests of the public at large, the repository of the power will ordinarily be bound or entitled to have regard to the interests of the individual before he exercises the power'.[11] That is, the requirement to afford natural justice is the rule, not the exception.

Brennan J then moved on to examine the relevant legislation. His Honour discounted the impact of the ADJR Act and instead focused on amendments to the Act itself since 1977. Brennan J stated as follows at paragraphs 30 and 31 of his judgment:

> [30] The insertion of ss 6A and 27(2A), however, makes it manifest that the question to be decided under s 18 is not simply whether the prohibited immigrant should be deported but whether he should be granted an entry permit and perhaps a permanent entry permit so that he ceases to be a prohibited immigrant with all the disabilities which that status entails. The complex of powers contained in ss 6, 6A, 7 and 18 are directed to the status and disposition of the immigrant. The affection of the immigrant's interests is of the very nature of those powers and the repository must have regard to those interests in exercising them. And if the legislature intended the Minister or his delegate to have regard to the interests of the prohibited immigrant, the legislature may be presumed to intend that the prohibited immigrant should be heard before those powers are exercised.

> [31] ... It follows that the nature of the power to be exercised is now somewhat different from what it was in 1977. As the complex of powers conferred by ss 6, 6A, 7 and 18 taken in conjunction with s 27(2A), now require the interests of the prohibited immigrant and his family to be taken into account, there is a substantial ground of distinction between the Act as it stood when it was construed in *Salemi (No. 2)* and *Ex parte Ratu* and the Act as it stood when the deportation orders in this case were made. The significance of the Minister's power to cancel a temporary entry permit is less in the 1983 context than it was in the Act as it stood in 1977. In my opinion, the Act as it stood at the time when the deportation orders were made did not displace the presumption

---

11   Supra n5 at paragraph 24 of the judgment of Brennan J.

that Parliament intended that an exercise of the complex of powers conferred by ss 6, 6A, 7 and 18 should be conditioned on observance of the principles of natural justice.

That is, Brennan J found that the Act itself required that the interests of a prohibited non-citizen must be taken into account before a deportation order was made. The presumption in favour of natural justice was not displaced, and it followed inevitably that a duty of procedural fairness was therefore imposed on the decision maker.

Codification of procedures in the *Migration Act*

Two significant amendments were made to the Act in the face of *Kioa* and similar decisions. The first was the *Migration Amendment Act 1989* ('the MAA 1989'), which came into effect on 19 December 1989, and the second was the *Migration Reform Act 1992* ('the MRA'), which came into effect on 1 September 1994. An entirely new set of regulations came into effect at the same time in each case. An important stated objective of both Acts was to reduce the scope for judicial review of migration decisions, by reducing the exercise of discretionary power by decision makers.

The *Migration Amendment Act 1989* and the *Migration (1989) Regulations*

The MAA 1989 was the first amendment to the *Migration Act 1958* that clearly set out, in legislation, the criteria for grant for visas and entry permits. The reforms were influenced in part by recommendations made by the Committee to Advise on Australia's Immigration Policies (CAAIP), chaired by Stephen Fitzgerald. CAAIP published its report (the 'Fitzgerald Report') in 1988.[12] The Fitzgerald Report formulated a draft model bill to take into account changing attitudes and practices, and to reflect a 'positive and forward-looking approach to immigration policy and administration'.[13]

The Fitzgerald Report noted that the previous migration legislation had been criticised for 'its indiscriminate conferral of uncontrolled discretionary decision-making powers'.[14] The report reinforced this criticism by stating that a major deficiency of the Migration Act was 'the broad and unstructured

---

12 *Immigration: A Commitment to Australia*, Report of the Committee to Advise on Australia's Immigration Policies, Australian Government Publishing Service, Canberra, 1988.
13 *Immigration: A Commitment to Australia – Legislation*, the Committee to Advise on Australia's Immigration Policies, Australian Government Publishing Service, Canberra, 1988.
14 Supra n12 at 112.

nature of discretionary powers', which 'created a great deal of uncertainty'.[15] To overcome this deficiency, the draft model bill formulated by CAAIP included a system where 'identifiable policies and criteria for decision-making will be clearly set out in statutory rules'.[16]

The codification of the visa and entry permit decision-making structure was discussed in paragraph 3 of the Explanatory Memorandum (EM) to the MAA 1989 as follows:

> [3] The Act also puts in place the means by which the broad discretions currently found in the Act will be exercised by reference to decision criteria to be prescribed in the Migration Regulations (the Regulations). Once criteria for a class of application have been prescribed a decision maker will be bound by them, as will both tiers of review (where the decision is one which is prescribed as reviewable). A decision will not be reviewable under the new two tier system unless decision criteria have been prescribed in the Regulations and the decision was made on the basis of those criteria.

The Minister for Immigration and Ethnic Affairs, Robert Ray, described the purpose of these amendments in his second reading speech as follows:[17]

> Currently the Minister for this portfolio has decision-making discretions which are totally unfettered. That is, the migration legislative scheme is essentially machinery legislation. It gives the Minister in this portfolio power to determine who can enter Australia and who must leave. There is no provision in this scheme for Parliamentary guidance of the exercise of the power. A Minister can make decisions on these matters virtually at his or her discretion. Thus, legally, a Minister has the power to determine and change policy in the immigration field as he or she wishes independent of the Parliament.
>
> Further, unlike any comparable area of administration, the decision-making powers conferred by the Act are vested in the Minister. The Minister thus has the power to reverse any decision made by an officer of the Department. This in turn can result in a Minister becoming involved in the minutiae of the portfolio, at the cost of developing overall policy in the depth which, in my view, is essential.

---

15   Ibid at 113.
16   Ibid at 112.
17   Senate Hansard, 5 April 1989 at 922–27.

The wide discretionary powers conferred by the Migration Act have long been a source of public criticism. Decision-making guidelines are perceived to be obscure, arbitrarily changed and applied, and subject to day-to-day political intervention in individual cases.

Accordingly I am proposing in this Bill a decision-making system in which policies governing entry to and stay in Australia will, for the first time, be spelt out in the migration legislative scheme. Parliament, then, through its powers of disallowance will be able to monitor those policies. I am also vesting most of the decision-making powers currently conferred on me in the Secretary of the Department ...

It is clear that the approach to the determination and expression of policy, to the reviewing of decisions, and to the overall determination and control of the size and composition of the entry of people into Australia, particularly the migrant intake, which flows from the present migration legislative scheme is no longer appropriate. The current legislative scheme reflects an era when the overall numbers of people entering Australia were far smaller than they are today, when the rights of individuals were not protected by administrative law, and the general administration of the Migration Act and the formulation of policy reflected the unfettered nature of the decision-making powers conferred by the Act.

Developments in administrative law and the need to control the flow of people into Australia in accordance with overall economic and social policies, have led to costly tensions between these objectives and the current legislative scheme ... This Bill resolves these tensions, and, further, gives Parliament power to monitor the changes in policy direction which inevitably emerge from day-to-day administration of the Migration Act.

The MAA 1989 was also noteworthy for introducing statutory merits review by an independent tribunal, created by the Act. Previously, decisions such as deportation orders could be reviewed by the AAT, but the MAA 1989 elected not to give the full immigration jurisdiction to the AAT, and instead created the Immigration Review Tribunal (IRT). Paragraph 2 of the EM to the MAA 1989 provided as follows:

[2] The Act is to be amended to provide for a statutory two-tier system of review of prescribed immigration decisions. The first tier of review will be conducted by specially authorised review officers within a unit in the Department of Immigration, Local Government and Ethnic Affairs (the Department) followed by appeals to an external review body called

the Immigration Review Tribunal (IRT). The present jurisdiction of the Administrative Appeals Tribunal in criminal deportation matters will not be affected. The IRT will operate independently of the Department and will have as its objective providing a mechanism of review that is fair, just, economical and quick.

The review unit within the Department was called the Migration Internal Review Office (MIRO), which existed until 1997. MIRO provided an informal review of an adverse decision, but was not an independent tribunal. Michael Chaaya, citing the Committee for the Review of the System for Review of Migration Decisions,[18] summed up some of the criticisms of MIRO in 1997 as follows:[19]

> MIRO itself has been criticised for its lack of independence from the Department of Immigration and Multicultural Affairs (DIMA). On the one hand, the MIRO staff are independent of the Departments primary decision makers and not subject to their control in the reassessment of individual cases. On the other hand, making this independence a functional reality is made difficult by the fact that it currently exists as an organisational unit of the Department. Other issues which have been identified as deficiencies in the internal merits review process include: the lack of a fresh look by MIRO; the delays in finalising applications; the absence of any oral hearing or direct communication between the review officer and the applicant; and the production of reasons which fail to adequately explain to the applicant the rationale for the decision.

MIRO was effectively abolished in 1999, when the IRT and MIRO were merged to form the Migration Review Tribunal (MRT). This was done by means of the *Migration Legislation Amendment Act (No. 1) 1998*, which came into effect on 1 June 1999.

The *Migration (1989) Regulations*, which also came into effect on 19 December 1989, were the first regulations to set out the criteria for grant of visas. To give an example of how the criteria were set out, Regulation 126 provided the criteria for grant of an Extended Eligibility (Spouse) Entry Permit:

> The following criteria are prescribed in relation to an extended eligibility (special circumstances) entry permit:
>
> (a)   the applicant is not the holder of a **visitor visa** or entry permit, or an illegal entrant (other than an illegal entrant referred to in subparagraph 25(1)(b)(i));

---

18   *Non-Adversarial Review of Migration Decisions: The Way Forward*, (1992) Australian Government Publishing Service, Canberra at 47–52.

19   Michael Chaaya, 'Proposed Changes to the Review of Migration Decisions: Sensible Reform Agenda or Political Expediency?' (1997) 19(4) *Sydney Law Review* 547.

(b) the applicant:

   (i) since arrival in Australia, has become the spouse of an Australian citizen or an Australian permanent resident and the relationship with his or her spouse is a genuine and continuing relationship; and

   (ii) satisfies public interest criteria and the prescribed health criteria specified in item 9 in Schedule 1.

The term 'extended eligibility (special circumstances) entry permit' was defined in Regulation 2 as including a number of entry permits, including an Extended Eligibility (Spouse) Entry Permit. The terms 'spouse' and 'de facto spouse' were also defined in Regulation 2. Although the terms 'class' and 'subclass' were not used in the 1989 Regulations in the same way they are today, Regulation 2 can be seen as providing for a 'class' of entry permits known as 'extended eligibility (special circumstances) entry permits', and the Extended Eligibility (Spouse) Entry Permit can be regarded as a subclass in that class.

The *Migration Reform Act 1992* and the *Migration Regulations 1994*

The Act and Regulations were put approximately into the form that we know them today by the *Migration Reform Act 1992* and the *Migration Regulations 1994*. By 1992, the government's objectives in codifying criteria for visas and entry permits and providing for independent merits review, namely a reduction in the number of cases proceeding to judicial review, were clearly not being realised, and a major rewriting of the Act was deemed to be required.

The Refugee Review Tribunal

One important legislative change that came about prior to the coming into effect of the MRA was the creation of the Refugee Review Tribunal (RRT) as an independent body to review all decisions relating to applications for refugee status. The RRT commenced operations on 1 July 1993, and when a decision was made to defer the commencement of the MRA until 1 September 1994, the provisions relating to the RRT were exempt from the deferral.[20]

---

20   See the *Migration Laws Amendment Act 1993*.

Universal visa requirement

Section 29 of the Act has the effect that all non-citizens in Australia must hold a visa that is in effect. Prior to 1 September 1994, some entrants to Australia (most importantly New Zealanders) were exempt from the requirement to hold a visa or entry permit, but this is no longer the case. New Zealanders can now apply for a Special Category Visa (SCV) in immigration clearance simply by presenting a valid New Zealand passport, and unless their behaviour or health is of concern, they will be granted a visa on the spot.

Prior the passage of the MRA, terms such as 'prohibited non-citizen' and 'illegal entrant' were used to describe persons who do not have a legal right to enter or remain in Australia. The newly inserted s 14(1) provided that a non-citizen in the migration zone who is not a lawful non-citizen is an unlawful non-citizen. This definition requires understanding of the term 'lawful non-citizen'. Section 13(1) of the Act precisely defines a 'lawful non-citizen' as a non-citizen in the migration zone who holds a visa that is in effect. A combined reading of these two provisions makes it clear that 'an unlawful non-citizen' is a person who is not a citizen of Australia and is in the Australian migration zone[21] without a valid visa.[22]

A person may become an 'unlawful non-citizen' in three different ways:

1. Entering Australia without a visa (such as 'unauthorised maritime arrivals').

2. Entering Australia with a valid visa which ceases by passage of time or because a specific event happens.

3. Entering Australia with a valid visa which is cancelled onshore.

Classes and subclasses

The Act and Regulations distinguish between a class and a subclass of visa. Subsection 31(1) of the Act provides that 'there are to be prescribed classes of visas', and s 45 of the Act makes it clear that a visa applicant must apply for a visa of a specified class. The prescribed classes of visas, along with the criteria for making a valid application for each class, are set out in Schedule 1 of the Regulations. Each Item of Schedule 1 also specifies one or more subclass in each class.

---

21 The 'migration zone' broadly consists of the area consisting of the States, the Territories, Australian resource installations and Australian sea installations. See s 5(1) of the *Migration Act 1958* for a detailed definition.

22 There are some exceptions for inhabitants of the Protected Zone, another term defined in s 5(1) of the Act, and which broadly covers the Torres Strait Islands.

While an applicant applies for a visa of a particular class, they are granted a visa of a particular subclass specified in that class. The criteria for the grant of each subclass are set out in Schedule 2 of the Regulations.

The Act itself also provides for a number of classes of visa, as specified by s 31(2) of the Act. Some visas created directly by the Act also have Schedule 1 and 2 criteria – for example, SCVs are created by s 32 of the Act, but are given the class designation TY by Item 1219 of Schedule 1, and constitute Part 444 of Schedule 2 (subclass 444 is the only subclass in class TY). On the other hand, the criteria for the grant of an Absorbed Person Visa (APV) are set out solely in s 34 of the Act.

Visas can be 'substantive' or otherwise. A substantive visa, as set out in s 5(1) of the Act, is a visa that is not a Bridging Visa (primarily granted to permit an applicant to remain lawfully in Australia while an onshore application is processed), a Criminal Justice Visa or an Enforcement Visa.

Validity and grant criteria

The Act also introduced the concept of validity of visa applications. Section 45 of the Act specifies criteria (many of which are expanded on in the Regulations) for making a valid visa application. The criteria for validity vary from class to class, but applications must use the specified form, pay the specified Visa Application Charge (VAC), and specify a class of visa in the application in order to be valid. The visa applicant must also usually, but not always, be in a specified location (that is, inside or outside Australia). If an application is invalid it is a legal nullity, and cannot even be considered by the Minister (s 47 of the Act). A finding that an application is invalid can be the subject of judicial review, but as it is not a decision on the application, it cannot be the subject of merits review.

Another ground on which an application is frequently found to be invalid is under ss 48 or 48A of the Act. Section 48 provides that a non-citizen who has had a visa refused in Australia, or a visa cancelled in Australia, and does not hold a substantive visa, cannot make a valid application for a visa, other than a protection visa or a class of visa prescribed by the Regulations (Regulation 2.12). Section 48A applies a similar principle to protection visa applications, although the Minister has the power under s 48B to permit a non-citizen to make a second application without leaving Australia.

As an aside, a number of court cases in the late 1990s and early 2000s involved visa applicants seeking to have their own visa applications declared invalid, often on the ground that their form had not been completed. For example,

Minister for Immigration and Multicultural Affairs v A[23] concerned an applicant for a protection visa who submitted a Form 866 in which the 'claims' section stated simply 'statutory declaration to follow'. The statutory declaration was never provided, and the Department refused the application. The applicant's solicitor then failed to apply for RRT review within time, leaving judicial review as the only available option. The Federal Court found that a substantial part of Form 866, in which the applicant was required to detail his or her claims for refugee status, was not completed, which meant that the form was not completed and the application was invalid. This meant that the Minister had no power to consider the application (see s 47 of the Act) and the refusal decision was also a legal nullity. This had the further result that the applicant had not had a visa refused in Australia, and was therefore not subject to either ss 48 or 48A of the Act.

Section 40 of the Act provides that the Regulations may prescribe criteria for the grant of a visa, including but not limited to whether the applicant is in Australia, outside Australia or in immigration clearance. A key provision of the Act is s 65(1), which provides as follows:

> After considering a valid application for a visa, the Minister:
>
> (a) if satisfied that:
>
> > (i) the health criteria for it (if any) have been satisfied; and
> >
> > (ii) the other criteria for it prescribed by this Act or the regulations have been satisfied; and
> >
> > (iii) the grant of the visa is not prevented by section 40 (circumstances when granted), 500A (refusal or cancellation of temporary safe haven visas), 501 (special power to refuse or cancel) or any other provision of this Act or of any other law of the Commonwealth; and
> >
> > (iv) any amount of visa application charge payable in relation to the application has been paid;
>
> is to grant the visa; or
>
> (b) if not so satisfied, is to refuse to grant the visa.

It is to be noted again that the Minister must consider all valid visa applications, must not consider invalid ones, and there is no discretion as to whether to grant the visa. The visa *must* be granted if all legislative criteria are met, and *must*

---

23   (1999) FCA 1679.

be refused otherwise. This does not necessarily mean that the visa will be granted *immediately* — for example, some visa classes are subject to 'caps' on the numbers that can be granted in any one program year (1 July – 30 June). As an example, assume that a person meets the criteria for grant of a subclass of visa that is included in a class subject to the 'cap and queue' provision in s 85 of the Act. If the cap has not yet been reached for the program year, the visa will be granted immediately. If the cap has been reached, the application will be set aside ('queued') and granted at the start of the next program year.

Finally on this point, the criteria for validity and grant are set out in Schedules 1 and 2 in the form of 'recipe cards'. That is, most Items of Schedule 1 and Parts of Schedule 2 follow the same format.

The normal format for an Item of Schedule 1 is as follows:

Heading — Item number XXXX, Class Description and Designation

Sub-item XXXX(1) — Specifies the form to be used

Sub-item XXXX(2) — Specifies the VAC (there may be more than one, depending on the nature of the application)

Sub-item XXXX(3) — Various matters, almost always including whether the application must be made inside or outside Australia, and whether the applicant must be inside or outside Australia.

The Schedule 2 recipe card looks like this:

Part Number (same as subclass number) XXX and Description

Sub-part XXX.1 — Any definitions specific to the Part

Division XXX.21 — Criteria to be met at the time of application by the primary applicant

Division XXX.22 — Criteria to be met at the time of decision by the primary applicant

Division XXX.31 — Criteria to be met at the time of application by any secondary applicants (family members)

Division XXX.32 — Criteria to be met at the time of decision by any secondary applicants (family members)

Part XXX.4 — Circumstances applicable to grant (usually the physical location of the applicant at the time of decision)

Part XXX.5 — Duration of the visa

Part XXX.6 – Conditions (if any). The conditions are specified by reference to an item of Schedule 8, which lists all conditions that can be imposed on visas.

Note that some newer subclasses (for example 186 and 187) have no specific 'time of application' and 'time of decision' criteria. It is yet to be seen whether new subclasses will continue to follow this drafting template or not.

Code of procedure for deciding visa applications

The MRA, when it fully came into effect, substantially renumbered and reordered the Act. One important provision of the MRA was the new Subdivision AB, which created a 'Code of Procedure' for Departmental processing of applications for visas (entry permits having been abolished by the MRA). Subdivision AB was intended to provide a clear procedure for dealing with applications, and that as long as this procedure was followed, primary decisions[24] could not be set aside on the basis of a failure to provide procedural fairness.

Judicial review

Applications for judicial review of Departmental decisions were dealt with by a new Part 8 of the Act. The key provision of the new Part 8 was s 476, which provided in part as follows:

(1) to subsection (2), application may be made for review by the Federal Court of a judicially reviewable decision on any one or more of the following grounds:

   (a) that procedures that were required by this Act or the regulations to be observed in connection with the making of the decision were not observed;

   (b) that the person who purported to make the decision did not have jurisdiction to make the decision;

   (c) that the decision was not authorised by this Act or the regulations;

   (d) that the decision was an improper exercise of the power conferred by this Act or the regulations;

---

24   A 'primary decision' is defined in s 476 of the Act as one that could be reviewed by one of the Tribunals, and excludes such decisions from the jurisdiction of the Federal Circuit Court. It should also be noted that primary decision can be subject to judicial review in the High Court, but this will rarely be an option worth pursuing because of the cost, unless the decision is otherwise unreviewable (for example, an offshore refusal decision without an Australian sponsor or nominator).

(e) that the decision involved an error of law, being an error involving an incorrect interpretation of the applicable law or an incorrect application of the law to the facts as found by the person who made the decision, whether or not the error appears on the record of the decision;

(f) that the decision was induced or affected by fraud or by actual bias;

(g) that there was no evidence or other material to justify the making of the decision.

(2) The following are not grounds upon which an application may be made under subsection (1):

(a) that a breach of the rules of natural justice occurred in connection with the making of the decision;

(b) that the decision involved an exercise of a power that is so unreasonable that no reasonable person could have so exercised the power.

The term 'judicially reviewable decision' was defined in s 475 of the Act, and included decisions made by the IRT, RRT or the AAT relating to visas. Primary decisions made by the Department were expressly excluded from that definition under s 475(2). At the same time, new Parts 5 and 7 of the Act essentially provided for independent merits review of all onshore decisions relating to visas. The clear intention was that applicants would pursue merits review *rather than* judicial review, but the end result was that many applicants pursued both.

The Explanatory Memorandum (EM) to the MRA elucidated on Part 8 as follows:

[44] In acknowledgement of the special nature of immigration decisions and as a result of the widened availability of merits review, the Reform Bill amends the Act to set down reformulated grounds of judicial review. To ensure procedural fairness, procedures for decision-making which embody the principles of natural justice have been set out in the Reform Bill.

[45] The specific codified procedures in the Reform Bill, and those to be set out in the *Migration Regulations*, replace the current uncertain rules with regard to natural justice and statutory criteria for decision-making will clarify the matters that must be considered in making a decision. An applicant will be able to appeal to the Federal Court if the codified

procedures and criteria have not been followed by decision makers, but a court appeal will only be permitted where the applicant has first pursued all merits review rights.

The then Minister for Immigration and Ethnic Affairs, Mr Hand, stated as follows in his second reading speech:[25]

> The measures I have announced so far will lead to greater precision in our efforts to control the border. Under the reforms, decision-making procedures will be codified. This will provide a fair **and** certain process with which both applicant **and** decision maker can be confident. Decision makers will be able to focus on the merits of each case knowing precisely what procedural requirements are to be followed. These procedures will replace the somewhat open-ended doctrines of natural justice **and** unreasonableness.
>
> The Reform Bill proposes significant extensions to the current system for review of migration decisions. Credible independent merits review will ensure that the Government's clear intentions in relation to controlling entry to Australia, as set out in the Migration Act, are not eroded by narrow judicial interpretations. Under the Reform Bill, the following people who are adversely affected by a decision will be entitled to independent merits review: onshore refugee claimants; onshore cancelled visa holders, except those cancelled at the border; onshore applicants for a visa, except those detected at the border; **and** an Australian sponsor of an offshore applicant for a visa.

Again, there was a clear assumption that the provision of independent merits review would have the effect that refused visa applicants would not go a step further and take their case to judicial review if not satisfied with the merits review.

There have been many changes made to the Act and Regulations since 1 September 1994, most notably the introduction of the concept of 'excised offshore places' and the privative clause in September 2001, and the imposition of sanctions on employers who hire non-citizens who are not legally entitled to work in Australia, along with a number of amendments to judicial review processes. However, the basic *structure* of the Act and Regulations has not changed since the MRA came into effect on 1 September 1994.

---

25   House of Representatives Hansard, Wednesday, 4 November 1992 at 2620.

The effect of 'outsourcing'

An issue that has attracted some attention since the mid-1990s is that of 'outsourcing' of the Department of Immigration's functions. Outsourcing is not always an easy concept to define. It is rare that a business enterprise or a government department will be an entirely self-contained unit – a migration agent, for example, will not attempt to set up their own ICT organisation, and will instead deal with existing mobile phone and internet providers for the ICT components of their business. However, when government departments start outsourcing the management or decision-making aspects of their 'business' to external bodies, there arises a different situation altogether.

One definition of outsourcing is 'an agreement in which one company contracts out a part of their existing internal activity to another company'.[26] This definition may raise more questions than answers – what exactly is 'internal activity', for example? One way of looking at the issue might be to regard a function as having been 'outsourced' when control of and responsibility for a particular function is shifted from one business to another, the latter typically having particular expertise in the outsourced function. This kind of thinking can be seen in another academic description of outsourcing:[27]

> In the early 1980s, 'outsourcing' typically referred to the situation where firms expanded their purchase of manufactured physical inputs, like car companies that purchased window cranks and seat fabrics from outside the firm rather than making them inside. But in 2004, outsourcing took on a different meaning. It now referred to a specific segment in the growing international trade in services. This segment consists of arm's-length, or ... 'long-distance' purchase of services abroad, principally, but not necessarily, via electronic mediums such as the telephone, fax and the Internet.

The situation becomes more legally complex when a government entity starts to outsource its functions. Section 65 refers to the 'Minister' as the person responsible for making a decision, although s 496 makes it clear that the Minister can delegate his or her responsibilities to Departmental officers (and indeed, as *Carltona Ltd v Commissioner of Works*[28] points out, government departments simply could not function otherwise). However, the question remains as to whether the Minister can delegate his or her decision-making powers under the Act to a private individual or organisation?

---

26   Ian McCarthy and Angela Anagnostou, 'The Impact of Outsourcing on the Transaction Costs and Boundaries of Manufacturing', (2004) 88 *International Journal of Production Economics* 61 at 68.
27   Jagdish Bhagwati, Arvind Panagariya and TN Srinivasan, 'The Muddle over Outsourcing', (2004) 18 *Journal of Economic Perspectives* 93 at 93.
28   (1943) 2 All ER 560.

Complications can also ensue when only purely 'corporate' functions, and not decision-making functions, are outsourced. For example, assume that the personnel functions of the Department are outsourced to a specialist human resources firm. How does that impact on the Department's obligations to its employees under the *Public Service Act 1999*, or under occupational health and safety legislation?

Outsourcing of functions within the immigration portfolio have been and are an increasing feature of departmental processes.

Outsourcing of the Department's information technology and communication functions

Outsourcing of the Department's ICT functions seems to date back at least as far as 1997 – within a year of the election of the Howard government. The Department's 1996–97 Annual Report stated as follows under 'Sub-Program 6.3: Information Technology':[29]

> In August 1997, a long-term strategic alliance was reached with the Computer Science Corporation (Australia) (CSC) to provide more effective application development to support cost-effective delivery of departmental programs. The Alliance is an innovative approach aimed at achieving value for the Commonwealth, providing access to a larger pool of skills and facilitating skills transfers.
>
> Senior management in the Department and the CSC worked to refine management arrangements and align teams and cultures. Working groups, chaired by departmental and CSC staff, were established to develop management guidelines and procedures for the Alliance, taking into account policies and practices of both organisations.
>
> The Alliance was critical to accelerating solutions to IT and associated business problems. Under the auspices of the Alliance, processes have been developed to align IT services more closely to corporate business priorities.

It appears from the Annual Report that the 1997 'alliance' was not a full outsourcing agreement, but rather a contract by which CSC provided assistance with the Department's existing ICT infrastructure.

---

29   http://www.immi.gov.au/about/reports/annual/1997-98/html/sub6_3.htm, extracted 8 September 1994.

However, a full outsourcing agreement was not long in coming. The Department's submission to the Senate Standing Committee on Finance and Public Administration, made on 21 February 2001, gave this history of the outsourcing arrangements:

1. BACKGROUND

1.1 Formation

The Cluster 3 Agreement commenced on 1 July 1998 for a five-year term with options for two further two-year extensions. The telecommunications component of the Cluster 3 Agreement was for a three-year term ... The overall value of the contract over 5 years is $160m.

1.2 Composition

- The Cluster 3 group of Commonwealth agencies comprises:

- Department of Immigration and Multicultural Affairs (DIMA),

- Australian Electoral Commission (AEC),

- Department of Finance and Administration (for services to Electorate Offices) (DOFA–EOS),

- Australian Government Analytical Laboratories (AGAL),

- Australian Surveying and Land Information Group (AUSLIG),

- Ionospheric Prediction Service (IPS),

- IP Australia (IPAus).

1.3 Services covered

CSC is the outsourced IT services provider to the Cluster. These services comprise a number of 'lines of service' including:

- Mainframe services,

- Midrange services,

- Desktop, local area network and Helpdesk services,

- Voice and Data network services, and

- Other IT Infrastructure services as required.

The outsourcing arrangement does not include Applications Development.[30]

The submission went on to state that a Contract Management Office had been established, with a staff of six, and explained that the Department would attempt to bind CSC by contract to a set of performance standards, and could penalise CSC under the contract for failing to meet those standards.[31] In theory, like any contract, the agreement could be terminated if CSC failed to meet its obligations.

Most of the submissions received by the Committee were broadly supportive of outsourcing of IT functions, although there were some arguments against it. Dr Leslie Willcocks of the University of Warwick in the UK provided a submission claiming that projected cost savings from outsourcing were rarely, if ever, realised.[32] Dr Mohammed Shamsul Haque of the University of Singapore pointed to a more fundamental objection, namely that '[p]olitical representatives can exercise some direct supervision over public agencies', but 'they do not have effective control over private sector vendors or contractors', regardless of the terms of the contract.[33]

The new arrangements were not without problems. There were major IT shutdowns in the first 12 months of the CSC contract, including a three-day shutdown of all computer functions in February 1999.

The Australian National Audit Office (ANAO), at least initially, also seemed to take a dim view of the success of IT outsourcing. On 6 September 2000, the ANAO handed down a report entitled 'Implementation of Whole-of-Government Information Technology Infrastructure Consolidation and Outsourcing Initiative'.[34] The ANAO noted that they had only two years' worth of data to examine, but stated nevertheless as follows:

Implementation of the IT Initiative has involved significant effort on the part of OASITO[35] and participating agencies. It involves the tendering of an unprecedented volume of business to industry in a limited period of time. Shortfalls in expected industry capacity and participation have been a significant factor in the need to revise and extend the

---

30 http://www.aph.gov.au/Parliamentary_Business/Committees/Senate/Finance_and_Public_Administration/ Completed%20inquiries/1999-02/it_outsourcing/~/link.aspx?id=44A7067B7C974BF4AC884E86AE360CDC&_ z=z, extracted 8 September 2014.

31 Ibid.

32 Ibid.

33 Ibid.

34 http://www.anao.gov.au/~/media/Uploads/Documents/2000%2001_audit_report_9.pdf, extracted 8 September 2014.

35 Office of Asset Sales and IT Outsourcing.

implementation schedule. Implementation of the Initiative by OASITO is now expected to be completed in 2001, some two years after the initial date; and to cost nearly three times as much as was originally budgeted.[36]

Despite the perceived problems, CSC's contract was renewed in 2006[37] and they are still the Department's ICT provider.

The Electronic Travel Authority

The Electronic Travel Authority (ETA), established in 1999 could be thought of as a semi-outsourced visa application system. In short, the ETA was the forerunner of today's electronic visitor visas. In a report entitled 'The Electronic Travel Authority' and released on 22 July 1999, the ANAO described the purpose of the ETA as follows:[38]

> The growth in international travel in recent years and the projected number of visitors expected for the Olympics in Sydney in 2000 presented DIMA with the challenge of handling large numbers of bona fide travellers while preventing entry of undesirable persons. The internationalisation of the economy and the consequent need of business to move readily in and out of Australia reinforced the need to facilitate entry for short-term visitors whilst maintaining border security needs.

In other words, the ETA was intended to provide for streamlined visitor and short-term business visa processing for nationals of certain declared countries and territories (such as Taiwan). The ANAO described the ETA process, in summary, as follows. A person holding a passport of one of the declared countries could go to an authorised travel agent, who would input their passport details to a Departmental system, known as the Movement Alert List (MAL),[39] to which they had access. The system would either grant an ETA, or refer the applicant to the Department – the agent had no authority to *refuse* an application. An ETA did not need to be evidenced, although a successful applicant could obtain a printout of the grant record if they wished.[40]

Much of the ANAO report was technical in nature, and need not be repeated here. However, the ANAO's main concerns involved the IT security of the ETA system, and the reliability of MAL, and in particular who had the authority

---

36 Ibid at p 14.
37 http://www.csc.com/au/ds/51298/51386-csc_australia_highlights, extracted 8 September 2014.
38 http://www.anao.gov.au/uploads/documents/1999-00_Audit_Report_3.pdf at paragraph 1.3 (p 29), extracted 8 September 2014.
39 MAL lists individuals with known criminal records, or other people whose presence in Australia could be a security concern.
40 Supra n38 at p 31.

to make entries on that database. A follow-up audit was released in 2007,[41] which was generally supportive of continued electronic visa applications and processing, although there were still some concerns about the reliability of MAL.

The ETA is an interesting example of a partially outsourced system that has been brought back within the Department. Electronic visas are now no longer applied for through travel agents or airlines, but through the Department's website itself. This is not because of any ideological shift on the part of successive governments, but because home internet connections are now much more readily accessible than in 1999. It is also now possible to apply not only for visitor and short-term business visas online, but also for a range of employer-sponsored visas and, since February 2014, partner visas.

Medical information processing

Medical examination for visa applicants is a function that has always been at least partly outsourced. Applicants who undertook medicals overseas have, for many years, been required to attend an examination with a local accredited medical practitioner known as a 'panel doctor', as it is simply impossible for the Department to employ a doctor in every country in which an immigration medical might be required. The background to the panel doctor system was explained to some extent by the Department in its submission to the Joint Standing Committee on Migration's Inquiry into Immigration Treatment of Disability in November 2009. The Department stated as follows:[42]

> Until the mid-1990s the then Department of Health, Housing and Community Services (DHHCS) played a more active role in terms of immigration assessments, as well as providing advice in terms of the health requirement. For example, 'designated examiners', the predecessors to panel doctors, were selected with the help of a Regional Medical Director (RMD) from DHHCS or upon the advice of the National Office of DHHCS. In 1992, there were, for example, two RMDs (one in Paris and one in Bangkok) who provided advice to DHHSC and the Department of Immigration, Local Government and Ethnic Affairs (DILGEA) on policy and procedural issues. The main focus of RMDs was the selection and supervision of 'designated examiners'.

The panel doctor system is still in place. It should be noted that panel doctors may not *reject* an applicant based on health criteria – if the panel doctor cannot 'clear' the applicant for migration, a decision must be made by a Commonwealth

---

41   http://www.anao.gov.au/uploads/documents/2007-08_Audit_Report_2.pdf, extracted 8 September 2014.
42   http://www.aph.gov.au/Senate/committee/legcon_ctte/migration_2009/submissions.htm at p 7, extracted 9 September 2014.

Medical Officer (CMO). See Regulation 2.25A of the Regulations. It might also be noted that the Health Assessment Service (HAS), which employed CMOs engaged in providing immigration health opinions, was transferred from the Department of Health and Family Services to the Department of Immigration in July 1997.[43]

What *has* been outsourced in more recent times is the function of conducting immigration medical examinations in Australia. At one time, medical examinations were undertaken by CMOs, and then by the Australian Government Health Service (AGHS). Health Services Australia (HSA) is the successor organisation to the AGHS, and was incorporated on 17 June 1997 under the *Corporations Act 2001*. HSA is also subject to the *Commonwealth Authorities and Companies Act 1997*. Functions, assets and liabilities of the Australian Government Health Service were transferred to HSA on 1 July 1997 under the *Hearing Services and AGHS Reform Act 1997*.[44] Therefore the switch from AGHS to HSA was really an example of corporatisation rather than true outsourcing – HSA was made up of the same people as AGHS, but were now employed by a government-owned business rather than an autonomous government department.

HSA was successful in retaining its contracted role in 2006, when it was awarded another contract that would run from May 2007 until May 2012.[45] However, from 28 June 2014 the role has been truly outsourced, with Bupa Medical Visa Services Ltd taking over the role as the onshore medical assessment provider.[46]

The detention services contract

By far the most controversial aspect of outsourcing by the Department is the outsourcing of management of Immigration Detention Centres (IDCs). This chapter will focus on the management of IDCs in Australia, and not those in Nauru and Papua New Guinea (PNG), which are the subject of separate arrangements, and in theory at least are under the jurisdiction of those respective national governments.

---

43   Department of Immigration and Multicultural Affairs Annual Report 1997–98. http://www.immi.gov.au/about/reports/annual/1997-98/html/sub1_3.htm, extracted 9 September 2014.

44   See Health Services Australia Annual Report 2000–01 at p 45. https://www.medibankhealth.com.au/files/editor_upload/File/annual/HSA_AR_2000-01.pdf, extracted 9 September 2014. See also Australian National Audit Office, 'Administration of the Health Requirement of the *Migration Act 1958*', Audit Report no 37 2006–07 at p 44. http://www.anao.gov.au/uploads/documents/2006-07_Audit_report_37.pdf, extracted 9 September 2014.

45   Department of Immigration and Citizenship Annual Report 2006–07 at p 59. http://www.immi.gov.au/about/reports/annual/2006-07/_pdf/annual-report-2006-07-complete.pdf.

46   http://www.immi.gov.au/News/Pages/new-services-provider.aspx and http://immi.gov.au/allforms/health-requirements/medical-serice-provider-changes.htm, both extracted 9 September 2014.

History

Prior to 1997, the day-to-day operations of IDCs were managed by Australian Protective Services (APS), a government body that had the task of providing security on Commonwealth premises. Work on a competitive tender for management of IDCs started almost as soon as the Howard government was elected in March 1996. The initial contract for IDC management was awarded to Australian Correctional Services Pty Ltd (ACS) with effect from November 1997, and the services 'on the ground' were performed by ACS's wholly owned subsidiary Australian Correctional Management Pty Ltd (ACM).[47] The contract was for an initial period of three years but was extended as a result of negotiations with ACM, a tender process, negotiations with the preferred tenderer and the formal contract transition period. The Detention Services Contract with ACM ran for six years.[48]

When the contract was re-tendered in 2003, Group 4 Falck Global Solutions Pty Ltd (G4S) emerged as the successful tenderer. The new contract was signed on 27 August 2003 and came into effect on 1 September 2003. G4S subsequently changed its name to Global Solutions Limited (Australia) Pty Ltd (GSL).[49] The Department claimed that the contract required GSL to 'provide a custodial service for people held in immigration detention and take responsibility for the security, custody, health and welfare of detainees delivered into its custody'[50] by the Department.

Prior to 2006, Specialist services such as health care and psychological treatment to detainees were provided under subcontractual arrangements through GSL. These services were removed from the GSL contract in October 2006. At that time, International Health and Medical Services (IHMS) and Professional Support Services (PSS) were engaged directly by the Commonwealth to deliver health care and psychological services respectively at IDCs.[51]

Finally, in 2009, the contract was re-tendered again, and this time more than one contractor was appointed. Serco Australia Pty Ltd was chosen as the detention services provider for IDCs and transport and escort services, while

---

47   Senate Standing Committee on Legal and Constitutional Affairs, 'Administration and operation of the *Migration Act 1958*', 2 March 1996, paragraph 7.4. http://www.aph.gov.au/Parliamentary_Business/Committees/Senate/Legal_and_Constitutional_Affairs/Completed%20inquiries/2004-07/migration/report/c07, extracted 10 September 2014.

48   Joint Standing Committee on Migration, 'Immigration detention in Australia: Facilities, Services and Transparency', 18 August 2009, paragraphs 3.7 and 3.8. http://www.aph.gov.au/parliamentary_business/committees/house_of_representatives_committees?url=mig/detention/report3/chapter3.htm, extracted 10 September 2014.

49   Ibid at paragraph 3.22.

50   Senate Legal and Constitutional References Committee, *Administration and operation of the Migration Act 1958* (March 2006), Parliament of the Commonwealth of Australia at 214.

51   Supra n48 at paragraph 3.24.

GSL was retained as the service provider in immigration residential housing and transit centres.[52] IHMS was contracted for the provision of a range of onsite primary health care services, including registered nurses, general practitioners and mental health professionals, as well as referrals to external services. This was despite the fact that the Labor government had gone to the 2007 election promising to end the outsourcing of IDC management.[53] These contracts expire in December 2014, and the Commonwealth issued a request for tender for these functions on 3 April 2014.[54] Tendering closed on 28 May 2014,[55] and the successful tenderer or tenderers have yet to be announced.

Structure

The Detention Services Contract (DSC) is a complex document. There is no public version of the contract available online. However, while the details of the DSC have been amended in each request for tender, the basic structure has remained the same. In short, the Department specifies a significant number of performance indicators, known as Immigration Detention Standards (IDSs), that the contractor must meet, and failure to meet those standards permits the Commonwealth to penalise the contractor by withholding a proportion of the payments due under the contract. A feel for the kind of obligations imposed by the DSC can be obtained from the Federal Court decision in *S v Secretary, Department of Immigration and Multicultural and Indigenous Affairs*,[56] which set out certain parts of the Commonwealth–GSL contract (as it stood prior to 2006) as follows:

---

52 'Residential housing' refers to a system of immigration detention whereby non-citizens (usually in family groups) are detained in houses, where they can cook their own meals and so on, although still supervised by Detention Services Officers. Immigration Transit Centres (ITCs) are similarly low-security environments designed for persons who are not expected to remain in detention for long periods of time. A description of residential housing and ITCs can be found in the Full Federal Court decision of *SBEG v Secretary, Department of Immigration and Citizenship (No. 2)* (2012) FCA 569 at paragraphs 39–54.
53   Ibid at paragraph 3.45; *The Age*, 'Labor breaks detention promise', 4 June 1999, http://www.theage.com. au/national/labor-breaks-detention-promise-20090119-7ku5.html, extracted 10 September 2014.
54   https://www.tenders.gov.au/?event=public.atm.showClosed&ATMUUID=793E960D-97FC-7C08-3316F483460D6262, extracted 10 September 2014.
55   Ibid.
56   (2005) FCA 549 at paragraph 35.

2.2.1.1 General

2.2.1.1.1 Detainees are able to access timely and effective primary health care, including psychological/psychiatric services (including counselling): • in a culturally responsive framework; and • where a condition cannot be managed within the facility, by referral to external advice and/or treatment.	(a) No substantiated instance of a detainee not having access to health care of this nature.
2.2.1.1.2 In establishing the health care service, the Services Provider: • ensures services are delivered by qualified, registered and appropriately trained health care professionals; • develops and implements a health care plan for each facility; and • draws on the advice, knowledge and experience of a health advisory panel.	(a) The Department is provided with evidence on a monthly basis that the health care service is available and accessible. (b) No substantiated instance of health care staff not being qualified, registered and appropriately trained. (c) No substantiated instance of the centre health plans not being implemented, effective or reviewed periodically. (d) No substantiated instance of advice of the health advisory panel not being drawn on.

2.2.3.4 Self-harm

2.2.3.4.1 The potential for detainees to self-harm is minimised, to the fullest extent possible.	(a) Evidence is provided to the Department that strategies are in place and implemented to minimise the potential for detainees to self-harm.

2.2.3.4.2 Detainees who self-harm or attempt self-harm are provided with medical assistance as soon as possible and, post-incident, with ongoing appropriate treatment including but not limited to psychological/psychiatric assessment and counselling.	(a) No substantiated instance of any such detainee not being provided with appropriate and timely treatment.

2.2.3.5 Hunger strikes

2.2.3.5.1 Hunger-striking detainees are provided with health care consistent with the law and standard medical and psychiatric practices, and commensurate with their needs, including, where required, medical treatment.	(a) The Department is provided with evidence that a strategy is in place and implemented for identifying whether detainees are taking adequate sustenance. (b) No substantiated instance of a hunger-striking detainee not being provided with health care in an appropriate, lawful, and timely way.
2.2.3.5.2 Post-incident and as required, detainees who have been on a hunger-strike have access to ongoing medical treatment, including but not limited to psychological/psychiatric assessment and counselling.	(a) No substantiated instance of a detainee who has been on a hunger strike not having access to ongoing medical treatment.

The fact that the Department felt it necessary to specifically provide for performance indicators relating to 'self-harm' and 'hunger strikes' in immigration detention speaks volumes by itself. Other performance indicators relate to matters ranging from provision of education to children to dealing with large-scale disturbances.

Criticism from government bodies

There has been significant and sustained criticism of the outsourcing of IDC management in the Parliament, media and academia. The Palmer Report[57] into

---

57   https://www.immi.gov.au/media/publications/pdf/palmer-report.pdf, extracted 11 September 2014.

the unlawful detention of Cornelia Rau made some significant adverse comments on the DSC. Cornelia Rau was an Australian permanent resident of German nationality who suffered from schizophrenia. She disappeared from a Sydney treatment centre and was ultimately detected months later in immigration detention at the Baxter IDC, having first been detained in Brisbane women's prison (as an immigration detainee). She had claimed to be a German tourist who had overstayed her visa, and was detained for that reason. As she gave a variety of names to corrections, Departmental and GSL staff, German authorities were unable to identify her. Ms Rau spent a significant amount of time in detention in isolation and 'management' facilities, because of repeated 'inappropriate' behavior, such as flirting with male guards, no doubt brought on by her psychiatric condition.

A summary of the Palmer Report's findings on the DSC was included in the Senate Standing Committee on Legal and Constitutional Affairs report, 'Administration and Operation of the *Migration Act 1958*', dated 2 March 1996[58] as follows:

> [7.19] One of the main findings in the Palmer Report was that the current detention services contract with GSL is 'fundamentally flawed and does not permit delivery of the immigration detention policy outcomes expected by the Government, detainees and the Australian people'. Indeed, the 'unduly rigid, contract-driven approach has placed impediments in the way of achieving many of the required outcomes' Since the performance management regime between DIMIA and GSL 'does not manage performance or service quality or risks in any meaningful way', the entire system is 'ill-conceived' and could 'never deliver to the Commonwealth the information on performance, service quality and risk management' that DIMIA had hoped it would.
>
> [7.20] Despite acknowledging that '(m)any of the ingredients seem to be there', the Palmer Report found that: ... the arrangements fall short in delivering an immigration detention environment that is required by the policy and described in the contract. It is too simple to just blame GSL or DIMIA: the situation is both complex and demanding.
>
> [7.21] Moreover: DIMIA does not seem to recognise that the nature of the contract determines behaviour. It is not enough to demand in the contract that the service provider act in partnership: there must be a basis for a real partnership that respects the rights and responsibilities of both parties.

---

58   Supra n47 at paragraphs 7.19–7.21.

The ANAO has made similar adverse findings against outsourcing arrangements for detention. The Joint Standing Committee summed up the ANAO's investigations as follows:

> [7.25] In 2003–04, the ANAO undertook the first stage (Part A) of a performance audit on the management of detention centre contracts. The report of the Part A audit, Audit Report No. 54, 2003–04, *Management of the Detention Centre Contracts – Part A* (the Part A Report), was released on 18 June 2004. It focused on DIMIA's management of the detention centre contracts with GEO.

> [7.26] In 2005–06, the second part of the performance audit (Part B) was conducted. The Part B audit report, Audit Report No. 1, 2005–06, *Management of the Detention Centre Contracts – Part B* (the Part B Report), was released on 7 July 2005. The objective of this second audit was 'to assess DIMIA's management of detention services through the contract, including the transition period and the implementation of lessons learned from the previous contract'.

> [7.27] The Part B audit conducted by ANAO did not separately examine the outcomes of the detention program itself, nor the inherent quality of the services provided. This audit examined DIMIA's management of the contractual arrangements for the delivery of detention services and related performance measures.[59]

The ANAO's findings were summed up as follows:[60]

> [7.29] The ANAO concluded in both the Part A Report and the Part B Report that DIMIA had been unable to articulate its requirements clearly for the provision of detention services under the contracts with its service providers. While acknowledging that a crucial issue in contractual arrangements is striking an appropriate balance between the degree of purchaser oversight of service delivery and the operational flexibility afforded to contracted parties, both reports highlighted serious deficiencies with this approach and emphasised that it is contingent upon the purchaser being able to clearly specify outputs, including appropriate service quality measures.

> [7.30] For example, the ANAO found serious flaws with the IDS, the related performance measures and contract monitoring conducted by DIMIA. The ANAO also found that DIMIA had not sufficiently articulated the roles and responsibilities of third parties in the delivery

---

59   Ibid at paragraphs 7.25–7.27.
60   Ibid at paragraphs 7.29–7.33.

of detention services; nor had it clearly specified mechanisms for the ongoing monitoring of third party arrangements for compliance with intended outcomes.

[7.31] In the Part A Report, the ANAO found that DIMIA's management of the detention arrangements 'suffered from a lack of clearly identified and articulated requirements'. The ANAO also found that DIMIA's management of the program, together with the delivery of services under the contract and the prioritisation of tasks, 'focused on risks that materialised, rather than systematic risk analysis, evaluation, treatment and monitoring'.

[7.32] ... [T]he Part B Report found that the detention services contract does not adequately specify key responsibilities and expectations for the level and quality of services, either by DIMIA or GSL. In particular, 'clear and consistent definitions are not provided for health standards that are central to detainee welfare' ...

[7.33] Rather than DIMIA actively enforcing the performance of GSL, the monitoring of GSL's compliance with its contractual obligations is carried out by an 'exceptions-based' approach. The focus of this approach is the reporting of 'incidents'; DIMIA assumes that detention services are being delivered satisfactorily at each immigration detention centre unless the reporting of an 'incident' (or repeated 'incidents') reveals a problem.[61]

Criticism from academics

The outsourcing of IDC management has also attracted withering criticism in the academic sphere. Much of the criticism has focused on the allegation that officers who provide physical security at IDCs, along with the corporate entities themselves, see themselves as managing prisoners and not immigration detainees. Michael Welch has written as follows:[62]

The persistence of criminal subjectivity is deeply embedded in Serco's institutional operations. In 2012, investigative journalists posted on-line a copy of Serco's training manual. The 400 page illustrated induction manual appears to be geared toward a maximum-security prison population rather than a detention center for asylum seekers. Detailed instructions demonstrate to staff members how to 'hit', 'strike', 'kick',

---

61 A system that obviously gives the Detention Services Provider an incentive to downplay the seriousness of 'incidents', or not report them at all.

62 Michael Welch, 'Economic Man and Diffused Sovereignty: A Critique of Australia's Asylum Regime', (2014) 61 *Crime, Law and Social Change* 81 at 90.

'punch' and 'jab' their fingers into detainee limbs and 'pressure points' to render them motionless. The 'control and restraint' techniques suggest a commitment to skill and expertise. The manual recommends the use of 'pain' to defend, subdue and control asylum seekers through straight punches, palm heel strikes, side angle kicks, front thrust kicks and knee strikes. Guards are told to target specific 'pressure points' in the manner of riot squad police to squeeze nerves as 'a valuable subject control option.'

Others have been more critical of the government, questioning its motives in outsourcing detention management in the first place. Michael Grewcock has claimed that the entire purpose of outsourcing IDC management was to allow the government to blame someone else when things went wrong in IDCs:[63]

Australia had turned to private enterprise to run its detention centres in part to insulate the government from criticism when things went wrong. The removal of direct ministerial control over the daily operation of detention centres not only allows governments to distance themselves from practices that might be condemned as abusive but also has a deadening effect on public discussion.

A number of other authors have pointed out the same problem. For example, Lynda Crowley-Cyr, points out that by setting out the IDSs in a contract rather than legislation, the Commonwealth hopes to shift liability on to the services provider. A detainee cannot sue on the contract between the Commonwealth and a private entity, and the Commonwealth appears to have hoped that any liability in tort would fall on the 'on the ground' services provider rather than itself.[64]

S v Secretary, Department of Immigration and Multicultural and Indigenous Affairs

S[65] was the first case to make it clear that the Commonwealth is unable to completely contract out its duty of care to immigration detainees. S and M were detainees who had spent around five years in detention, culminating in being detained at the Baxter IDC at Port Augusta. Each sued the Secretary of the Department and the Commonwealth on the basis that 'the Commonwealth has breached its duty to ensure that reasonable care is taken of S and M in detention in relation to the treatment of their respective psychiatric conditions'.[66] Importantly, S and

---

63   Michael Grewcock, 'Border Crimes: Australia's War on Illicit Migrants', Sydney: Institute of Criminology at 6.
64   Lynda Crowley-Cyr, 'Contractualism, Exclusion and "Madness" in Australia's Outsourced Wastelands', (2005) 5 *Macquarie Law Journal* 81.
65   Supra n56.
66   Ibid at paragraph 5.

M did not seek to argue that individual medical practitioners were negligent, but instead argued that their psychiatric damage could be 'ascribed to systemic defects in the manner in which mental health services are provided in Baxter, which defects are responsible for the deterioration in the medical conditions of S and M with resultant increase in risk of self-harm or suicide'.[67]

Finn J in the Federal Court made his views clear right from the first paragraph of the judgment, when he stated that '[t]hese two applications are a predictable consequence of the decisions of the High Court in *Al Kateb v Godwin* (2004) 208 ALR 124 and *Behrooz v Secretary, Department of Immigration and Multicultural and Indigenous Affairs* (2004) 208 ALR 271'.[68] The central feature of the decision, however, was that the Commonwealth was unable to shift responsibility for the welfare of detainees, and liability in tort if that responsibility is breached, from itself to a private contractor. Finn J summed up at paragraphs 257–259 as follows:

> [257] In each of these matters the facts speak for themselves. It was the Commonwealth's duty to ensure that reasonable care was taken of S and M who, by reason of their detention, could not care for themselves. That duty required the Commonwealth to ensure that a level of medical care was made available to them which was reasonably designed to meet their health care needs including psychiatric care. They did not have to settle for a lesser standard of mental health care because they were in immigration detention.

> [258] Given the known prevalence of mental illness amongst the over 100 long-term detainees at Baxter, and the likely needs of S and M in particular at least since their participation in December 2004 roof top protest and hunger strike, the level of psychiatric service made available to S and M was, and remained, clearly inadequate. Where there was an obvious need to take steps to provide timely psychiatric service after the protest, none were taken. The Commonwealth ought to have appreciated that to rely upon the two monthly visits of [psychiatrist] Dr Frukacz resulted in inadequate service provision in the circumstances. This was no fault of Dr Frukacz. The Commonwealth neglected to take steps to inform itself of this inadequacy. Its conduct contributed to the progressive deterioration of the applicants over several months.

> [259] The Commonwealth entered into a complex outsourcing arrangement for the provision of mental health services which left it to contractors and subcontractors to determine the level of services to be supplied. The hallmarks of these arrangements were devolution

---

67 Ibid.
68 Supra n56.

and fragmentation of actual service provision. The service provision was so structured that there was a clear and obvious needs for regular and systematic auditing of the psychological and psychiatric services provided if the Commonwealth was to inform itself appropriately as to the adequacy and effectiveness of these services for which it bore responsibility. There has to date been no such audit. The Commonwealth has put into place monitoring and working procedures to deal essentially with the immediate and the ad hoc, though these did not avail S and M up to these hearings. The Commonwealth now foreshadows more by way of auditing and monitoring. Nonetheless, it is difficult to avoid the conclusion that the Commonwealth's own arrangement for outsourcing health care services itself requires review. Its aptness is open to real question.

It might also be noted that, armed with this decision, the parents of Shayan Badriae, a then 11-year-old boy who had suffered serious psychiatric injury in immigration detention, sued the Commonwealth for negligence in 2005. After around 40 days of a trial, during which the Commonwealth attempted to set up a 'wicked stepmother' defence (i.e. arguing that Shayan's injuries were the fault of his stepmother, based mainly on the fact that Shayan's younger half-sister, the natural child of Shayan's stepmother, presented no psychiatric injuries), the Commonwealth suddenly settled the matter for an undisclosed sum.[69]

It appears that the outsourcing of detention services fragments the responsibility for services to detainees, places them in the care of people who believe they are dealing with maximum security prisoners, encourages the provider to cover up its mistakes, and is not even effective in shifting liability in tort to the service provider. Its continuing existence can only be explained in terms of the blame-shifting motivation suggested by Grewcock and others.

---

69   For an account of the Badriae case, see Jacquie Everett, *The Bitter Shore*, Pan MacMillan Australia, 2008.

Chapter 3. Primary Decision-Making Procedures under the *Migration Act 1958* and *Migration Regulations 1994*

This chapter will examine decision-making procedures for primary decisions and the role of policy in the Department and the Tribunals. This chapter also includes two appendices, outlining two significant new pieces of legislation – the *Migration Amendment (Character and General Visa Cancellation) Act 2014* and the *Migration and Maritime Powers Legislation Amendment (Resolving the Asylum Legacy Caseload) Act 2014*.

Part 1 – Decision-making at the primary level

Visa application procedures

The reasons *why* the *Migration Act 1958* was amended with effect from 1 September 1994 to set out a detailed 'code of procedure' rather than relying on the common law principles of natural justice were examined in Chapter 2. The 'code of procedure' for making primary (Departmental) decisions[1] can be found in Part 2, Division 3, Subdivision AB of the Act. Subdivision AB consists of ss 51–64 of the Act, which are entitled as follows:

51A. Exhaustive statement of natural justice hearing rule

52. Communication with Minister

54. Minister must have regard to all information in application

55. Further information may be given

56. Further information may be sought

57. Certain information must be given to applicant

58. Invitation to give further information or comments

59. Interviews

---

1   The Act usually refers to the 'Minister' as the decision maker. Subsection 496(1) provides that '[t]he Minister may, by writing signed by him or her, delegate to a person any of the Minister's powers under this Act'. In practice, unless the Act specifically refers powers to the Minister personally, those powers are delegated to Departmental officers.

60. Medical examination

61. Prescribed periods

62. Failure to receive information not require action

63. When decision about visa may be made

64. Notice that visa application charge is payable

Until 2014, Subdivision AB applied only to visa applications made within Australia at the primary level. Different provisions of the Act apply to matters such as cancellations (see, for example, Subdivisions C and D of Part 2, Division 3 of the Act) and requests for Ministerial intervention.

Some of these provisions can be dealt with quite quickly.

- Section 52 requires that an applicant for a visa communicate with the Minister (through his or her delegates in the Department) in writing.

- Section 54 requires the Minister to consider all information that is actually before him or her in relation to the visa application when making the decision. Importantly, when read with s 55, it becomes clear that this includes information that was received after a time limit imposed by the Minister, but which the Minister has in fact received prior to making the decision.

- Subsection 55(1) permits an applicant to send further information to the Minister, prior to a decision being made, as he or she sees fit. Subsection 55(2) provides that the Minister is not required to delay making a decision past any deadline given to the applicant simply because the applicant may intend to provide further information.

- Section 56 allows the Minister to seek further information from the applicant. If the information is received prior to a decision being made, the Minister must consider it.

- Section 59 provides that an applicant must make 'every reasonable effort to be available for, and attend, an interview', and that the Minister does not have to request a face-to-face interview – a phone interview, for example, may suffice.

- Section 60 permits the Minister to require an applicant to attend a medical examination.

- Section 62 provides that if the Minister invites an applicant to provide information and it is not received by the deadline, he or she does not have to make any additional effort to obtain the information.

- Section 64 deals with notices of demand for a second stage of the Visa Application Charge (VAC).

Section 57

Section 57 of the Act is the 'adverse information' provision, and amounts to a codification of the principle expressed in *Kioa v West*.[2] That is, s 57 requires the Department to disclose to the applicant any and all information that it holds that could be a reason to refuse the application, and allow the applicant to comment on it.

The kind of information that must be disclosed is set out in s 57(1), which provides as follows:

> In this section, **relevant information** means information (other than non-disclosable information) that the Minister considers:

> (a) would be the reason, or a part of the reason, for refusing to grant a visa; and

> (b) is specifically about the applicant or another person and is not just about a class of persons of which the applicant or other person is a member; and

> (c) was not given by the applicant for the purpose of the application.

That is, the information must be adverse, be specific to the applicant in some way, and not information provided by the applicant themselves. The usual kind of information that is covered by s 57(1)(b) is information that relates to the conditions in a country, which would be most frequently relevant in an application for a protection visa.[3]

Application of Section 57

Until 2014, s 57(3) placed an important limitation on the application of s 57 to visa applications. This subsection provided as follows:

> This section does not apply in relation to an application for a visa unless:

> (a) the visa can be granted when the applicant is in the migration zone; and

> (b) this Act provides, under Part 5 or 7, for an application for review of a decision to refuse to grant the visa.

That is, s 57 did not apply to a visa application unless the application could be granted while the applicant is in Australia, and was subject to merits review in the case of refusal.

---

2   (1985) 159 CLR 550.

3   See for example *Wu v Minister for Immigration and Multicultural and Indigenous Affairs* (2003) FCA 1249 at paragraphs 22 and 23.

Subsection 57(3) was raised squarely in the High Court case of *Saeed v Minister for Immigration and Citizenship*.[4] *Saeed* concerned an application for a subclass 175 (Skilled – Independent) visa outside Australia. As there was no Australian sponsor involved in the application, Ms Saeed was not entitled to merits review of any refusal decision, meaning that s 57(3) had the effect that s 57 did not apply to her.

Ms Saeed's visa was refused on the basis that some of her employer references were regarded by the Department as fraudulent.[5] This information was never put to Ms Saeed, and the first time she heard of the Department's suspicions was in the refusal letter. She retained counsel in Australia and applied for review in the High Court, in its original jurisdiction under s 75(v) of the Constitution. The Minister argued that s 57(3) meant that s 57 did not apply to Ms Saeed, and that the Department therefore had no obligation to inform her of its suspicions prior to the decision. The High Court agreed that s 57 did not apply, but found that the common law rules of natural justice *did* apply. The 'exclusive statement' provision in s 51A of the Act did not assist the Minister, because Ms Saeed was not covered by s 57 at all. Therefore, the Department should have followed the *Kioa* principle, and informed her of the adverse information and given her the opportunity to comment prior to making a decision.

In response, Parliament passed the *Migration Legislation Amendment Bill (No. 1) 2014*. Schedule 6, Part 1, Clause 2 of the Bill repealed s 57(3). The result is that the *Saeed* ruling has been reversed, and both onshore and offshore applications are now subject to s 57.

Non-disclosable information

Another potentially controversial element of s 57 is the provision that 'non-disclosable information' is not to be disclosed. This term is defined in s 5(1) of the Act as follows:

> 'non-disclosable information' means information or matter:
>
> (a) whose disclosure would, in the Minister's opinion, be contrary to the national interest because it would:
>
>> (i) prejudice the security, defence or international relations of Australia; or
>>
>> (ii) involve the disclosure of deliberations or decisions of the Cabinet or of a committee of the Cabinet; or

---

4   (2010) HCA 23.
5   'Bogus documents' in the wording of s 103 of the Act.

(b) whose disclosure would, in the Minister's opinion, be contrary to the public interest for a reason which could form the basis of a claim by the Crown in right of the Commonwealth in judicial proceedings; or

(c) whose disclosure would found an action by a person, other than the Commonwealth, for breach of confidence;

and includes any document containing, or any record of, such information or matter.

It is a recognised principle of administrative law that a decision maker does not have to disclose the exact document containing adverse information, or every single detail of that information. It is sufficient that the 'substance' or 'gist' of the information is disclosed to the applicant.[6] In some cases it could be positively dangerous to disclose, for example, the name of a complainant to an applicant. However, the obligation to provide the substance of adverse information is still strong. For example, in *VEAL v Minister for Immigration and Multicultural and Indigenous Affairs*[7] the High Court found that the applicant should have been given the substance of an anonymous 'dob-in' letter, even when the MRT had expressly disavowed any reliance on it.

Of all the provisions of the definition of 'non-disclosable information', probably only subparagraph (a)(ii) is clear and unambiguous. Terms such as 'security interests' of Australia obviously refer to something of exceptional magnitude, but the exact scope of subparagraph (a)(i) has yet to be tested by the courts.[8]

Paragraph (b) of the definition appears to have been litigated very rarely, if at all. The Department's LEGEND database states simply that information is non-disclosable if disclosure would 'in the Minister's opinion, be contrary to the public interest', which does not appear to be an accurate summary of paragraph (b). It is likely that we will have to wait for further elucidation from the courts.

The scope of the equitable duty for breach of confidence, referred to in paragraph (c) of the definition, was summed up by Gummow J in *Corrs Pavey Whiting and Byrne v Collector of Customs (Vic)*[9] as follows:

It is now settled that in order to make out a case for protection in equity of allegedly confidential information, a plaintiff must satisfy certain criteria. The plaintiff: (i) must be able to identify with specificity, and not merely in global terms, that which is said to be the information in

---

6 See for example *Muin v Refugee Review Tribunal* (2002) 190 ALR 601.

7 (2005) 222 ALR 411.

8 It is notable that in *Minister for Immigration and Multicultural Affairs v Jia* (2001) 205 CLR 507 that the High Court gave the Minister exceptional latitude in determining what was in the 'national interest', almost to the point of finding the issue to be non-justiciable.

9 (1987) 14 FCR 434, cited with approval in *VEAL*, supra n7.

question; and must also be able to show that (ii) the information has the necessary quality of confidentiality (and is not, for example, common or public knowledge); (iii) the information was received by the defendant in such circumstances as to import an obligation of confidence; and (iv) there is actual or threatened misuse of that information: *Saltman Engineering Co Ltd v Campbell Engineering Co* (1948) 65 RPC 203 at 215; *Commonwealth v John Fairfax and Sons Ltd* (1980) 147 CLR 39 at 50-51; *O'Brien v Komesaroff* (1982) 150 CLR 310 at 326-328. It may also be necessary, as Megarry J thought probably was the case (*Coco v A N Clark (Engineers) Ltd* [1969] RPC 41 at 48), and as Mason J (as he then was) accepted in the Fairfax decision was the case (at least for confidences reposed within government), that unauthorised use would be to the detriment of the plaintiff.

In other words, it appears that to found an action for breach of confidence, the information must be specific, have a 'quality of confidentiality' (meaning that by its nature it should not be readily disclosed), given in a confidential manner (e.g. a private letter rather than a Facebook post), and there is some kind of threat to the confidentiality of the information.[10] In particular, it will be a rare situation where the identity of an informant is not 'non-discloseable information'.[11]

Sections 58 and 61

Section 58 of the Act permits the Minister to ask an applicant for further information under s 56, or to make comment on adverse information under s 57, and impose time limits on responding. The Minister may require the applicant to respond by writing, phone or at a face-to-face interview. The time period for responding must be specified in the invitation. Section 58 also permits regulations to be made prescribing the time in which an applicant must respond to an invitation, and these prescribed periods are set out in Regulation 2.15 of the *Migration Regulations 1994*.

Section 61 deals with other prescribed time periods, relating to matters such as time limits in which applications for visas of specified classes must be made. No regulations appear to have been made under this section.

Section 63

This section is entitled 'When decision about visa may be made'. Subsection 63(2) relates to invitations to give information under s 56, and s 63(3) relates to invitations to comment on adverse information under s 57. Both subsections

---

10   A somewhat more generous (to the government) interpretation has been given by the High Court in *MIAC v Kumar* (2009) HCA 10; 238 CLR 448.

11   *Minister for Immigration and Citizenship v Kumar* (2009) 238 CLR 448.

provide that the Minister may not proceed to a decision after giving such an invitation until the information is received, the applicant informs the Minister that he or she does not have or will not provide the information, or the deadline has passed. Subsection 63(4) deals with requests for the payment of a second stage VAC, and provides that a decision must not be made until the VAC is paid, the applicant informs the Minister that he or she cannot or will not pay it, or the deadline imposed for payment passes.

Decision-making and notification

Section 65 of the Act provides, in effect, if the Minister is satisfied that if an applicant meets all criteria for the grant of a visa it must be granted, and otherwise must be refused. The Minister's satisfaction depends on the submission of evidence by an applicant that they do in fact meet all legislative criteria for the grant of a visa.

Section 66 deals with notification of decisions. Subsection 66(1) refers to notification of decisions by prescribed means, a provision which has been broadly superseded by the insertion into the Act of ss 494A–494D,[12] which are now the main provisions dealing with notification of primary decisions. The most important of these provisions are ss 494B and 494C, the former of which specifies the means by which the Minister can give a document to a person, and the latter providing details of when a document is taken to have been received by the recipient. For example, s 494B(4) provides that the Minister may send a document (including a decision record) to a person by means of pre-paid post to the last address *provided* by the person for receiving documents, provided that the document is sent within three working days of the date of the document. Subsection 494C(4) then provides as follows:

> If the Minister gives a document to a person by the method in subsection 494B(4) (which involves dispatching the document by prepaid post or by other prepaid means), the person is taken to have received the document:
>
> (a) if the document was dispatched from a place in Australia to an address in Australia – 7 working days (in the place of that address) after the date of the document; or
>
> (b) in any other case – 21 days after the date of the document.

The purpose of deemed notification provisions is obvious – to ensure that an applicant cannot avoid service of an adverse decision, and therefore avoid

---

12   By means of the *Migration Legislation Amendment (Electronic Transactions and Methods of Notification) Act 2001*.

compliance action. Note that applications for review must be made within a specified time after notification of a decision,[13] which means that, although failure to notify an applicant of a decision does not invalidate the decision itself,[14] it will have the effect that an applicant's period in which to apply for review will not start to run until he or she has been correctly notified. In some cases, large numbers of notifications have been found to be defective, meaning that some applicants have been able to remain in Australia for years before having to lodge an application for merits review.[15]

Finally, s 66(2) imposes a duty on the Minister to provide reasons for a refusal decision in relation to applications that are subject to merits review. This subsection provides as follows:

> Notification of a decision to refuse an application for a visa must:
>
> (a) if the grant of the visa was refused because the applicant did not satisfy a criterion for the visa – specify that criterion; and
>
> (b) if the grant of the visa was refused because a provision of this Act or the regulations prevented the grant of the visa – specify that provision; and
>
> (c) unless subsection (3) applies to the application – give written reasons (other than nondisclosable information) why the criterion was not satisfied or the provision prevented the grant of the visa; and
>
> (a) if the applicant has a right to have the decision reviewed under Part 5 or 7 or section 500 – state:
>
> (i) that the decision can be reviewed; and
>
> (ii) the time in which the application for review may be made; and
>
> (iii) who can apply for the review; and
>
> (iv) where the application for review can be made.

Subsection 66(3) has the effect that if a visa cannot be granted onshore, and cannot be reviewed by the MRT or RRT, reasons for a refusal need not be provided.

Subsection 66(2) has, perhaps surprisingly, not been the subject of litigation. However, the 'reason for reasons' is that a person affected by an adverse decision

---

13   For the Migration Review Tribunal, see s 347(1)(a) of the Act and Regulation 4.10 of the Regulations.
14   See s 66(4) of the Act.
15   See as one example *Srey v Minister for Immigration and Multicultural and Indigenous Affairs* (2003) FCA 1292.

will not know whether there are grounds for review without reasons for that decision. In *Beale v Government Insurance Office of NSW,* Meagher JA stated that:[16]

> Perhaps the primary reason for an obligation on courts to provide reasons is the fact that a party seeking an appeal may generally only appeal where the trial judge has made an error of law. The absence of reasons or insufficient reasons may not allow an appeal court to determine whether the trial judge's verdict was or was not based on an error of law or an appealable error.

That is, the Minister's reasons must be adequate for the purpose of deciding whether to pursue review of that decision.

Cancellation procedures

Cancellation procedures are distributed throughout the Act, and differ according to the cancellation power being employed. The examination of cancellation procedures will therefore be necessarily brief, but it should be noted that:

- Since the repeal of s 20 of the *Education Services (Overseas Students) Act 2000* in 2013 there is now nothing that can trigger an automatic cancellation of a student visa under Subdivision GB of the Act. An essential prerequisite for such cancellation was that an s 20 ESOS Act notice was issued to a student – see s 137J of the Act.

- Nearly all cancellations are discretionary, meaning that even if the grounds for cancellation exist, the Minister does not *have* to cancel the visa in most cases. However, s 116(3) of the Act provides that '[i]f the Minister may cancel a visa under subsection (1), the Minister must do so if there exist prescribed circumstances in which a visa must be cancelled', and these circumstances are set out in subregulation 2.43(2) of the Regulations. However, even mandatory cancellations require the Minister to make a decision – they are not *automatic.*

- Finally, most cancellation powers cannot be exercised until the Minister gives the visa holder an opportunity to comment on whether a cancellation ground exists, or why, if a ground *does* exist, the visa should not be cancelled regardless. However, there are a number of 'cancel first and ask questions later' provisions in the Act, these being ss 128, 133A(3), 133C(3), 134A–134B and 501(3).

---

16   (1997) 48 NSWLR 430 at 441, cited with approval by *SZKLO v Minister for Immigration and Citizenship* (2008) FCA 735 at paragraph 19. The 'reason for reasons' provided by these cases are similar to those provided by the Supreme Court of Canada in *Newfoundland and Labrador Nurses' Union v Newfoundland and Labrador (Treasury Board)* (2011) SCC 62.

The cancellation powers in s 501 of the Act will be discussed in the part of this chapter dealing with that section.

Subdivision C

The key provision of Subdivision C of Part 2 Division 3 of the Act is s 109, which provides for cancellation of a visa if any of the grounds of 'non-compliance' in ss 101–105 are made out. In short, ss 101–105 of the Act apply to provision of incorrect information to the Department, whether in a visa application (s 101), a passenger card (s 102) or by means of a 'bogus document' (s 103). A non-citizen is also required to give particulars of changes of circumstances (s 104) or previously provided incorrect information to the Department (s 105). Failure to comply with these requirements permits the Minister to give a Notice of Intention to Consider Cancellation (NOICC) to the visa holder. The visa holder may then dispute that there are grounds for cancellation, or admit non-compliance and argue that the visa should not be cancelled in any event (ss 107 and 108). The NOICC must be specific in setting out claimed non-compliance – *Zhong v Minister for Immigration and Citizenship*[17] found that '[i]t is not enough to generically claim that the visa holder has breached a section of the Act without giving particulars of the facts and circumstances which are said to give rise to the possible breach of the particular section'. The Minister may then decide whether to cancel the visa under s 109.

Section 109 is unique amongst the general cancellation powers in that there are *legislative* criteria that the Minister must consider before cancelling a visa under that section. Regulation 2.41 lists a large number of factors that the Minister must consider, some of the more important being the nature of the correct information or genuine document (paragraphs 2.41(a) and (b)), the circumstances in which the non-compliance occurred (paragraph 2.41(d)), and the immigration history and general character of the visa holder (paragraphs 2.41(f)–(j)). It is important to note that the Minister must consider *all* of the factors in Regulation 2.41 before making a cancellation decision.[18]

Subdivisions D and E

Subdivision D of Part 2 Division 3 of the Act is, rather unimaginatively, entitled 'Visas may be cancelled on certain grounds'. The key provision is s 116(1), which provides as follows:

> Subject to subsections (2) and (3), the Minister may cancel a visa if he or she is satisfied that:

---

17   (2008) FCA 507 at paragraph 80.
18   *Minister for Immigration and Citizenship v Khadgi* (2010) FCAFC 145.

(a) the decision to grant the visa was based, wholly or partly, on a particular fact or circumstance that is no longer the case or that no longer exists; or

(aa) the decision to grant the visa was based, wholly or partly, on the existence of a particular fact or circumstance, and that fact or circumstance did not exist; or

(b) its holder has not complied with a condition of the visa; or

(c) another person required to comply with a condition of the visa has not complied with that condition; or

(d) if its holder has not entered Australia or has so entered but has not been immigration cleared – it would be liable to be cancelled under Subdivision C (incorrect information given by holder) if its holder had so entered and been immigration cleared; or

(e) the presence of its holder in Australia is or may be, or would or might be, a risk to:

    (i) the health, safety or good order of the Australian community or a segment of the Australian community; or

    (ii) the health or safety of an individual or individuals; or

(f) the visa should not have been granted because the application for it or its grant was in contravention of this Act or of another law of the Commonwealth; or

(fa) in the case of a student visa:

    (i) its holder is not, or is likely not to be, a genuine student; or

    (ii) its holder has engaged, is engaging, or is likely to engage, while in Australia, in conduct (including omissions) not contemplated by the visa; or

(g) a prescribed ground for cancelling a visa applies to the holder.

The 'prescribed grounds' are set out in subregulation 2.43(1) and are too numerous to list here. Subsection 116(3) provides that '[i]f the Minister may cancel a visa under subsection (1), the Minister must do so if there exist prescribed circumstances in which a visa must be cancelled', and these mandatory cancellation grounds are set out in subregulation 2.43(2) as follows:

• If the visa held by the non-citizen in question is a subclass 050, 070, 200, 201, 202, 203, 204, 449, 785, 786 or 866, the visa must be cancelled if 'the holder of the visa is a person whose presence in Australia may be directly or indirectly associated with the proliferation of weapons of mass destruction'.

- If the non-citizen holds any other visa, the mandatory cancellation grounds are:

  o the holder of the visa is a person whose presence in Australia may be directly or indirectly associated with the proliferation of weapons of mass destruction or is otherwise contrary to Australia's foreign policy interests; or

  o the person has been 'declared' under the *Autonomous Sanctions Regulations 2011*; or

  o the person that has been assessed by the Australian Security Intelligence Organisation to be directly or indirectly a risk to security.

It can therefore been seen that cancellation is only mandatory in very particular and serious circumstances. Note, however, that s 116(3) cancellation is not *automatic*, meaning that the processes described below must still be followed. All other grounds under s 116 are discretionary.

The process for cancelling a visa under s 116 is set out in Subdivision E of the Act, and is very similar to s 109. A NOICC must first be served on the visa holder, as required by s 119, detailing the grounds under which cancellation is being considered, and inviting the visa holder to respond. The visa holder may argue either that the alleged ground does not exist, or concede that the alleged ground exists but argue that the visa should not be cancelled regardless (the latter of which will be pointless if mandatory cancellation under s 116(3) is being considered). The Minister may not make a decision until the visa holder responds to the notice, informs the Minister that he or she does not intend to respond, or the time given for responding expires (s 124). The Minister must then notify the visa holder of his or her decision in accordance with s 127 and Regulation 2.55.

It is important to note that a permanent visa may not be cancelled under s 116 if the holder is in Australia, and was immigration cleared on his or her last entry — see s 117(2) of the Act. However, a permanent visa holder who is not in Australia can have their visa cancelled under s 128.

Subdivision F

Subdivision F of Division 3, Part 2 of the Act is linked to Subdivision D, but the processes for cancellation are substantially different. Section 128 of the Act provides as follows:

If:

(a) the Minister is satisfied that:

  (i) there is a ground for cancelling a visa under section 116; and

  (ii) it is appropriate to cancel in accordance with this Subdivision; and

(b) the non-citizen is outside Australia;

the Minister may, without notice to the holder of the visa, cancel the visa.

That is, a visa may be cancelled under s 128 without prior notice to a visa holder. The only conditions on such cancellation are that the visa holder falls within a ground specified in s 116, that he or she is outside Australia, and that s 128 cancellation is 'appropriate'. Exactly what 'appropriate' is intended to mean in unclear, but in *Singh v Minister for Immigration*,[19] the Federal Magistrates Court (as it was then known) found that cancellation under s 128 was not appropriate because the Department could, if it had permitted the visa holders to re-enter Australia, have begun cancellation proceedings under s 109. That is, cancellation under s 128 will not be appropriate if another ground of cancellation, which requires prior notice in the form of a NOICC, is available.[20]

While a visa can be cancelled under s 128 without prior notice to the former holder, the cancellation can be revoked at the request of the applicant. Section 129 requires the Minister to notify the former visa holder of an s 128 cancellation, and as part of that notice, invite the former holder to argue that there were no grounds for the cancellation, or that the Minister should not have cancelled the visa regardless. If a response is received within a prescribed time, the Minister must then make a decision as to whether to revoke the cancellation (s 131). If the cancellation is revoked, the former holder is taken to have been granted that visa on the date of revocation (s 133(1)). In other words, revocation is not retrospective in effect.

The 'prescribed periods' for the purposes of s 129 are set out in Regulation 2.46, a provision that is worth setting out in full:

(a) if the former holder of the visa is outside Australia when he or she is given a notice of the cancellation – 28 days;

---

19 (2006) FMCA 1163.
20 Note, however, a very different approach in *Hu v MIMIA* (2004) FCAFC 63, in which it was found that it is up to the applicant to demonstrate that the decision maker failed to consider a relevant matter, or took an irrelevant factor into account, in deciding whether to use the s 128 power as opposed to s 116, for example.

    (b) if he or she is in Australia when he or she is given notice of the cancellation:

        (i) if he or she wishes the cancellation to be reconsidered while he or she is in Australia – 5 minutes; or

        (ii) if he or she wishes the cancellation to be reconsidered while he or she is outside Australia, and he or she departs Australia as soon as possible after being given a notice of the cancellation – 28 days;

    beginning when the former holder of the visa is given a notice of the cancellation.

Paragraph 2.46(b)(i), which sees the former visa holder given a grand total of five minutes to make a case for revocation of their cancellation, applies as follows. Assume that a visa holder has their visa cancelled under s 128 while outside Australia. They then attempt to return to Australia prior to receiving this notice. This means that the first that the former holder will hear of the cancellation is when they are refused immigration clearance on the basis that they do not hold a visa that is in effect. If the former holder wishes to make a case for revocation while remaining in Australia, they have only five minutes to do so. The obvious intention of this provision is to encourage (or even force) the former holder to depart Australia and seek to have the cancellation revoked from overseas.[21]

Section 140

Section 140 deals with 'consequential cancellation' – that is, cancellation of a visa held by person B where person A's visa has already been cancelled, and person B relied on person A in some way for the grant of their visa. Section 140 provides as follows:

    (1) If a person's visa is cancelled under ss 109 (incorrect information), 116 (general power to cancel), 128 (when holder outside Australia), 133A (Minister's personal powers to cancel visas on section 109 grounds), 133C (Minister's personal powers to cancel visas on section 116 grounds) or 137J (student visas), a visa held by another person because of being a member of the family unit of the person is also cancelled.

---

21   This scenario is much less likely today given that the Department's international computer network would prevent most people getting on a plane to Australia if their visa had been cancelled.

(2) If:

    (a) A person's visa is cancelled under ss 109 (incorrect information), 116 (general power to cancel), 128 (when holder outside Australia), 133A (Minister's personal powers to cancel visas on section 109 grounds), 133C (Minister's personal powers to cancel visas on section 116 grounds) or 137J (student visas); and

    (b) another person to whom subsection (1) does not apply holds a visa only because the person whose visa is cancelled held a visa;

the Minister may, without notice to the other person, cancel the other person's visa.

(3) If:

    (a) a person's visa (the **cancelled visa**) is cancelled under any provision of this Act; and

    (b) person is a parent of another person; and

    (c) the other person holds a particular visa (the **other visa**), that was granted under s 78 (child born in Australia) because the parent held the cancelled visa;

    (d) the other visa is also cancelled.

(4) If:

    (a) a visa is cancelled under subsection (1), (2) or (3) because another visa is cancelled; and

    (b) the cancellation of the other visa is revoked under s 131, 133F, 137L or 137N;

the cancellation under subsection (1), (2) or (3) is revoked.

There are a number of significant provisions of s 140:

- Subsections 140(1) and (2) apply only to cancellations under the specifically mentioned provisions and not (for example) ss 134, 134Q or 501.
- Cancellation under s 140(1) is automatic. A person falls within s 140(1) if they are a secondary visa holder (a member of the primary visa holder's family unit), and the primary visa holder's visa has been cancelled.
- Cancellation under s 140(2) is discretionary, but no prior notice of the cancellation is required. A common situation of a person falling within s 140(2) is if they were granted a partner visa on the basis of being the spouse

or de facto partner of an Australian permanent resident, and that permanent resident's visa has been cancelled.

- Subsection 140(3) applies only to visas granted to children born in Australia, and is also automatic. Section 78 of the Act provides that a child born in Australia will be taken to hold the same visa as his or her parent(s).

- Subsection 140(4) applies to revocation of cancellations, and is also automatic. In any situation where the primary person successfully seeks revocation of their cancellation, the cancellation of any other persons who were cancelled under ss 140(1)–(3) is also revoked.

It is also worth noting that if a cancellation decision is set aside by a tribunal or a court, the cancellation decision is a legal nullity, the result being that the cancellation is taken never to have occurred.[22] This means that if a primary person successfully seeks review of their cancellation decision, anyone whose visa was cancelled under s 140 as a result of that cancellation will also have their visa restored, as this means that there was no primary cancellation decision on which the s 140 delegate could have based their decision. Further, a person whose visa is cancelled under s 140(2) can make an application for review independent of the primary person under s 338(3) of the Act.[23]

Specialised cancellation powers

There are a number of cancellation powers in the Act that apply only to certain kinds of visas.

Cancellation of business visas – Section 134

Section 134 of the Act applies specifically to 'business visas', a term that is defined in s 5(1) of the Act and Regulation 2.50 of the Regulations. Subsection 134(1) provides that the Minister may cancel a business visa if the visa holder has not obtained a substantial ownership interest in an Australian business, is not contributing to the daily management of the business, or does not intend to continue carry out these tasks. Subsection 134(2) then specifies that the Minister must *not* cancel a business visa if the applicant has made a 'genuine effort' to carry out these roles and responsibilities.

Similarly to Regulation 2.41, s 134(3) sets out a number of factors that the Minister must take into account in deciding whether a person has made a 'genuine effort' to meet the requirements of a business visa. These include such matters as business plans drawn up by the visa holder, capital transferred into

---

22   See for example *Ruddock v Taylor* (2005) 221 ALR 32.
23   See for example *Re Liu, Yi Meng* (2004) MRTA 1393. In fact such a person *must* make an independent application, since Regulation 4.12 does not allow combined applications for review of cancellation decisions.

Australia, whether there are any Australian partners in the business, and so on. Subsection 134(4) is a consequential cancellation provision similar to s 140(1) of the Act (although s 134(4) is mandatory and not automatic), but s 134(5) prohibits consequential cancellation if such cancellation would result in 'extreme hardship' to such a person. Further, under s 134(9), a business visa can only be cancelled under s 134 if a notice of intention to cancel was given to the holder under s 135 within three years of the date of an onshore grant, or within three years of the visa holder's entry to Australia in the case of an offshore grant.

Section 135 requires the Minister to notify the visa holder of intended cancellation by means of a NOICC, and must consider any representations made by the visa holder. Uniquely, under s 135(4), if the time specified in the notice ends more than three years after the date of onshore grant or the visa holder's entry to Australia, the Minister has only 90 days after receiving representations, being informed that no representations will be made, or the time limit to respond passing, to make a cancellation decision – if he or she fails to do so, the visa must not be cancelled. It is significant that cancellation under s 134 (and s 137Q, see below) is not covered by an 'exhaustive statement of the natural justice hearing rule' and therefore the common law rules of natural justice apply.

Cancellation of regional sponsored employment visas – Section 137Q

Section 137Q of the Act deals specifically with 'Regional Sponsored Employment Visas', which are defined in s 137Q(3) and in Regulation 2.50AA. Subsections 137Q(1) and (2) provide as follows:

Employment does not commence

(1) The Minister may cancel a regional sponsored employment visa held by a person if:

    (a) the Minister is satisfied that the person has not commenced the employment referred to in the relevant employer nomination within the period prescribed by the regulations; and

    (b) the person does not satisfy the Minister that he or she has made a genuine effort to commence that employment within that period.

Employment terminates within 2 years

(2) The Minister may cancel a regional sponsored employment visa held by a person if:

    (a) the Minister is satisfied that:

(i)   the person commenced the employment referred to in the relevant employer nomination (whether or not within the period prescribed by the regulations); and

(ii)   the employment terminated within the period (the **required employment period**) of 2 years starting on the day the person commenced that employment; and

(b)   person does not satisfy the Minister that he or she has made a genuine effort to be engaged in that employment for the required employment period.

Again, it is a key issue whether the person made a 'genuine effort' to commence or remain in the relevant regional employment. There is no equivalent of s 134(3) in s 137Q, and this phrase appears not to have been the subject of litigation. The MRT has found, however, that dismissal because of a complaint about unfair working conditions constitutes a 'genuine effort' to remain in employment.[24] Like an s 134 cancellation, s 137Q cancellation requires a NOICC, provision of time to respond to the NOICC, and notification of the final decision by the Minister (ss 137R and 137S of the Act). There is also a provision for automatic cancellation under s 137T for any visa held by another person because of being a member of the family unit of the person whose visa has been cancelled under s 137Q.

Notification of cancellation decisions

Notification of cancellation decisions (whether a NOICC, a notice of cancellation or a response to a request for revocation) is governed not by ss 494A–494D of the Act, but by Regulation 2.55. Regulation 2.55 is structured in a similar manner to those sections, by specifying means of notification and then the time at which a person is taken to have received notice of the document, but with one important difference. Subregulation 2.55(3), when referring to the visa holder's address, refers to the *last known address* held by the Department, not the last address specifically provided by the visa holder. That is, if a non-citizen provides address A to the Department as an address for service, but the Department becomes aware (by whatever means) that he or she actually resides at address B, the Department must send a refusal notification to address A, but must send a cancellation notice to address B. Other than that, the notification provisions of Regulation 2.55 are very similar to those in ss 494A–494D.

It may be that there is some residual uncertainty about uncertainty as to whether the Minister can choose to use s 494B even in a cancellation case, but there is authority in the Federal Magistrates Court supporting the view that Regulation 2.55

---

24   *Re 1405726* (2014) MRTA 1915.

is the appropriate provision.[25] PAM – Notification Requirements paragraph 9.9 also advises that Regulation 2.55 should be used 'in order for the department to benefit from the deemed receipt provisions'.

Section 501

Section 501 of the Act is entitled 'Refusal or Cancellation of Visa on Character Grounds', and as the title suggests, includes both a refusal ground and a cancellation power. It is now almost the sole ground for removing non-citizens with criminal convictions or similar character problems from Australia, and the criminal deportation provisions in ss 200 and 201 of the Act are now very rarely used (and will therefore not be discussed in this chapter). The main reason for this is that s 201 of the Act applies only to permanent residents with less than ten years residence in Australia (not including time spent in prison), but s 501 can apply to any non-citizen.

Specific powers

Powers requiring provision of natural justice

The primary refusal power can be found in s 501(1). It is headed 'Decision of Minister or Delegate – Natural Justice Applies' and provides that '[t]he Minister may refuse to grant a visa to a person if the person does not satisfy the Minister that the person passes the character test'. Two features are immediately apparent:

- Refusal under s 501(1) requires some sort of prior notice to the visa holder. While the procedures for serving a s 501 NOICC are set out in policy and not legislation, the Act *does* prevent refusal under s 501(1) without some kind of warning.

- The person must satisfy the Minister that he or she passes the character test. That is, there is an onus of proof of some kind on the applicant to prove their good character. In most cases, the Department will accept a police clearance as evidence of good character, but as will be seen in the discussion of the meaning of the term 'character test', this will not always be the case.

Subsection 501(2) falls under the same heading as s 501(1), and provides as follows:

> The Minister may cancel a visa that has been granted to a person if:

---

25 *Matete v Minister for Immigration and Citizenship* (2008) FMCA 573 at [13] and *Choi v Minister for Immigration and Citizenship* (2008) FMCA 1717 at [46].

(a) the Minister reasonably suspects that the person does not pass the character test; and

(b) the person does not satisfy the Minister that the person passes the character test.

That is, s 501(2) cancellation cannot proceed unless the Minister (or delegate) has a reasonable suspicion that the person does not pass the character test, and cannot proceed to cancel the visa unless the person fails to satisfy him or her that they do in fact pass the test. Again, this involves some sort of communication with the visa holder in order to give them the opportunity to show that they pass the character test.

Unlike the other cancellation powers in the Act, the procedures to be followed under ss 501(1) and (2) are primarily set out in policy, not the legislation. The common law rules of natural justice therefore apply.[26] Sending an s 501(1) notice is covered by ss 494B and 494C, while an s 501(2) NOICC is covered by Regulation 2.55. However, the content of such notices is covered by a dedicated chapter of the Procedures Advice Manual (PAM). The PAM states that the following information should be included in a ss 501(1) or (2) notice:[27]

- advice as to the alleged activities that brings the person within the scope of the character test. For cases based on the person's substantial criminal record reference to the source document/s (usually criminal history or other official records of conviction) is sufficient;

- the evidence or information that the department has to support this, and the source of this evidence;

- an invitation to comment on the case against them, and present arguments and evidence that the claimed grounds for not passing the character test do not exist and/or that there are other reasons as to why their visa should not be cancelled or visa refused; and

- the manner in which the person/holder is to respond to the NOICR/NOICC, and how long they have to provide the response.

It is also notable that the Minister *may* refuse or cancel a visa under ss 501(1) or (2) if the person fails the character test. Once again, refusal or cancellation is discretionary. A refusal or cancellation under s 501(1) is reviewable by the Administrative Appeals Tribunal if it is made by a delegate, but not if it is made by the Minister personally – s 500(1)(b).

---

26 *Minister for Immigration and Multicultural and Indigenous Affairs v George* (2004) FCAFC 276.

27 PAM3, 'Section 501 – The Character Test, Visa Refusal and Cancellation', section 35. https://legend. immi.gov.au/Migration/2014/25-09-2014/legend_current_mp/Pages/_document00001/_level%20100006/_ level%20200069/_level%20300186/level%20300187.aspx#JD_A066-40pt41Thedecisionmakingprocess.

Refusal or cancellation without prior notice

Subsection 501(3), on the other hand, permits the Minister, acting personally, to cancel or refuse a visa for failure to meet the character test without prior notice to the non-citizen. Subsection 501(5) clearly provides that the 'rules of natural justice' and Subdivision AB of Division 3 Part 2 of the Act do not apply to an s 501(3) decision. Paragraph 501(3)(d) provides that the Minister may only act in this manner if 'the Minister is satisfied that the refusal or cancellation is in the national interest', but courts have been historically reluctant to attempt to define this phrase.[28] Even *Minister for Immigration and Citizenship v Haneef*,[29] a case in which the Full Federal Court was scathingly critical of a s 501(3) cancellation, the court did not take issue with the Minister's construction of what was in the 'national interests' of Australia.

A decision made by the Minister under s 501(3) is not reviewable by the Administrative Appeals Tribunal (AAT), but may be revoked, in accordance with s 501C of the Act. Subsection 501C(3) requires the Minister, after making the decision, to inform the non-citizen of the reasons for the decision, and give him or her the opportunity to argue for revocation of the decision. The decision may only be revoked if 'the person satisfies the Minister that the person passes the character test' in accordance with s 501(4)(b) – that is, the Minister has no discretion to revoke the cancellation if the person fails the character test.

Sections 501A–501CA

Section 501A also provides the Minister with a personal power, this time to set aside a positive finding by a Departmental delegate or the AAT and instead refuse or cancel a visa under s 501. Curiously, the Minister can seemingly decide whether or not to provide natural justice to a person in this position – a decision made under s 501A(2) requires the provision of natural justice, and a decision under s 501(3) does not, and there is no other clear delineation between them. Again, the Minister can only make such a determination in the national interest – ss 501A(2)(e) and 501A(3)(d). An s 501A decision may also be revoked under s 501C.

Subsection 501(3A) provides as follows:

> The Minister must cancel a visa that has been granted to a person if:

> (d) the Minister is satisfied that the person does not pass the character test because of the operation of:

---

28 See for example *Minister for Immigration and Multicultural Affairs v Jia* (2001) 205 CLR 507 and *Gbojueh v Minister for Immigration and Citizenship* (2012) FCA 288.

29 (2007) FCAFC 203.

  (i)   (6)(a) (substantial criminal record), on the basis of paragraph (7) (a), (b) or (c); or

  (ii) paragraph (6)(e) (sexually based offences involving a child); and

(e) the person is serving a sentence of imprisonment, on a full-time basis in a custodial institution, for an offence against a law of the Commonwealth, a State or a Territory.

Section 501CA requires the Minister (not necessarily acting personally) to notify a person whose visa is cancelled under s 501(3A) of that cancellation and permit them to make submissions as to why the cancellation should be revoked. The revocation power is found in s 501CA(4). However, s 501BA permits the Minister, now acting personally, to set aside a revocation and substitute a decision not to revoke the cancellation.

Sections 501E and 501F

Section 501E of the Act is a provision similar to s 48, in that a person who has a visa cancelled or refused may not make another valid application onshore, other than a Protection Visa or a visa prescribed under s 501E(2)(b). (At present, no visas are prescribed under this paragraph.) Section 501F provides that if a person's visa is refused or cancelled under s 501, then any undecided visa applications are refused and any other visa held by the non-citizen is also cancelled.

The character test

The term 'character test' is defined in s 501(6). This is a lengthy provision, but is worth setting out in full.

For the purposes of this section, a person does not pass the **character test** if:

(a) the person has a substantial criminal record (as defined by subsection (7)); or

(aa) the person has been convicted of an offence that was committed:

  (i)   while the person was in immigration detention; or

  (ii) during an escape by the person from immigration detention; or

  (iii) after the person escaped from immigration detention but before the person was taken into immigration detention again; or

(ab) the person has been convicted of an offence against section 197A; or

(b) the Minister reasonably suspects:

(i) that the person has been or is a member of a group or organisation, or has had or has an association with a group, organisation or person; and

(ii) that the group, organisation or person has been or is involved in criminal conduct; or

(ba) the Minister reasonably suspects that the person has been or is involved in conduct constituting one or more of the following:

(i) an offence under one or more of sections 233A to 234A (people smuggling);

(ii) an offence of trafficking in persons;

(iii) the crime of genocide, a crime against humanity, a war crime, a crime involving torture or slavery or a crime that is otherwise of serious international concern;

whether or not the person, or another person, has been convicted of an offence constituted by the conduct; or

(c) having regard to either or both of the following:

(i) the person's past and present criminal conduct;

(ii) the person's past and present general conduct;

the person is not of good character; or

(d) in the event the person were allowed to enter or to remain in Australia, there is a risk that the person would:

(i) engage in criminal conduct in Australia; or

(ii) harass, molest, intimidate or stalk another person in Australia; or

(iii) vilify a segment of the Australian community; or

(iv) incite discord in the Australian community or in a segment of that community; or

(v) represent a danger to the Australian community or to a segment of that community, whether by way of being liable to become involved in activities that are disruptive to, or in violence threatening harm to, that community or segment, or in any other way; or

(e) a court in Australia or a foreign country has:

  (i) convicted the person of one or more sexually based offences involving a child; or

  (ii) found the person guilty of such an offence, or found a charge against the person proved for such an offence, even if the person was discharged without a conviction; or

(f) the person has, in Australia or a foreign country, been charged with or indicted for one or more of the following:

  (i) the crime of genocide;

  (ii) a crime against humanity;

  (iii) a war crime;

  (iv) a crime involving torture or slavery;

  (v) a crime that is otherwise of serious international concern; or

(g) person has been assessed by the Australian Security Intelligence Organisation to be directly or indirectly a risk to security (within the meaning of section 4 of the *Australian Security Intelligence Organisation Act 1979*); or

(h) an Interpol notice in relation to the person, from which it is reasonable to infer that the person would present a risk to the Australian community or a segment of that community, is in force.

Otherwise, the person passes the **character test**.

The term 'substantial criminal record' is defined in s 501(7) as follows:

For the purposes of the character test, a person has a **substantial criminal record** if:

(a) the person has been sentenced to death; or

(b) the person has been sentenced to imprisonment for life; or

(c) the person has been sentenced to a term of imprisonment of 12 months or more; or

(d) the person has been sentenced to 2 or more terms of imprisonment, where the total of those terms is 12 months or more; or

(e) the person has been acquitted of an offence on the grounds of unsoundness of mind or insanity, and as a result the person has been detained in a facility or institution; or

(f)   the person has:

(i)   been found by a court to not be fit to plead, in relation to an offence; and

(ii)   the court has nonetheless found that on the evidence available the person committed the offence; and

(iii)   as a result, the person has been detained in a facility or institution.

Significant guidance on the interpretation of ss 501(6) and (7) is given in Direction 65, a Ministerial direction made under s 499 of the Act. Direction 65 will be considered in more detail in the section on Departmental policy.

Part 2 – The role of policy in departmental decision-making

Like most administrative decision makers, immigration officers rely on policy to support their understanding of legislation. In practice, many junior Departmental decision makers rely exclusively on the PAMs and other policy instructions to make their decision. Many decision makers in high-volume and low-complexity areas are, or at least were prior to 2007, simply unaware that the Act and Regulations existed, and made their decisions solely on the basis of policy instructions.

It is not an error of law for administrative decision makers to consider and have regard to formally promulgated policy. However, if policy conflicts with legislation, it is of no effect.[30] A Canadian case illustrates this principle well. In *Ramoutar v Canada (Minister of Employment and Immigration)*[31] decision makers in Citizenship and Immigration Canada (CIC) were faced with a policy document that required officers assessing applications for spouse visas to have evidence 'beyond reasonable doubt' that the relationship was genuine before being able to grant a spouse visa. As the *Immigration Act*[32] contained no such requirement, CIC could not lawfully apply this policy, and the decision in question was therefore set aside by Federal Court of Canada. Even when policy is consistent with legislation, it must not be applied 'inflexibly' – instead, decision makers must always be aware of the possibility of an exceptional case where the policy should not be applied.[33] As noted above, junior Departmental officers fall into this trap very frequently.

---

30   See as one example *Green v Daniels* (1977) 13 ALR 1.
31   (1993) 3 FCR 370.
32   RSC 1985, c 1–2.
33   *British Oxygen Co Ltd v Minister of Technology* (1971) AC 610; *Yong v Minister for Immigration and Multicultural Affairs* (2000) FCA 1391.

The Department of Immigration utilises two main kinds of policy documents — directions under s 499 of the Act, and the PAMs. These will now be considered in turn.

Section 499 directions

An s 499 direction is a sort of 'uber-policy' direction that takes precedence over all other policy, but not, of course, legislation. Subsection 499(1) provides that '[t]he Minister may give written directions to a person or body having functions or powers under this Act if the directions are about: (a) the performance of those functions; or (b) the exercise of those powers' and s 499(2A) provides that '[a] person or body must comply with a direction under subsection (1)'. The reference to 'a body' is significant, as this has the effect that a review tribunal must also follow any and all relevant s 499 directions.[34]

Whether the Minister, acting personally, is himself or herself bound by an s 499 direction is an interesting question. The Minister would appear to be 'a person' exercising powers under the Act and Regulations. However, the Federal Court has found, in *Misiura v Minister for Immigration and Multicultural Affairs*[35] and *WASB v Minister for Immigration and Citizenship*[36] that the Minister is not bound by an s 499 direction, although departure from a relevant direction without prior notification to an applicant could amount to a failure to afford procedural fairness.[37]

Direction 65

The best known, and by some distance the most litigated (when one includes its predecessors), s 499 direction is Direction 65, which is intended to provide guidance on the exercise of powers under ss 501(1) and (2) of the Act. Direction 65, which came into effect on 22 December 2014, is the latest in a series of s 499 directions concerned with the character provisions of the Act, and replaced Direction 55, which had come into effect on 25 July 2012.

Direction 65 itself states that the direction is divided into four parts (inclusive of a Preamble) and two annexes.

Direction 65 provides guidance on both the meaning of the character test, and the factors that must be taken into account in determining whether the

---

34   See for example *Williams v Minister for Immigration and Border Protection* (2014) FCA 674 at paragraph 93.
35   (2001) FCA 133.
36   (2013) FCA 1016.
37   Ibid at paragraph 48.

discretion to refuse or cancel a visa should be exercised. For example, Part A identifies the following as the 'primary considerations' in deciding whether to cancel the visa of a non-citizen who fails the character test:

- Protection of the Australian community from criminal or other serious conduct.

- The best interests of minor children in Australia.

- The 'expectations of the Australian community'.

The first point requires the decision maker to consider the seriousness of the person's conduct and their risk of recidivism, while the third is concerned with whether the nature of the offence itself would lead Australians to believe that the person should not be permitted to form part of the Australian community. The issue of the best interests of any children requires the decision maker to consider matters such as:

(a) The nature and duration of the relationship between the child and the person.

(b) The extent to which the person is likely to play a positive parental role in the future.

(c) The impact of a person's prior and future conduct on the child.

(d) The likely effect separation from the person would have on the child.

(e) Other persons who fill the parental role in relation to the child.

(f) Any known views of the child.

(g) Evidence of child abuse or neglect including evidence of physical or emotional trauma arising from the persons conduct.

The 'best interests of the child' criterion is, of course, taken directly from the decision of the High Court in *Minister for Immigration and Ethnic Affairs v Teoh*,[38] which was in turn based on Australia's ratification of the Convention on the Rights of the Child.

Part A then goes on to identify the following 'other considerations' that decision makers must take into account:

- International non-refoulement obligations – examines Australia's obligations under international instruments such as the Convention on the Status of Refugees and the Convention Against Torture, and requires the decision

---

38   (1995) 183 CLR 273.

maker to consider whether returning the non-citizen to their home country could breach these obligations.

- Strength, nature and duration of the person's ties to Australia – this factor requires the decision maker to balance the non-citizen's ties to Australia with the gravity of their conduct, and in some way determine whether the person is now 'Australia's problem'.[39]

- Impact on Australian business interests – only relevant where 'visa cancellation would significantly compromise the delivery of a major project or delivery of an important service in Australia'.

- Impact on victims in Australia.

- Extent of impediments if removed – this factor is focused on the impediments that a person may face in their 'home' country, such as their age and health, language or cultural barriers, and social or medical support.

Direction 65 also gives guidance on the interpretation of the character test itself, and is most valuable in determining the meaning of possibly subjective provisions of s 501(6) such as those found in s 501(6)(d)(iii), (iv) and (v).

Paragraph (1)(d) of Direction 65 is clearly aimed at individuals such as the Holocaust-denying 'historian' David Irving, who was famously refused a visa on multiple occasions in the early 1990s.[40] The note under this paragraph is very likely aimed at radical religious (mainly Muslim) clerics.

Direction 65 is deliberately broad in scope and is intended to catch a wide range of people with controversial or extremist views, although s 501(6)(d)(iii)–(v) of the Act have appear to have been applied infrequently.[41]

Part C of Direction 65 did not appear in earlier versions, because it relates to new s 501(3A) of the Act, which *requires* the Minister to cancel a visa where the non-citizen has a 'substantial criminal record' and is currently imprisoned in Australia. Under s 501CA, such a person may request the Minister to revoke

---

39   See for example *Nystrom v Minister for Immigration and Multicultural and Indigenous Affairs* (2005) FCAFC 121 at paragraph 29.

40   See for example *Irving v Minister for Immigration, Local Government and Ethnic Affairs* (1993) 115 ALR 125.

41   Exact statistics on grounds of s 501 refusals and cancellations are hard to come by. The Departmental 2012–13 Annual Report states as follows at 165:

    In 2012–13, the minister or his delegate made 1092 character decisions under section 501. These decisions comprised 65 refusals (20 onshore, 45 offshore), 139 cancellations and 888 cases either not refused or not cancelled. For this latter group, standard practice is for the department to issue formal warnings.

See http://www.immi.gov.au/about/reports/annual/2012-13/pdf/2012-13-diac-annual-report.pdf, extracted 6 October 2014.

the cancellation. The factors that must be considered in deciding a revocation request are substantially identical to those that must be considered in relation to ss 501(1) and (2).

Other directions

It is notable that some s 499 directions are expressly intended to apply to review tribunals. For example, Direction 57, contains a section which relates to order of processing of protection visa applications, and applications for review of Departmental decisions, provides as follows.

The s 499 directions that are in effect as of January 2015 are as follows:

- General Direction No 9 (signed 21/12/1998) – Criminal Deportation[42]
- Direction No 47 of 2010 (signed 04/07/2010) – Required health assessment
- Direction No 49 (signed 05/01/2011) – Order for considering and disposing of visa applications under section 91 of the *Migration Act*
- Direction No 51 (signed 02/10/2012) – Strip search of immigration detainees
- Direction No 52 (signed 14/10/2011) – Priority processing for standard business sponsors with accredited status
- Direction No 53 (signed 03/11/2011) – Assessing the genuine temporary entrant criterion for student visa applications
- Direction No 54 (signed 25/06/2012) – Order of consideration – Certain skilled migration visas
- Direction No 56 (signed 21/06/2013) – Consideration of Protection Visa applications
- Direction No 57 (signed 25/06/2013) – Order of consideration of Protection Visas
- Direction No 58 (signed 1 August 2013) – Exercise of powers by Fair Work Inspectors
- Direction No 59 – Powers concerning the entry of persons to Immigration Detention Centres
- Direction No 60 – Screening procedures in relation to immigration detainees
- Direction No 61 – Guidelines for considering cancellation of student visas for non-compliance with student visa condition 8202 (or for the review of such cancellation decisions) and for considering revocation of automatic

---

42   It is interesting that this direction is still in effect, as criminal deportation is now a very rarely used power.

cancellation of student visas[43] (or for the review of decisions not to revoke such cancellations)

- Direction No 62 – Order for considering and disposing of Family Stream visa applications

- Direction No 63 – Bridging E visas – Cancellation under section 116(1)(g) – Regulation 2.43(1)(p) or (q)

- Direction No 64 (signed 9/12/2014) – Priority for considering and disposing of applications for specified visas made by persons who reside, or have resided, in an Ebola Virus Disease affected country

- Direction No 65 (signed 22/12/2012) – Visa refusal and cancellation under s 501

It is notable that many s 499 directions deal with the exercise of the few remaining discretionary powers or subjective considerations, such as the 'genuineness' of a student visa applicant (no. 53), cancellation and deportation powers (nos 9, 55, 61 and 63), exercise of inspection or search powers (nos 51, 58, 59, 60), or the order in which visa applications are to be processed (nos 49, 54 and 57).

The Procedures Advice Manual

The second kind of policy document regularly referred to by Departmental officers is the Procedures Advice Manual (PAM). The PAM is a comprehensive document providing advice on the exercise many provisions of the Act and Regulations, and is far too extensive to be the subject of detailed examination here. The PAMs are subordinate to legislation and s 499 directions, but are (with the possible exception of Direction 65) probably the most frequently consulted source of policy.

Like s 499 directions, the PAMs will be most useful to decision makers, and the most controversial, when dealing with the exercise of subjective terms or discretionary powers. To that end, this chapter will consider a particular example of PAM policy – guidance on the interpretation of the term 'beyond the control of the applicant' in Condition 8503, as set out in Schedule 8 of the Regulations.

Condition 8503

Section 41 of the Act is entitled 'Conditions on Visas'. Subsection 41(1) states that the Regulations may provide that visas are subject to specified conditions. Paragraph 41(2)(a) of the Act then provides as follows:

---

43 Note that automatic cancellation of student visas no longer occurs, as s 20 of the *Education Services for Overseas Students Act 2000* was repealed in 2013.

(2) Without limiting subsection (1), the regulations may provide that a visa, or visas of a specified class, are subject to:

(a) a condition that, despite anything else in this Act, the holder of the visa will not, after entering Australia, be entitled to be granted a substantive visa (other than a protection visa, or a temporary visa of a specified kind) while he or she remains in Australia.

Condition 8503, set out in Schedule 8 of the Regulations, is an example of a condition described in s 41(2)(a). It provides that '[t]he holder will not, after entering Australia, be entitled to be granted a substantive visa, other than a protection visa, while the holder remains in Australia'.[44]

Section 46 of the Act is entitled 'Valid Visa Application'. Subsection 46(1A) provides as follows:

Subject to subsection (2), an application for a visa is invalid if:

(a) the applicant is in the migration zone; and

(b) since last entering Australia, the applicant has held a visa subject to a condition described in paragraph 41(2)(a); and

(c) Minister has not waived that condition under subsection 41(2A); and

(d) the application is for a visa of a kind that, under that condition, the applicant is not or was not entitled to be granted.

The effect of s 46(1A) is that a non-citizen who holds a visa that is subject to a s 46(2)(a) condition may not make a valid application for a visa onshore, unless the condition is waived by the Minister. The waiver provision is then set out in s 41(2A) of the Act:[45]

The Minister may, in prescribed circumstances, by writing, waive a condition of a kind described in paragraph (2)(a) to which a particular visa is subject under regulations made for the purposes of that paragraph or under subsection (3).

The 'prescribed circumstances' for the purposes of s 41(2A) are set out in subregulation 2.05(4) of the Regulations, which relevantly provides as follows:

---

44 In *Sevim v Minister for Immigration & Multicultural Affairs* (2001) FCA 1597 the applicant made the argument that Condition 8503 is not the same condition as the condition created by s 41(2)(a), an argument comprehensively rejected by Gray J at paragraph 33.
45 Subsection 41(3) is a provision that permits the Minister to impose conditions, by regulation, on visas, other than the conditions specifically set out in s 46(2).

For subsection 41(2A) of the Act, the circumstances in which the Minister may waive a condition of a kind described in paragraph 41(2)(a) of the Act are that:

(a) since the person was granted the visa that was subject to the condition, compelling and compassionate circumstances have developed:

   (i) over which the person had no control; and

   (ii) that resulted in a major change to the person's circumstances.

PAM commentary

Section 19 of the PAM chapter entitled 'Reg 2.05 — Conditions applicable to visas — Waiver of 'no further application' conditions' sets out the following examples on situations in which an individual's circumstances will be regarded as 'compelling and compassionate':

1. Medical unfitness to travel.

2. Death or serious illness of a close family member.

3. Significant hardship.

4. War or natural disaster in the visa holder's home country.

5. Closure of an educational institution or the inability of that institution to continue to provide a course (in the case of a student visa holder).

6. The applicant has Australian government support and certain other factors apply.

Under 'significant hardship', the PAM relevantly states as follows:

It is *not* intended that the following would in themselves constitute such a change in circumstances:

- marriage to an Australian resident
- failure to complete a course
- pregnancy.

Section 20 of the PAM deals with 'circumstances not beyond the applicant's control'. The only such situations listed are pregnancy and failure to complete a course (for student visa holders). Pregnancy as an issue is dealt with briefly, as follows:

Pregnancy in itself would not be grounds for a waiver. If the visa holder was pregnant at the time their visa was granted they do not satisfy the 'changed circumstances' requirement for a waiver and other visa options should be explored. Women who become pregnant while in Australia would generally need to have evidence that they are unable to leave Australia – see section 19.2 Unfitness to travel.

Is the PAM inconsistent with the Act and Regulations?

There has to be a reasonable argument that the blanket prohibition on decision makers interpreting pregnancy as a situation beyond the control of the expectant mother is *ultra vires* the legislation. This is for the following reasons:[46]

- The MRT has at times found that pregnancy is a situation beyond the control of the woman concerned, although not in relation to a Condition 8503 waiver.[47]

- The statement that pregnancy is not a situation beyond the control of the mother *after* it occurs implicitly assumes the availability of abortion. However, except for the Australian Capital Territory, there is no such thing as 'abortion on demand' in Australia.

- Even where abortion *is* lawful, such an action may be contrary to the religion or conscience of the expectant mother.

Migration series instructions

There was, until 2007, a third source of policy, this being the Migration Series Instructions (MSIs). The MSIs were generally based around a particular issue rather than a particular piece of legislation. For example, one of the better known MSIs was MSI 371, which came into effect on 2 December 2002.[48]

MSI 371 was concerned alternative forms of immigration detention, such as hospitals, police stations and residential housing. This MSI was notable for a number of matters:

---

46 For more details, see Alan Freckelton, 'The Application of Condition 8503 of the *Migration Regulations 1994* to Pregnant Visa Holders', (2014) 58 *Immigration Review Bulletin* 828.

47 *Re Young Ok Kim* [2001] MRTA 4412, 26 September 2001; *Re Lu Si Ning* (2003) MRTA 0223, 17 January 2003 (both relating to s 116(3) of the Act and paragraph 2.43(2)(b) of the Regulations). Courts have generally been less sympathetic to this argument – see *Auva'a, in the matter of an application for a Writ of Prohibition and Certiorari and Declaratory and Injunctive Relief against Vanstone* (2003) FCA 1506 and *Emeish v Minister for Immigration and Multicultural and Indigenous Affairs* (2005) FMCA 1308.

48 Australian Human Rights Commission, '*BZ and AD v Commonwealth of Australia (Department of Immigration and Citizenship)* – Report into breaches of privacy, arbitrary detention, the right for the child to be treated with humanity and with respect for the inherent dignity of the human person and the failure of the Commonwealth to treat the best interests of the child as a primary consideration', (2012) AusHRC 55 at 51.

- It required women and children to be removed from Immigration Detention Centres (IDCs) and relocated to residential housing as soon as practicable.

- It was drafted in the space of a month in response to Parliamentary pressure on the Minister, including from the government's backbench[49].

Most of the MSIs were absorbed into the PAMs from 2007 onwards. Interestingly, no trace of MSI 371 appears to remain. There also appears to be no trace of the MSI online.

The purpose of policy and fettering of administrative decision-making

It can be seen that the purpose of departmental policy is to prescribe, or perhaps impose, a particular way of interpreting a subjective consideration or discretionary power, in order to provide some uniformity in the approach of decision makers. Section 499 directions have some kind of legislative backing, and the Act itself requires that decision makers have regard to relevant s 499 directions when making their decisions. As long as a s 499 direction does not conflict with the legislation, there is no dispute that decision makers must abide by it.

The PAMs are in a different situation, as there is no legislative authority for their existence. It is obviously not a good thing for the Department or visa applicants if decision makers can simply adopt any idiosyncratic interpretation of the Act and Regulations that they wish. Australian courts and tribunals do not dispute that consistent interpretation and application of legislation by departments and tribunals is desirable.[50]

However, at what point does a policy become a fetter on an administrative decision maker, noting that it is an individual (or a position within a department, which can only be held by an individual) who is the delegated decision maker, not the department itself? Lord Denning noted as follows in *Sagnata Investments Ltd v Norwich Corporation*:[51]

> I take it to be perfectly clear now that an administrative body, including a licensing body, which may have to consider numerous applications of a similar kind, is entitled to lay down a general policy which it proposes to follow in coming to its individual decisions, provided always that

---

49   The drafters of MSI 371, of which an author of this text was one, were prohibited by the Minister's office from referring to 'long' or 'lengthy' periods of detention. Instead, the linguistic atrocity 'not short periods of detention' had to be used.

50   See for example *Re Drake and Minister for Immigration and Ethnic Affairs (No 2)* (1979) 2 ALD 634 at 639.

51   (1971) 2 QB 614 at 626.

it is a reasonable policy which it is fair and just to apply. Once laid down, the administrative body is entitled to apply the policy in the individual cases which come before it. The only qualification is that the administrative body must not apply the policy so rigidly as to reject an applicant without hearing what he has to say. It must not 'shut its ears to an application'. The applicant is entitled to put forward reasons urging that the policy should be changed, or saying that in any case it should not be applied to him. But, so long as the administrative body is ready to hear him and consider what he has to say, it is entitled to apply its general policy to him as to others.

In two similar cases, the Supreme Court of Canada found that an administrative decision-making body was entitled to hold meetings of its members to discuss difficult cases and provide guidance, but the key issue is whether there is any pressure (formally or informally) on the decision maker to decide an application contrary to his or her own conscience or interpretation of the law.[52] If the same principle was applied in Australia, one would imagine that a large number of Departmental decisions could be struck down (assuming they were the subject of judicial review in the first place), as from experience the pressure on junior decision makers to follow policy is immense, and as previously noted many are actually unaware of the existence of the legislation.

Like many other matters in administrative law, policy-making is about a balance – consistency but not uniformity. It would be perfectly proper, for example, for the PAMs to state that pregnancy should not *normally* be considered a matter beyond the control of an expectant mother, as this formulation would leave the door open for consideration of the exceptional case of conscientious or religious objection to abortion, for example. The Canadian approach appears to be the desirable one – evidence of pressure to conform to a certain interpretation of legislation *at all costs* is evidence of fettering, not merely an approach to achieving the desirable goal of consistency.

---

52 *International Woodworkers of America, Local 2–69 v Consolidated Bathurst Packaging Ltd* (1990) 1 SCR 282; *Tremblay v Quebec (Commission des Affaires Sociales)* (1992) 1 SCR 952.

Appendix 1 – *The Migration Amendment (Character and General Visa Cancellation) Act 2014*

The *Migration Amendment (Character and General Visa Cancellation) Act 2014* ('the MACGVC Act') was given Royal Assent on 10 December 2014 and came into effect partly on that day and partly the next day[53]. The MACGVC Act makes significant amendments to the visa cancellation and character provisions of the *Migration Act 1958*.

Amendments to the character test

The amendments to the *Migration Act* made by the MACGVC Act are intended to strengthen the powers to refuse to grant, or to cancel, a visa on character grounds by inserting additional grounds on which a person will not pass the character test. These include:

- That the Minister reasonably suspects that the person has been or is a member of a group or organisation, or has had or has an association with a group, organisation or person that has been or is involved in criminal conduct, whether or not anyone has been convicted of an offence.

- The Minister reasonably suspects that the person has been or is involved in conduct constituting an offence of people-smuggling or an offence of trafficking in persons as described in the Migration Act, or the crime of genocide, a crime against humanity, a war crime, a crime involving torture or slavery or a crime that is otherwise of serious international concern, whether or not any convictions have resulted.

- A court in Australia or a foreign country has convicted the person of one or more sexually based offences involving a child, or found the person guilty of such an offence, or found a charge against the person proved for such an offence without recording a conviction.

- The person has, in Australia or a foreign country, been charged with or indicted for one or more of the crime of genocide, a crime against humanity, a war crime, a crime involving torture or slavery, or a crime that is otherwise of serious international concern.

- The person has been assessed by the Australian Security Intelligence Organisation (ASIO) to be directly or indirectly a risk to security.

---

53   See s 2 of the MACGVC Act and http://www.comlaw.gov.au/Details/C2014A00129, retrieved 3 February 2014.

- An Interpol notice in relation to the person is in force (from which it is reasonable to infer that the person would present a risk to the Australian community or a segment of that community).

It would appear that many of these grounds had already been covered by s 501. Someone who has been charged with or is suspected of involvement in crimes against humanity, for example, would fall within ss 501(6)(c)(ii) or possibly 501(6)(d)(iv), regardless of whether they have been convicted of any offence. In the fairly unlikely event that a person charged with a sexual offence against a child escapes conviction despite the facts of the case being proved, they could also fall within s 501(6)(c)(ii).

The real change may be to the 'association' requirement, which is found in an amended s 501(6)(b). The amended s 501(6)(b) provides as follows:

The Minister reasonably suspects:

(i) that the person has been or is a member of a group or organisation, or has had or has an association with a group, organisation or person; and

(ii) that the group, organisation or person has been or is involved in criminal conduct.

That is, mere membership of certain groups would suffice for the Minister to find that the person is not of good character. In some cases, this may not be a problem – if a person is a member of a criminal gang, for example, they are highly unlikely to be of good character. However, what about membership of organisations such as the Liberation Tigers of Tamil Eelam (LTTE), a group that has humanitarian and paramilitary wings? The Supreme Court of Canada has recently moved away from the view that mere membership of a group can reflect on an applicant's character, and has instead found that examination of individual circumstances is always required.[54] This amendment seems designed to head off such a finding in Australia. Paragraph 41 of Schedule 1 of the Explanatory Memorandum (EM) makes this quite clear by stating that '[t]here is no requirement that there be a demonstration of special knowledge of, or participation in, the suspected criminal conduct by the visa applicant or visa holder'.

Other character-related amendments

- Providing that in the event that a person were allowed to enter or to remain in Australia, there is a risk (as opposed to a significant risk) that the person

---

54   *Ezokola v Canada (Citizenship and Immigration)* (2013) SCC 40.

would engage in any of the conduct referred to in subparagraphs 501(6)(d)(i)–(v) of the Migration Act;

- ○ This is a potentially problematic amendment. What is a 'significant risk'? Paragraph 46 of Schedule 1 of the EM states that the intention of this amendment is 'that the level of risk required is more than a minimal or trivial likelihood of risk, without requiring the decision maker to prove that it amounts to a significant risk', but the Act simply refers to a 'risk', which could be interpreted as 'more than zero risk'. Such an interpretation could be used to exclude nearly anyone.

- Providing that a person has a substantial criminal record (and so does not pass the character test) if the person has been sentenced to two or more terms of imprisonment where the total of those terms is 12 months (rather than two years or more, as is currently the case).

- Providing that a person has a substantial criminal record (and so does not pass the character test) if a court has found the person unfit to plead in relation to an offence but the court has found that the person committed the offence, and as a result the person has been detained in facility or institution.

This amendment seems to be already covered by the definition of 'substantial criminal record' in s 501(7)(e) of the Act. However, paragraph 67 of Schedule 1 of the EM states that '[s] 501(7)(e) has been found to be inadequate as it does not capture a person who has received, for example, an indicative or non-punitive order of imprisonment or detention, and consequently has not been 'acquitted' of the offence'.

- Clarifying that if a person has been sentenced to two or more terms of imprisonment to be served concurrently (whether in whole or in part), the whole of each term is to be counted in working out the total of the terms.

- Clarifying that for the purposes of the character test, a sentence or a conviction imposed on a person is only to be disregarded if both the person has been pardoned in relation to the conviction concerned, and the effect of that pardon is that the person is taken never to have been convicted of the offence.

This is an odd amendment, as a pardon rarely has the effect that the person has never been convicted. This was an important point in the Lorenzo Ervin litigation in 1997, when a US citizen who had received an executive pardon after serving 20 years of a life sentence for hijacking was nevertheless regarded as having a substantial criminal record.[55]

---

55   *Re Minister for Immigration and Multicultural Affairs Ex parte Ervin* (1997) HCATrans 213 (10 July 1997) and HCATrans 214 (11 July 1997). *Ervin* ultimately did not go to trial, as the Minister withdrew the cancellation of his visa.

- Inserting a new mandatory ground for the cancellation without notice of a visa under s 501 of the Migration Act that will apply where:

  o the person is serving a full-time sentence of imprisonment for an offence against the law of the Commonwealth, a State or a Territory; and

  o the Minister is satisfied that the person has a substantial criminal record.

  And clarifying that a decision to cancel a visa under this new mandatory ground for cancellation is not a decision that is reviewable by the Administrative Appeals Tribunal.

- Providing that where this new power to cancel a visa is exercised, the Minister, acting personally, or a delegate of the Minister may revoke the cancellation if satisfied that the person passes the character test or there is another reason why the cancellation should be revoked (new s 501CA);

  This provision is similar to the cancellation without notice and revocation provisions that currently exist in ss 501(3)–(5) and 501C. A mandatory character cancellation provision is uncommon in Australian law, and mandatory character cancellation without prior notice is unprecedented. Anyone serving a sentence of 12 months more *must* have their visa cancelled, under new s 501(3A), and will not receive prior notice of this cancellation. While many people in this situation will be serving time for very serious offences, it is not hard to envisage situations where mandatory cancellation is undesirable, whether because there are some kind of mitigating circumstances in relation to their imprisonment, or because they are Australian in all but name (a *Nystrom*[56]-type situation).

- Providing that decisions of a delegate of the Minister not to revoke the cancellation of a visa of a non-citizen who is in prison is a decision that is reviewable by the Administrative Appeals Tribunal.

- Providing that where the cancellation of the visa of a person in prison has been revoked by a delegate of the Minister or the AAT, the Minister may, acting personally, set aside that revocation decision and cancel the visa if satisfied that the person does not pass the character test and the cancellation of the visa is in the national interest.

  This power of the Minister is similar to the powers that currently exist in s 501A. One wonders what the point of giving a delegate or the AAT the power to set aside a refusal to revoke a cancellation is, if the Minister can just turn around and revoke that revocation.

---

56   Supra n38.

- Clarifying that a decision under s 65 of the *Migration Act* to refuse to grant a protection visa on character grounds is a decision that is reviewable by the AAT.

- Inserting a new power for the Minister to require the head of an agency of a State or Territory to disclose to the Minister personal information about a person whose visa may be cancelled under s 501 of the *Migration Act*, subject to certain specified exceptions.

- Clarifying that a person who holds a permanent visa that was granted by the Minister acting personally is not excluded from entering Australia or being in Australia under s 503 of the *Migration Act*.

- Clarifying that the prohibition in s 501E of the *Migration Act* on making an application for a visa (which applies to a person in respect of whom a decision was made under ss 501, 501A or 501B) does not apply to a person who was granted a permanent visa by the Minister acting personally.

Non-character matters

Finally, the MACGVC Act makes a number of amendments not relating to character provisions, including the following:

- Clarifying that the Minister may cancel a visa under s 116(1)(a) of the *Migration Act* in circumstances where a decision to grant the visa was based, wholly or partly, on a particular fact or circumstance that did not exist (as well as where the decision was based on a particular fact or circumstance that no longer exists). This has been done by inserting s 116(1)(aa), which applies where a fact or circumstance *never* existed.

  This will be another amendment acclaimed by law students. Paragraph 116(1)(a) is currently interpreted as meaning that the Minister may only cancel a visa under this provision if a particular fact *no longer* exists, not that it *never* existed.

- Clarifying that the Minister may cancel a visa under s 116(1)(e) of the *Migration Act* if the presence of its holder in Australia is or may be, or would or might be, a risk to the health, safety or good order of the Australian community or a segment of the Australian community, or the health or safety of an individual or individuals.

- Inserting into s 116 of the *Migration Act* a new ground for cancellation of a visa if the Minister is not satisfied as to the visa holder's identity.

- Inserting into section 116 of the *Migration Act* a new ground for cancellation of a visa if the Minister is satisfied that incorrect information (that is not covered by Subdivision C of Division 3 of Part 2) was given by or on behalf of the visa holder to the Department and the incorrect information was taken into account in or in connection with making a decision that enabled the person to make a valid application for a visa or a decision to grant a visa to the person.

Paragraph 20 of Schedule 2 of the EM explains this new s 116(1AB) as follows:

> The purpose of new subsection 116(1AB) of the *Migration Act* is to provide that incorrect information must not be given to the Department at any time, not just where the information is provided as part of a person's visa application as required in Subdivision C of Division 3 of Part 2 of the *Migration Act*. For example, the new cancellation ground would apply where incorrect information is given which informs the grant of a visa which does not require an application to be made or which is granted through ministerial intervention, or incorrect information given during an administrative process in relation to the *Migration Act* for the purpose of responding to Australia's international obligations to the person under a relevant International Instrument.

- Clarifying that s 117(2) of the *Migration Act* (which prevents the Minister from cancelling a permanent visa where the visa holder is in the migration zone and was immigration cleared on last entering Australia) does not apply to the new grounds for cancellation of a visa in s 116 set out above;

This amendment will not be popular with law students, or Departmental decision makers. Subsection 117(2) was originally quite clear, that s 116 cannot be used to cancel a permanent visa onshore. It will now become a very complex piece of legislation.

- Inserting a new Subdivision into Division 3 of Part 2 of the *Migration Act* that contains new personal powers of the Minister to cancel visas on the grounds in ss 109 and 116 of the *Migration Act* where a decision was made not to cancel the visa on those grounds and the Minister is satisfied that those grounds exist and that it would be in the public interest to cancel the visa (new ss 133A and 133C of new Subdivision FA).

This is astonishing. Whether one is in favour of provisions like ss 501A or not, there is at least some objective reason for them. When one looks at AAT decisions like *Le Geng Jia and Minister of Immigration and Multicultural Affairs*,[57] in which the AAT found that a convicted rapist was a person of good character by blaming the victim for her rape, one can come to the conclusion that 'something had to be done' about the AAT's interpretation of the character provisions of the Act. Further, people who are subject to s 501 cancellation are frequently a 'threat' of some kind to the Australian community. However, there is simply no evidence that provisions like the new ss 133A and 133C are necessary. The Minister even has the choice as to

---

57   (1996) AAT 236.

whether the non-citizen should receive prior notification of the cancellation – see ss 133A(1) and (3). Even the EM can offer little justification for these provisions, stating as follows in paragraph 42 of Schedule 2:

> Ultimately, the community holds the Minister responsible for decisions within his portfolio, even where those decisions have resulted from merits review. Therefore, it is appropriate that the Minister have the power to be the final decision maker in the public interest.

If we are going to accept this argument, then all applications should be decided personally by the Minister and all merits review should be abolished. Who knows, we might be swamped by people working illegally or getting details of their passenger cards incorrect otherwise.

- Inserting a provision whereby the Minister may revoke a decision made by the Minister personally to cancel a visa under new Subdivision FA of Division 3 of Part 2 of the *Migration Act* if the Minister is satisfied that the ground for cancelling the visa does not exist.

Again, this is similar to the existing ss 501(3) and 501C.

- Clarifying that a decision that was made personally by the Minister to cancel a visa under ss 109, 116 or 140(2) of the *Migration Act* is not reviewable by the MRT.

- Providing that a decision to cancel a visa that is made under new ss 133A or 133C of the *Migration Act* is not reviewable by the MRT.

- Clarifying that any decision to cancel a protection visa that is made personally by the Minister is not reviewable by the RRT.

Given that 'it is appropriate that the Minister have the power to be the final decision maker in the public interest', it is hardly surprising that merits review of decisions made under ss 109, 116 (by the Minister personally), 133A or 133C are not merits reviewable. The provision that a personal protection visa cancellation by the Minister is also not reviewable (new s 411(2)(aa) of the Act) is just a logical extension of this concept.

- Clarifying that a decision of a delegate of the Minister to cancel a bridging visa held by a non-citizen who is in immigration detention because of that cancellation is reviewable by the MRT.

This appears to have always been the intention in any event.

Appendix 2 – The *Migration and Maritime Powers Legislation Amendment (Resolving the Asylum Legacy Caseload) Act 2014*

The *Migration and Maritime Powers Legislation Amendment (Resolving the Asylum Legacy Caseload) Act 2014* ('the MMPLA Act') was introduced into the House of Representatives on 25 September 2014 and passed by the House on 22 October 2014. It was then introduced into the Senate on 28 October 2014 and passed, after some amendments, on 4 December 2014.[58] The Bill received Royal Assent on 15 December, and commenced in accordance with s 2 of the MMPLA Act. The proclamation referred to in that section does not appear to have yet been made.

The MMPLA Act has imposed far-reaching changes to the *Migration Act* and the *Maritime Powers Act 2013* in relation to the treatment and processing of applicants for refugee status in Australia. In effect, the intention of the Bill is to remove any domestic effect of the Convention on the Status of Refugees, and replace all references to the Convention in the *Migration Act* with a statutory definition of 'refugee'. The MMPLA Act also reintroduces Temporary Protection Visas (TPVs), creates a new Safe Haven Enterprise Visa (SHEV), introduces a new 'fast track' procedure to the RRT, and amends the powers of officers to apprehend suspected intended unauthorised arrivals and sea and take them to countries with which Australia has arrangements for refugee processing.

Removal of reference to the convention

One crucial effect of the MMPLA Act is to remove all references to the Convention on the Status of Refugees from the *Migration Act*. The term 'refugee' is now defined in new s 5H of the Act as follows:

(1) For the purposes of the application of this Act and the regulations to a particular person in Australia, the person is a **refugee** if the person:

    (a) in a case where the person has a nationality – is outside the country of his or her nationality and, owing to a well-founded fear of persecution, is unable or unwilling to avail himself or herself of the protection of that country; or

---

58 http://www.aph.gov.au/Parliamentary_Business/Bills_Legislation/Bills_Search_Results/Result?bId=r5346.

(b)   in a case where the person does not have a nationality – is outside the country of his or her former habitual residence and owing to a well-founded fear of persecution, is unable or unwilling to return to it.

(2)   Subsection (1) does not apply if the Minister has serious reasons for considering that:

(a)   the person has committed a crime against peace, a war crime or a crime against humanity, as defined by international instruments prescribed by the regulations; or

(b)   the person committed a serious non-political crime before entering Australia; or

(c)   the person has been guilty of acts contrary to the purposes and principles of the United Nations.

The terms 'well-founded fear of persecution' is defined in new s 5J, while 'membership of a particular social group' is defined in ss 5K and 5L. The term 'particularly serious crime' is defined in s 5M. Significantly, a 'well-founded fear of persecution' requires that the risk of persecution apply across all areas of the person's home country. As noted in the Explanatory Memorandum (EM) to the MMPLA Act, the implication of this amendment is that asylum seekers will not be eligible for protection in Australia if they can safely and legally relocate to a 'safe part' of their home country upon return.[59]

It is immediately obvious that the new s 5H reproduces Articles 1A(2) and 1F of the Convention to a significant extent. What then is the purpose of removing references to the Convention? Paragraph 1167 of the Explanatory Memorandum to the MMPLA Act states that '[n]ew subsection 5H(1) is intended to codify Article 1A(2) of the Refugees Convention, as interpreted in Australian case law, into Part 1 of the *Migration Act*', which may mean that the purpose of the amendment is to 'freeze' the law at the date the Act comes into effect, and prevent courts from applying any future overseas developments in Australia.

'Internal flight'

As noted above, one major change to the way in which refugee status will be interpreted in Australia relates to the 'internal flight alternative', or 'internal relocation principle'. Very broadly, this principle means that an asylum seeker should first seek protection within their own country, prior to seeking refugee

---

59   New s 5J(1)(c) of the Act, paragraph 1181 of the EM to the MMPLA Act. The EM can be found at: http://www.aph.gov.au/Parliamentary_Business/Bills_Legislation/Bills_Search_Results/Result?bId=r5346.

status overseas. A classic example of a case where the internal relocation principle was applied was *Singh (Manjit) v Minister for Immigration and Multicultural Affairs*,[60] in which the applicant was a suspected member of a Sikh separatist group in Punjab. The Punjab government had given the chief of police, one KPS Gill, more or less free rein to crush such groups, resulting in severe persecution of suspected members in Punjab. Gill had no authority in the rest of India, and Mr Singh was therefore regarded as being safe elsewhere in India. However, Australian courts had frequently found that relocation must be 'reasonable', in the sense that the applicant would actually be able to make a life for themselves outside their previous region of residence.

The MMPLA Act removes the 'reasonableness of relocation' requirement. Paragraphs 1182 and 1183 of the EM provide as follows:

> 1182. Although the internal relocation principle is not explicitly provided for in the Refugees Convention, in the decision of *SZATV v Minister for Immigration and Citizenship* (2007) 233 CLR 18 (*SZATV*), the High Court has held that the text of the Refugees Convention supports the internal relocation principle and is part of Australian law. The High Court has further found that if it is reasonable for an asylum seeker to relocate to another part of their country of nationality, then their fear of persecution is not well-founded and they will not meet the definition of a refugee in the Refugees Convention. Australia has applied the internal relocation principle consistent with this interpretation.

> 1183. While the Government will continue to adopt the internal relocation principle in the new statutory framework relating to refugees, it is the Government's intention that the principle will no longer encompass the consideration of whether the relocation is reasonable in light of the individual circumstances of the person. The Government considers that in interpreting the reasonableness element into the internal relocation principle, Australian case law has broadened the scope of the principle to take into account the practical realities of relocation. For example, as a result of cases such as *SZATV* and *Randhawa v MILGEA* (1994) 52 FCR 437, when assessing internal relocation options, decision makers are now required to consider aspects such a potential diminishment in quality of life or financial hardship which may result from the relocation. As such aspects fall short of the type of harm which amounts to persecution, the Government considers these to be irrelevant to the assessment of a **well-founded fear of persecution**. For these reasons, it is the Government's intention that new paragraph 5J(1)(c) not be read down by reference to such notions of reasonableness'.

---

60   (2000) FCA 705.

New s 5J(1)(c) of the Act is most likely a direct response to the recent High Court decision in *Minister for Immigration and Border Protection v SZSCA*,[61] in which the court found that a member of a particular social group does not have to fundamentally change their behavior if they relocate within a country. That is, if 'internal protection' comes at the price of fundamental change to their lives and livelihoods, it is not in fact protection and the applicant can still avail themselves of refugee status. This shows that the MMPLA Act does not merely 'freeze' Australian refugee law, but fundamentally changes it in some areas.

Temporary protection visas

The MMPLA Act makes a number of amendments to the *Migration Act* (and, somewhat unusually, the *Migration Regulations 1994*) to reintroduce TPVs to the legislative scheme. New s 35A provides for classes of visas called 'permanent protection visas' (s 35A(2) of the Act) and 'temporary protection visas' (s 35A(3)). New Item 1403 of Schedule 1 of the Regulations sets out the validity criteria for a TPV application, and the following new paragraph 1401(3)(d) is added to Item 1401:

> An application by a person for a Protection (Class XA) visa is valid only if the person:
>
> (i)   does not hold, and has not ever held, a Subclass 785 (Temporary Protection) visa, including such a visa granted before 2 December 2013; and
>
> (ii)   does not hold, and has not ever held, a Temporary Safe Haven (Class UJ) visa; and
>
> (iii) does not hold, and has not ever held, a Temporary (Humanitarian Concern) (Class UO) visa; and
>
> (iv)   held a visa that was in effect on the person's last entry into Australia; and
>
> (v)   is not an unauthorised maritime arrival; and
>
> (vi)   was immigration cleared on the person's last entry into Australia.

The Schedule 2 criteria for TPVs are set out in new Part 785, while Part 866 is amended to remove any reference to the Refugees Convention.

The most striking part of the reintroduction of TPVs is that certain visa applications that are undecided at the date that the MMPLA Act comes into

---

61   (2014) HCA 45.

effect will be 'converted' into TPV applications. New s 45AA(1) provides that an undecided and valid application may be converted into a new kind of application, and s 45AA(3) provides as follows:

> For the purposes of this Act, a regulation (a **conversion regulation**) may provide that, despite anything else in this Act, the pre-conversion application for the pre-conversion visa:
>
> (a)   is taken not to be, and never to have been, a valid application for the pre-conversion visa; and
>
> (b)   is taken to be, and always to have been, a valid application (a **converted application**) for a visa of a different class (specified by the conversion regulation) made by the applicant for the pre-conversion visa.

New Regulation 2.08F is a 'conversion regulation', and subregulations 2.08F(1) and (2) provide as follows:

> (1)   For section 45AA of the Act, despite anything else in the Act, a valid application (a **pre-conversion application**) for a Protection (Class XA) visa made before the commencement of this regulation by an applicant prescribed by subregulation (2) is, immediately after this regulation starts to apply in relation to the application under subregulation (3):
>
> (a)   taken not to be, and never to have been, a valid application for a Protection (Class XA) visa; and
>
> (b)   taken to be, and always to have been, a valid application for a Temporary Protection (Class XD) visa, made by the prescribed applicant.
>
> (2)   The following are prescribed applicants:
>
> (a)   an applicant who holds, or has ever held, any of the following visas:
>
> (i)   a Subclass 785 (Temporary Protection) visa granted before 2 December 2013;
>
> (ii)   a Temporary Safe Haven (Class UJ) visa;
>
> (iii) a Temporary (Humanitarian Concern) (Class UO) visa;
>
> (b)   an applicant who did not hold a visa that was in effect on the applicant's last entry into Australia;

(c) an applicant who is an unauthorised maritime arrival;

(d) an applicant who was not immigration cleared on the applicant's last entry into Australia.

The retrospective intent of Regulation 2.08F can clearly be seen in subregulation 2.08F(3):

> This regulation starts to apply in relation to a pre-conversion application immediately after the occurrence of whichever of the following events is applicable to the application:
>
> (a) if, before the commencement of this regulation, the Minister had not made a decision in relation to the pre-conversion application under section 65 of the Act—the commencement of this regulation;
>
> (b) in a case in which the Minister had made such a decision before the commencement of this regulation—one of the following events, if the event occurs on or after the commencement of this regulation:
>
> > (i) the Refugee Review Tribunal remits a matter in relation to the pre-conversion application in accordance with paragraph 415(2)(c) of the Act;
> >
> > (ii) the Administrative Appeals Tribunal remits a matter in relation to the pre-conversion application in accordance with paragraph 43(1A)(c) of the *Administrative Appeals Tribunal Act 1975* (as substituted in relation to an RRT-reviewable decision by section 452 of the Act);
> >
> > (iii) a court quashes a decision of the Minister in relation to the pre-conversion application and orders the Minister to reconsider the application in accordance with the law.

That is, if an applicant applies for a Protection Visa prior to the MMPLA Act coming into effect, is refused, this decision is affirmed by the RRT or AAT, and the applicant is successful at judicial review, the remitted application will be dealt with as an application for a TPV and not a permanent visa. This kind of retrospectivity appears to be unprecedented in Australia.

The government's repeated attempts to reintroduce TPVs make no sense in terms of 'stopping the boats' – in that sense, they simply do not work. Given that

TPVs first came into effect at the end of October 1999, it is preferable to compare the figures for 2000 against those for 2001 to see whether the introduction of TPVs had any impact on the number of unauthorised boat arrivals or asylum-seekers in Australia. The following table also looks at the years 1992 and 1993, the former being the year that Division 4B was inserted into the *Migration Act*.

Jurisdiction	1992	1993	% Change	2000	2001	% Change
Australia (unauthorised boat arrivals)*	216	81	-266.67	2,939	5,516	+187.68
Australia (asylum claims)**	6,000	7,500	+12.50	13,000	12,000	-8.33
Total OECD***	2,650,000	2,500,000	-1.06	1,755,000	1,700,000	-3.23

*   Janet Phillips and Harriet Spinks, *Boat Arrivals in Australia since 1976*, Commonwealth Parliamentary Library, 24 January 2012 at 18.

**   Timothy Hatton, *Seeking Asylum: Trends and Policies in the OECD*, Organisation for Economic Co-Operation and Development (2011) at 80; http://www.cepr.org/pubs/books/cepr/Seeking_Asylum.pdf

***   Ibid at 16 and 76.

Australia saw a huge *increase* in the number of UMAs in 2001 from 2000, despite modest falls in the number of asylum applications in both Australia and the OECD.

Mary Crock and Daniel Ghezelbash have argued that the Pacific Solution was the direct or at least most substantial cause of the significant reduction in unauthorised boat arrivals from 2002, but that immigration detention and TPVs had no impact.[62] Why is this the case? One explanation was given by the then ALP shadow Minister for Immigration, Mr Burke, who directly blamed the TPV regime for the drowning of 353 mostly women and children asylum seekers in the SIEV X disaster of 2001, claiming that 'the reason (the women and children) went to a people smuggler and found themselves on SIEV X was that dad wasn't able to be reunited with them'.[63] The reintroduction of TPVs only makes sense as a form of punishment of unauthorised boat arrivals.

'Fast-track' RRT processing

The MMPLA Act introduces a form of 'fast-track' processing by a body to be referred to as the Immigration Assessment Authority (IAA). A number of new definitions are inserted into s.5(1) of the Act, and it is convenient to start with the terms 'fast-track applicant' and 'fast-track decision':

---

62   Mary Crock and Daniel Ghezelbash, 'Do Loose Lips Bring Ships? The Role of Policy, Politics and Human Rights in Managing Unauthorised Boat Arrivals', (2010) 19 *Griffith Law Review* 238.

63   'Border Policies Caused Deaths, says Labor', *The Age*, 17 October 2006. See also Crock and Ghezelbash, supra n63 at 262.

fast track applicant means:

(a) a person:

    (i) who is an unauthorised maritime arrival and who entered Australia on or after 13 August 2012; and

    (ii) to whom the Minister has given a written notice under subsection 46A(2) determining that subsection 46A(1) does not apply to an application by the person for a protection visa; and

    (iii) who has made a valid application for a protection visa in accordance with the determination; or

(b) a person who is, or who is included in a class of persons who are, specified by legislative instrument made under paragraph (1AA)(b).

fast track decision means a decision to refuse to grant a protection visa to a fast track applicant, other than a decision to refuse to grant such a visa:

(c) because the Minister or a delegate of the Minister is not satisfied that the applicant passes the character test under section 501; or

(d) relying on:

    (i) subsection 5H(2); or

    (ii) subsection 36(1B) or (1C); or

    (iii) paragraph 36(2C)(a) or (b).

'Fast-track applicants' are then separated into 'excluded fast track review applicants' and 'fast track review applicants' as follows:

excluded fast track review applicant means a fast track applicant:

(a) who, in the opinion of the Minister:

    (i) is covered by section 91C or 91N;[64] or

    (ii) has previously entered Australia and who, while in Australia, made a claim for protection relying on a criterion mentioned in subsection 36(2) in an application that was refused or withdrawn; or

---

64   Broadly speaking, these sections apply to non-citizens covered by agreements between Australia and safe third countries (s 91C) and those who have a right of residence in safe third countries (s 91N).

(iii) has made a claim for protection in a country other than Australia that was refused by that country; or

(iv) has made a claim for protection in a country other than Australia that was refused by the Office of the United Nations High Commissioner for Refugees in that country; or

(v) makes a manifestly unfounded claim for protection relying on a criterion mentioned in subsection 36(2) in, or in connection with, his or her application; or

(vi) without reasonable explanation provides, gives or presents a bogus document to an officer of the Department or to the Minister (or causes such a document to be so provided, given or presented) in support of his or her application; or

(b) who is, or who is included in a class of persons who are, specified by legislative instrument made under paragraph (1AA)(a).

A 'fast track review applicant' is a fast track applicant who is not an excluded fast track review applicant'. The term 'manifestly unfounded claim' is not defined in the MMPLA Act, but paragraph 722 of the EM states as follows:

> This provision is intended to capture those fast track applicants who have put forward claims that are without any substance (such as having no fear of mistreatment), have no plausible basis (such as where there is no objective evidence supporting the claimed mistreatment) or are based on a deliberate attempt to deceive or abuse Australia's asylum process in an attempt to avoid removal. It is the Government's position that such persons should not have access to merits review because the nature of their claims are so lacking in substance that further review would waste resources and unnecessarily delay their finalisation.

New s 411(2)(c) provides that 'fast track decisions' are not RRT-reviewable decisions. The MMPLA Act then inserts a new Division 7A, which creates the IAA. It is notable that a 'fast track review applicant' does not need to make an application for review to the IAA – instead, s 473CA provides that '[t]he Minister must refer a fast track reviewable decision to the Immigration Assessment Authority as soon as reasonably practicable after the decision is made'. Interestingly, the MMPLA does not seem to expressly state that fast track reviewable decisions made in relation to excluded fast track review applicants must not be referred to the IAA, although this is strongly implied by new s 473BC, which states that '[t]he Minister may, by legislative instrument, determine that a specified fast track decision, or a specified class of fast track decisions, in relation to an excluded fast track review applicant should be reviewed under this Part'.

Another striking feature of the IAA, especially when compared to the RRT, is that the IAA must usually make its decisions 'on the papers'. This is the requirement of new s 473DB, although s 473DC permits the IAA to make inquiries, and s 473DD provides that the IAA may consider new information if it is 'satisfied that there are exceptional circumstances to justify considering the new information'. Further, s 473DF permits the IAA to invite an applicant to an 'interview' (not a 'hearing'). It is also notable that s 473DB(2) provides that the IAA may make a decision on a referred application at any time after the referral.

Paragraph 891 of the EM explains the purpose of s 473DB and following sections as follows:

> The purpose of this amendment is to describe what the limited merits review function of the IAA entails. The intention is for the IAA to review a fast track reviewable decision by only considering the review material provided to the Authority by the Secretary of the Department. The IAA is not required to accept or request new information or interview the referred applicant. This is however subject to Subdivision C – Additional information which sets out the limited circumstances in which the IAA may consider new information for the purposes of making a decision in relation to a fast track reviewable decision.

In the meantime, excluded fast track applicants are excluded from any merits review of their decision at all, and will no doubt go straight to judicial review, in the High Court in its original jurisdiction. The High Court will find itself back in a pre-*S157*[65] situation in relation to such applicants, where the High Court will find itself as the only court that can hear such applications.

Safe haven enterprise visas

The MMPLA Act also introduces a new class of visa, to be known as a 'Safe Haven Enterprise Visa' (SHEV). The legislation relating to SHEVs is appended to this chapter.

The purpose of a SHEV is described in new s 35A(3B) of the Act as 'to provide protection and to encourage enterprise through earning and learning while strengthening regional Australia'. The Minister's second reading speech on the MMPLA Act described the purpose and operation of the SHEV as follows:[66]

---

65   *Plaintiff S157/2002 v Commonwealth* (2003) 211 CLR 476.
66   House of Representatives Hansard, 25 September 2014 at 10546.

However, consistent with this government's principles of rewarding enterprise and its belief in a strong regional Australia, a new visa, the Safe Haven Enterprise Visa, will also be created. The Safe Haven Enterprise Visa will be will be open to applications by those who have been processed under the legacy caseload and are found to be refugees. I stress that that does not relate to people who may seek to come to Australia in the future by this method. They of course are subject to offshore processing and resettlement, as well as our turn-back measures and other arrangements.

The SHEV, as it is known, will be an alternative temporary protection visa to the TPV and encourages enterprise through earning and learning in regional areas. IMAs[67] granted a SHEV will be required to confine themselves to designated region – either a state or territory government or local government area, or an employer in a regional area can request to be designated. This would be identified through a national self-nomination process. No region would be required to compulsorily participate in such a scheme. The visa will be valid for five years and, like the TPV, will not include family reunion or a right to re-enter Australia. SHEV holders will be targeted to designated regions and encouraged to fill regional job vacancies, where they exist, and will have access to the same support arrangement as a TPV holder.

SHEV holders who have worked in regional Australia without requiring access to income support for $3\frac{1}{2}$ years will be able to apply and if they meet eligibility requirements be granted other onshore visas – for example, a family or skilled visa as well as temporary skilled and student visa. However, I stress: they will not be able to apply for a permanent protection visa.

New Item 1404 of Schedule 1 of the *Migration Regulations* prescribes the validity criteria for a Class XE (SHEV) visa, and paragraph 1404(3)(d) provides that to make a valid application for a SHEV, the applicant must hold or have held a TPV, SHEV, Temporary Safe Haven (TSH) visa or a Temporary Humanitarian Concern (THC) visa, or be an unlawful non-citizen of a specified kind. There is no requirement that an applicant have been granted any of these visas, or entered Australia, prior to any specified date, although subparagraph 1404(3)(d)(i) refers to 'holds, or has ever held, a Temporary Protection (Class XD) visa or a Subclass 785 (Temporary Protection) visa, including such a visa granted before 2 December 2013' (author's emphasis). Sub-item 1404(4) provides that

---

67   Illegal Maritime Arrivals.

'[t]he Minister may, by legislative instrument, specify a regional area for the purposes of these regulations', but no such instrument has yet been drafted. It remains to be seen whether any such instrument will be made.

Schedule 2 criteria are set out in new Part 790, and clause 790.511 specifies the validity period of a SHEV as follows:

> Temporary visa permitting the holder to travel to, enter and remain in Australia until:
>
> (a) if the holder of the temporary visa (the **first visa**) makes a valid application for another Subclass 790 (**Safe Haven Enterprise**) visa within 5 years after the grant of the first visa—the day when the application is finally determined or withdrawn; or
>
> (b) in any other case—the end of 5 years from the date of grant of the first visa.

The key provision, however, is probably new Regulation 2.06AAB. Subregulation 2.06AAB(1) sets out a list of visa subclasses for which a SHEV holder or former holder can validly apply. Subregulation 2.06AAB(2) then provides that a SHEV holder of former holder can only make a valid application for a visa specified in subregulation 2.06AAB(1) in the following circumstances:

> For the purposes of paragraph 46A(1A)(c) of the Act, an applicant for a visa who currently holds, or has ever held, a **safe haven enterprise** visa must, for a period or periods totalling 42 months (which need not be continuous) while the visa is (or was) in effect, satisfy one of the following requirements:
>
> (a) the applicant does not receive any social security benefits determined under subregulation (3), and is engaged in employment, as determined under that subregulation, in a regional area specified under subclause 1404(4) of Schedule 1;
>
> (b) the applicant is enrolled in full-time study at an educational institution, as determined under subregulation (3), in a regional area specified under subclause 1404(4) of Schedule 1;
>
> (c) the applicant satisfies a combination of the requirements in paragraph (a) and paragraph (b), at different times.

Subregulation 2.06AAB(3) simply provides that '[t]he Minister may, by legislative instrument, make a determination for the purposes of paragraphs (2)(a) and (b)', and again no such draft legislative instrument has been revealed. It can be seen that unless a notice is made under sub-item 1404(4) of Schedule 1 of the Regulations, it will be impossible for any applicant to meet the requirements for making a valid application for a SHEV, and this may well be the intention of the government.

Children born in Australia

Schedule 6 of the MMPLA Act makes a number of amendments that apply to children born in Australia to unauthorised maritime arrivals. New s 5AA(1A) provides that such children are also taken to be unauthorised maritime arrivals, while new s 5AA(1AA) provides that children born to unauthorised maritime arrivals in offshore processing countries are also unauthorised maritime arrivals. These provisions appear to reflect the existing law as set out in *B9/2014 v Minister for Immigration*[68] (the 'baby Ferouz' case), a decision which is under appeal. However, Part 2 of Schedule 6 makes it clear that Schedule 6 is intended to operate retrospectively, a decision which is clearly meant to head off any successful appeal against the *B9/2014* decision.

Actions taken at sea

Schedule 1 of the MMPLA Act relates to the ability of officers authorised under the *Maritime Powers Act 2013* to interdict vessels at sea and take them to another country, regardless of whether there is an agreement with the particular country in place. It restricts the court's capacity to invalidate government actions at sea, provides that the rules of natural justice do not apply to certain key actions, and suspends Australia's international obligations in the context of powers exercised under the *Maritime Powers Act*. Specifically, the Bill removes the reference in the *Maritime Powers Act* to the limitation of the exercise of powers outside Australia in accordance with international law. Instead, the MMPLA Act provides that such officers are not required to consider Australia's international obligations (including, for example, the principle of *non-refoulement*), or the international obligations or domestic law of another country in making their decisions.

It is worth pointing out that these provisions do appear to leave the door open for serious violations of the Refugees Convention and the UN Convention on the Laws of the Sea (UNCLOS), amongst other rules of international law. For example, the Refugee Council of Australia, in its submission to the Senate Legal and Constitutional Affairs Committee's consideration of the MMPLA Act, stated as follows at paragraphs 1.3 and 1.4:[69]

---

68   (2014) FCCA 2348.
69   http://www.refugeecouncil.org.au/r/sub/1410-Legacy-Caseload.pdf, extracted 4 December 2014.

[1.3] These amendments seek to empower the Minister to detain and transfer people on the high seas even though the Australian Government does not have these powers under the law of the sea nor under the various conventions, covenants and international instruments of human rights. On the high seas or within the Exclusive Economic Zone or the contiguous zone, vessels are governed by the principle of freedom of the seas. Only the flag state can intercept and exert jurisdiction on vessels in these zones, except where the vessel is engaged in piracy, the slave trade or is stateless.[70] As such, interception and detention of vessels in these zones is a violation of the United Nations Convention on the Law of the Sea (UNCLOS). As set out, these amendments would give Australia unbridled power to detain and transfer people on the high seas without consideration of *non-refoulement* obligations or in breach of its obligations under the law of the sea. Furthermore, the Minister would have the power to detain people and transfer them to another country without the consent of the other country and without an assessment of whether the people being transferred have protection claims against that country.

[1.4] RCOA is particularly troubled by amendments which create the risk of people facing arbitrary and prolonged detention without any scrutiny by Parliament or the courts. Given that the Australian Government would not confirm publicly that it had detained and held 157 asylum seekers in June 2014 until the commencement of a High Court case,[71] RCOA is worried that people will face prolonged detention or even be *refouled* without public knowledge. Additionally, as Professor Ben Saul points out, such detention may constitute incommunicado military detention – also described as enforced disappearance – something which is prohibited under the Rome Statute of the International Criminal Court.[72]

Again, the current government clearly has a mindset against international law. While it is true that international law is often internally contradictory and at times incomprehensible, the UNCLOS and the Refugees Convention are two conventions that are reasonably well-drafted and the UNCLOS in particular has been generally adhered to by its signatories. There appears to be no justification for ignoring it.

---

70   UNCLOS art 110(1). Furthermore, a stateless vessel only allows for the right to visit, and this right does not extend to a right to tow a boat to another part of the sea. See Guy S Goodwin-Gill and Jane McAdam, *The Refugee in International Law* (Oxford University Press, 3rd ed, 2007) 271.

71   *JARK and Ors v Minister for Immigration and Border Protection and Anor (2014)* HCATrans 150; *CPCF and Ors v Minister for Immigration and Border Protection and Anor* (2014) HCATrans 153.

72   Ben Saul, 'Australia has probably broken the law, but it will get away scot-free', *Crikey*, July 2014, available at: http://www.crikey.com.au/2014/07/04/australia-has-probably-broken-the-law-but-will-get-away-scot-free.

Chapter 4. Merits Review of Migration Decisions

Part 1 – History of merits review of migration decisions in Australia

Beginnings – the Administrative Appeals Tribunal (AAT)

Unlike judicial review, which has a history dating back at least as far as Henry II of England, merits review, in Australia, began in the 1970s. The first Australian body to have jurisdiction in relation to review of migration decisions was the Administrative Appeals Tribunal (AAT), which was brought into being by the *Administrative Appeals Tribunal Act 1975* ('the AAT Act') and commenced operations in 1977. Some of the very early AAT decisions on migration cases, such as *Re Becker and Minister for Immigration and Ethnic Affairs*[1] and, in particular, *Re Drake and Minister for Immigration and Ethnic Affairs*[2] are still good authority on the nature of merits review and the role of a review body. However, until 1992 the AAT did not have the power to make a final determination on a criminal deportation matter – instead it could only make a recommendation that an applicant not be deported.[3] However, it is interesting to note that the Minister went against an AAT recommendation on only two occasions prior to 1986.[4] Today, the AAT retains jurisdiction in migration matters only in the areas of criminal deportation (which is now rarely applied),[5] refusals and cancellations made by delegates under s 501 of the Act[6], cancellation of business visas under s 134 of the Act,[7] citizenship matters and regulation of the migration agents' profession.[8]

---

1   (1977) 1 ALD 158.
2   (1979) 2 ALD 634.
3   See s 180A of the *Migration Act 1958* as it stood prior to 1992, and s 43(1)(c)(ii) of the AAT Act. This was one of very few areas of law in which the AAT could not make a conclusive and determinative decision.
4   Mary Crock and Laurie Berg, *Immigration, Refugees and Forced Migration – Law, Practice and Policy in Australia*, Federation Press, 2011 at paragraph 18.08.
5   Paragraph 500(1)(a) of the *Migration Act 1958*.
6   Paragraph 500(1)(b) of the *Migration Act 1958*.
7   Section 136 of the *Migration Act 1958*.
8   Section 52 of the *Australian Citizenship Act 2007*.

Internal review

The first review mechanisms specifically for immigration decisions were purely administrative in nature, and not based in legislation. Crock and Berg describe the first review body, the Immigration Review Panels (IRPs), as follows:[9]

> Formal review of the merits of certain general migration decisions was instituted in January 1982 with the creation of the quasi-independent [IRPs], which also operated as a recommendatory body for the Minister. There was no statutory basis for any of these non-statutory review bodies or the work they performed. Cases were reviewed on paper[10] and applicants could neither correspond with these bodies nor adduce oral evidence, although the IRPs could, at their discretion, take evidence if they regarded such steps as essential for their deliberations.

Crock and Berg also point out that, like the MIRO,[11] the IRPs were criticised for their lack of independence from government. In 1985, the Administrative Review Council (ARC) estimated that around 88 per cent of IRP decisions affirmed the original decision.[12]

The IRPs became a source of controversy in the late 1980s, when the Ombudsman investigated the legality of a $240 review fee imposed in 1987.[13] The Minister was forced to concede that the fee, which again lacked any legislative authority, was being collected illegally.[14] The government's response was to require applicants who were unsuccessful at first instance to reapply and have the new applications be considered under the Regulation Second Application Scheme, which acted, confusingly enough, as if it *was* a merits review body.[15] This situation was obviously untenable in the longer term.

The Migration Review Office (MIRO) and Immigration Review Tribunal (IRT)

As noted in in previous chapters the *Migration Amendment Act 1989* ('the MAA 1989') introduced statutory merits review by an independent tribunal, created by the Act. Paragraph 2 of the Explanatory Memorandum (EM) to the MAA 1989 provided as follows:

---

9   Supra n4 at paragraph 18.10.
10   In other words, without any oral hearing of the applicant.
11   See Chapter 2.
12   ARC *Report no 25: Review of Migration Decisions*, Australian Government Publishing Service, 1985.
13   Department of Immigration and Ethnic Affairs, *Review '88* (DIEA, 1988) at 67–69.
14   Senator Robert Ray, Senate Hansard 3 March 1989 at 412.
15   Crock and Berg, supra n4 at paragraph 18.12.

The Act is to be amended to provide for a statutory two-tier system of review of prescribed immigration decisions. The first tier of review will be conducted by specially authorised review officers within a unit in the Department of Immigration, Local Government and Ethnic Affairs (the Department) followed by appeals to an external review body called the Immigration Review Tribunal (IRT). The present jurisdiction of the Administrative Appeals Tribunal in criminal deportation matters will not be affected. The IRT will operate independently of the Department and will have as its objective providing a mechanism of review that is fair, just, economical and quick.

Note the phrase 'fair, just, economical and quick' in the EM.

Unlike the IRPs, both the MIRO and the IRT were backed by legislation, having been introduced by the MAA 1989. Michael Chaaya described the roles of the MIRO and IRT as follows in 1997:[16]

A. Migration Internal Review Office

MIRO is currently a unit within the Department of Immigration and Multicultural Affairs designed as the first tier of merits review of certain migration decisions. Under Part 5, Division 2 of the *Migration Act* 1958 MIRO officers stand in the position of the original decision maker and re-assess the application to see whether they think it was the correct or preferable decision (subsection 341(1)[17]). In making a review determination, a MIRO officer can decide to either affirm the decision; vary the decision; remit the matter for reconsideration; or set the decision aside (subsection 341(2)). If the decision is affirmed, the applicant is advised of the reasons for the decision and whether any further merits review is available at the IRT level (section 343). It is also important to note that the use of MIRO by aggrieved applicants comes at a cost of $500.00. The objective of MIRO is to provide internal merits review which is fair, just, easily understandable, quick and cost efficient.

B. Immigration Review Tribunal (IRT)

The IRT is the second tier of the migration merits review system which conducts independent final merits review of certain decisions. These include decisions made by MIRO, or certain visa cancellation decisions

---

16   Michael Chaaya, 'Proposed Changes to the Review of Migration Decisions: Sensible Reform Agenda or Political Expediency?' (1997) 19(4) *Sydney Law Review* 547 at 548–49.

17   These references are to the section numbers after renumbering by the *Migration Reform Act 1992*, which came into effect on 1 September 1994.

and decisions to keep non-citizens in immigration detention.[18] The IRT s statutory objective is to provide a mechanism of review that is fair, just, economical, informal and quick (section 353). In pursuit of this objective, the Tribunal adopts informal and non-legalistic review procedures which are not bound by the rules of evidence, legal forms or technicalities associated with the traditional adversarial hearing. An application fee of $850.00 is required to commence an IRT application. In making its decision, the IRT has determinative powers and thus may affirm a decision under review; remit the matter for reconsideration; vary a decision; or set it aside and substitute a new decision (subsection 349(2)). Applicants to the IRT do not have a legal right to be represented by a lawyer or advocate but are able to seek advice in order to prepare their application.

Despite the criticisms levelled at the MIRO in particular,[19] the IRT and the MIRO were welcome developments in so far as they gave legislative backing to review of immigration decisions. For the first time, applicants had a right to reasons for decisions and, in most cases before the IRT, an oral hearing. However, there were some restrictions on the jurisdiction of the MIRO and IRT, as Crock and Berg explain.[20]

> The legislation governing IRT review was unusual in the curious mix of procedural discretion and substantive constraints of the law governing the grant of visas. In spite of broad powers given to the tribunal to determine its own procedures,[21] its ability to decide appeals 'according to substantial justice and the merits of a case' was subject always to the legislation governing its decision-making. Neither the MIRO nor IRT could go outside the terms of the Act or Regulations.[22] Under what was s 118(3), the tribunal was forbidden from 'purporting to grant an entry permit on humanitarian grounds'. Section 116 ensured that the tribunal had no discretion to extend the time for hearing appeals and could not consider appeals lodged out of time. The apparent obligation to grant applicants a hearing where a 'favourable' decision could not be made on the papers under s 129 could also be illusory as the phrase 'decision favourable to the applicant' was defined to include decisions mandated by the legislation.

---

18   Which is now of course mandatory – see s 189 of the *Migration Act*.
19   See Chapter 2.
20   Crock and Berg, supra n4 at paragraph 18.16.
21   Compare this to the current, highly prescriptive, Parts 5 and 7 of the *Migration Act 1958*.
22   Section 349 of the Act, prior to 1 July 1999. It could be argued that if the MIRO and IRT *could* go outside the Act, they would not be exercising a *review* function, but an entirely new power.

Many of these provisions criticised by Crock and Berg remain in the current Parts 5 and 7 of the Act.

MIRO was effectively abolished in 1999, when the IRT and MIRO were merged to form the Migration Review Tribunal (MRT). This was done by means of the *Migration Legislation Amendment Act (No 1) 1998*, which came into effect on 1 June 1999.

The Refugee Review Tribunal (RRT)

One important legislative change that came about prior to the coming into effect of the *Migration Reform Act 1992* ('the MRA') was the creation of the Refugee Review Tribunal (RRT) as an independent body to review all decisions relating to applications for refugee status. The RRT commenced operations on 1 July 1993, and when a decision was made to defer the commencement of the MRA until 1 September 1994, the provisions relating to the RRT were exempt from the deferral.[23]

Prior to the creation of the RRT, review of refugee decisions was carried out by an informally constituted body, the Refugee Status Review Committee (RSRC), which was similar in many ways to the IRPs. Savitri Taylor described the working of the RSRC as follows:[24]

> The Refugee Status Review Committee (RSRC) was a body which failed to be independent in any relevant sense. A community representative nominated by the Refugee Council of Australia (RCOA) was a member of the RSRC, together with representatives of the Department of Foreign Affairs and Trade (DFAT), the Attorney-General's Department and DIEA. A representative of UNHCR attended meetings in an advisory capacity ...

> Not only were three-quarters of the RSRC's membership representatives of the executive government, the DIEA representative on an RSRC panel was also the person who chaired the panel. This arrangement meant that a representative from the very department that made the primary-stage decision was in a position to control the discussions of the RSRC as well as being in a position to vote on the recommendation to be made to the Minister's delegate ... [T]he RSRC held its meetings in the absence of the claimant and certainly never gave the claimant an oral hearing ...

> It appears that, at RSRC meetings, genuine and lengthy discussion took place on points of disagreement. The discussion was genuine in

---

23 See the *Migration Laws Amendment Act 1993*.
24 Savitri Taylor, 'The Right to Review in the Australian Onshore Refugee Status Determination Process: Is it an Adequate Procedural Safeguard Against Refoulement?', (1994) 22(2) *Federal Law Review* 300 at 315–17.

the sense that members were known to go into a meeting sometimes without a clear view as to what the recommendation should be and to form a view as a consequence of the discussion or to go into a meeting with a particular view of a case only to change their view in the light of additional information or different perspectives provided by other members of the group or the UNHCR representative. On the other hand, the DIEA representative would, one imagines, have internalised the same organisational values as the primary decision maker and would probably also have felt subtly pressured to vindicate the primary decision.

It is important to consider whether a tribunal constituted by legislation is in any better position to guarantee independence than a purely administrative body like the RSRC.

The legislation creating the RRT was modelled significantly on that for the IRT. It is notable that there was only ever one tier of merits review for decisions relating to refugee status, as opposed to two for most other kinds of applications. That aside, the powers and the procedural responsibilities of the RRT were very similar to those originally given to the IRT, in that no adverse decision can be made without offering the opportunity for a hearing, hearings are constituted by a single member without a representative of the Department present, and its decisions are judicially reviewable.

The Migration Review Tribunal (MRT) and Codes of Procedure

As noted earlier, the MRT replaced both the MIRO and the IRT with effect from 1 July 1999. Senator Kemp, representing the Minister in the Senate, stated as follows in his second reading speech for the *Migration Legislation Amendment Bill (No 1) 1998* on 12 November 1998:[25]

> Under the changes introduced by this bill, the single tier review will be conducted by a new external review body, the Migration Review Tribunal.
>
> The Migration Review Tribunal will be required to conduct fair, impartial and expeditious review of migration decisions, at lower cost to the Australian taxpayer. This will be achieved through the introduction of more streamlined and flexible review decision-making processes.

The major change brought about by the 1998 Act, however, was the introduction of the codes of procedure for the MRT and RRT. Prior to 1 July 1999, the IRT and

---

25   Senate Hansard, 12 November 1998 at 213.

RRT had few express procedural obligations other than requiring the tribunal to offer the applicant a hearing if it could not make a positive decision 'on the papers'. The conduct of the IRT's and RRT's hearings was left up to the tribunals themselves, although reviews were to be conducted according to 'substantial justice and the merits of the case',[26] and in a manner that was 'fair, just, informal and quick'.[27] The purpose of the codes of procedure was explained by the Minister, Mr Ruddock, in his Second Reading Speech as follows:[28]

> The bill also includes certain safeguards for applicants by introducing a code of procedure for both the Migration Review Tribunal and the Refugee Review Tribunal which is similar to that already applying to decisions made by the department. This code includes such matters as the giving of a prescribed notice of the timing for a hearing, and a requirement that applicants be given access to, and time to comment on, adverse material relevant to them.

What is much more likely is that the codes were intended to be a complete and exhaustive statement of the tribunals' procedural obligations, and thereby displace the common law rules of natural justice. The Minister made this argument in respect of Subdivision AB of the Act in the case of *Re Minister for Immigration and Multicultural Affairs; Ex parte Miah*,[29] only for the High Court to rule that as Subdivision AB did not (at the time) specifically state that the common law rules of natural justice had been replaced, Subdivision AB did not have that effect, and the common law rules continued to exist alongside the code of procedure. The government's response was the *Migration Legislation Amendment (Procedural Fairness) Act 2002*, which inserted a number of provisions into the Act (most importantly for these purposes ss 51A, 357A and 422B) stating that the relevant part of the Act is an 'exhaustive statement of the requirements of the natural justice hearing rule in relation to the matters it deals with'. The Full Federal Court has ruled that s 422B at least is effective in displacing the common law requirements of natural justice.[30]

The MRT and RRT codes of procedure are now extremely complex, and important provisions such as s 424A (the RRT's duty to disclose adverse information) have generated huge amounts of litigation.

Finally, the AAT, MRT, RRT and a number of other Commonwealth merits review bodies are scheduled to merge with effect from 1 July 2015.[31] The *Tribunals*

---

26 Originally s 166C of the Act for the RRT, now set out in ss 353(1) (MRT) and 420(1) (RRT).

27 Now set out in ss 353(2)(b) (MRT) and 420(2)(b) (RRT) of the Act.

28 House of Representatives Hansard, 2 December 1998 at 1122.

29 (2001) 206 CLR 57.

30 *SCZIJ v Minister for Immigration and Multicultural Affairs* (2006) FCAFC 62.

31 http://www.ag.gov.au/LegalSystem/AdministrativeLaw/Pages/Commonwealthtribunalreform.aspx, extracted 7 November 2014.

Amalgamation Bill 2014, before the Senate at the time of writing, proposes the amalgamation of all the Commonwealth tribunals into one, but the procedures of what will become the Migration and Refugee Divisions of the new tribunal will remain mostly unchanged from the procedures for the MRT and RRT.

Part 2 – Nature of merits review

Review tribunals are part of the executive

First and foremost, it is important to note that MRT, RRT and AAT (and other review tribunals such as the Social Security Review Tribunal) are part of the executive and not the judiciary. The nature of judicial power will be discussed in more detail in later chapters, but for now it is sufficient to note that the MRT and RRT are deliberately *not* constituted as courts, and in fact ss 353(2)(a) and 420(2)(a) make it clear that they are not bound by the rules of evidence.

Unlike a court, the MRT and RRT make the 'correct and preferable' decision on an application before them.[32] The tribunals make an entirely new (*de novo*) decision on the basis of all the evidence before them, including new evidence that may not have been before the Departmental decision maker.[33] The MRT and RRT act on an 'inquisitorial' basis, meaning that the presiding member asks questions of the applicant and his or her adviser without hearing from the Minister, as opposed to a court, which with rare exceptions hears both sides of an argument with a judge making the decision.

A good example of the manner in which a merits reviewer is intended to act can be found in the UK case of *Huang v Secretary of State for the Home Department*.[34] Ms Huang, a failed applicant for humanitarian stay in the UK, applied for review the Home Department's decision to an 'adjudicator', as permitted by s 65 of the *Immigration and Asylum Act 1999*. That Act permitted a further appeal to the Court of Appeal from the adjudicator's findings on a question of law. Lord Bingham, writing for the House of Lords, found that the adjudicator, by focusing on whether there was an error in the original decision, did not fulfil their role. His Lordship stated that:[35]

> It remains the case that the judge is not the primary decision maker ... The appellate immigration authority, deciding an appeal under section 65,

---

32   *Drake v Minister for Immigration and Ethnic Affairs* (1979) 24 ALR 577 at 591.
33   See for example *Sok v Minister for Immigration and Citizenship* (2008) HCA 50.
34   (2007) 2 AC 167.
35   Ibid at paragraph 13.

is not reviewing the decision of another decision maker. It is deciding whether or not it is unlawful to refuse leave to enter or remain, and it is doing so on the basis of up to date facts.

That is, the appellate authority had acted in too 'judicial' a manner in this case, and should have considered Mrs Huang's case *de novo* rather than simply examining the primary decision maker's decision for any errors. It is a *court* that is prohibited from engaging in 'merits review'.

A similar decision was made by the Federal Court of Canada on 22 August 2014. In *Huruglica v Minister of Citizenship and Immigration*[36] Phelan J found that the Refugee Appeal Division (RAD) of the Immigration and Refugee Board (IRB) had erred when it found that a decision of the Refugee Protection Division (RPD) refusing the applicant refugee status was not unreasonable and therefore could not be set aside. Phelan J stated as follows at paragraph 47:

> Unlike judicial review, the RAD, pursuant to subsection 111(1)(b),[37] may substitute the determination which 'in its opinion, should have been made'. One precondition of exercising this power is that the RAD must conduct an independent assessment of the application in order to arrive at its own opinion. It is not necessary, in order to trigger this remedial power, that the RAD must find error on some standard of review basis.

This has given rise to two significant arguments about the tribunals' constitution and processes. Firstly, even though a review tribunal is not a court, must it be able to demonstrate its independence from government in order for its decisions to be upheld? Secondly, if the tribunals are supposed to follow an inquisitorial model, what is their duty to make inquiries of their own volition?

Institutional bias

It has been argued on multiple occasions that the review tribunals are not truly independent of government, and that their decisions are therefore affected by 'institutional bias' against applicants. For example, Savitri Taylor, as long ago as 1994, referred to the RRT as 'a supposedly independent administrative tribunal',[38] her argument was that the Minister's ability to issue a conclusive certificate, under what is now s 411(3) of the Act, in a particular case meant that the RRT lacked independence. Interestingly, no such conclusive certificate has

---

36   (2014) FC 799.
37   Of the *Immigration and Refugee Protection Act 2001* SC 2001, c 27.
38   Taylor, supra n24 at 310.

ever been issued, and the mere rumour that such a certificate could be issued in one case led the RRT to refer the matter to the AAT for the only time in its history.[39]

Another argument that the MRT and RRT lack true independence arises from the way members are appointed and retained. Crock and Berg explain the argument as follows:[40]

> The central problems with the regime, in our view, are the assumptions made that tribunal members are independent of government, and that they are neutral arbiters of the cases brought before them. In practice, tribunal members have been affected by what might be termed loosely 'politics' both in the manner of appointment/reappointment and (on occasion) in their decision-making. Where members have been appointed from within the bureaucracy and/or have been appointed on relatively short-term contracts the pressure to toe the government line can be considerable.

The concept of institutional bias within the Department and the tribunals has been around for a long time, but seems to have been used successfully only once. In *Mok v Minister for Immigration, Local Government and Ethnic Affairs*[41] three Cambodian asylum seekers who were refused entry permits by the Department (in the days before the commencement of the RRT) applied for judicial review, primarily on the basis that the Prime Minister, Mr Hawke, had made comments on national television to the effect that Cambodian boat arrivals were not refugees, would not be granted permanent residence in Australia, and that he would act 'forcefully' to ensure that applications for refugee status were refused.[42] Keely J in the Federal Court found that such statements, despite the efforts of successive immigration ministers to disown them, meant that all of the refusal decisions were affected by apprehended bias.

One other successful claim of institutional bias involved a Departmental *officer*, but not an immigration decision. *Phillips v Disciplinary Appeal Committee of the Merit Protection Review Agency*[43] involved an appeal against the decision of a committee to discipline Mr Phillips under the *Public Service Act* in relation to

---

39   *SRPP and Minister for Immigration and Multicultural Affairs* [2000] AAT 878. This case involved an applicant who had fled East Timor before independence, and rumours around the Department at the time (personally heard by the author) were that the Minister would issue the first ever s 411(3) certificate to prevent the RRT from hearing the matter. The RRT circumvented the rumoured conclusive certificate by exercising its power under Division 8 of Part 7 of the Act to refer the matter to the AAT, a power that has never been exercised before or since.

40   Supra n4 at paragraph 18.37.

41   (1993) 47 FCR 1.

42   Ibid at paragraph 19.

43   (1994) 34 ALD 758.

public comments he made that were critical of the Department. John McMillan, now the Commonwealth Information Commissioner, explains the case as follows:[44]

> Mr Phillips was an officer of the Department who was the subject of a disciplinary inquiry arising from public statements he had made that were critical of the Department. The Court held that the inquiry was flawed by reason of the participation of a Departmental nominee on the inquiry panel, as envisaged by the legislation. Although there was no evidence to suggest actual bias or animosity by the Departmental nominee, it was enough that he came from a Department in which senior officers were evidently troubled by Mr Phillips's behaviour. The Court reasoned that members of the public would reasonably apprehend bias by supposing that the Departmental nominee had career aspirations and a desire to be granted a public service efficiency bonus, and would thus lean towards the views of his senior officers, to the detriment of Mr Phillips.

In other words, the mere presence of a Departmental officer on the committee, despite the fact that this was permitted by the *Public Service Act*, was enough to find a reasonable apprehension of bias on the part of the entire committee.

This argument has been unsuccessful otherwise, even in relation to judicial appointments. For example, in *Forge v Australian Securities and Investments Commission*[45] the High Court refused to set aside a judgement of the Supreme Court of NSW despite the presence on the bench of 'acting judges', who had been appointed for a period of 12 months. A similar conclusion was reached in *Northern Australia Aboriginal Legal Aid Service v Bradley*,[46] in relation to the appointment of acting magistrates in the Northern Territory. It is therefore not surprising that Australian courts have yet to overturn a finding of the MRT or RRT on the basis that the presiding member's appointment lacked permanence.

The High Court has also made it clear that administrative tribunal does not have the same independence from government as a court,[47] and circumvention of an administrative tribunal's decision will not necessarily amount to an abuse of power. In *Minister for Immigration and Multicultural Affairs v Jia*[48] the AAT

---

44   John McMillan, 'Recent Themes in Judicial Review of Federal Executive Action', (1996) 24(2) *Federal Law Review* 347 at 362.

45   (2006) HCA 44. For an explanation of this decision see Anna Dziedzic '*Forge v Australian Securities and Investments Commission*: The *Kable* Principle and the Constitutional Validity of Acting Judges', (2007) 35(1) *Federal Law Review* 129.

46   (2004) 218 CLR 146.

47   The Supreme Court of Canada came to the same conclusion in *Ocean Port Hotel Ltd v British Columbia (General Manager, Liquor Control and Licensing Branch)* [2001] 2 SCR 781, despite the existence of s 7 of the *Charter of Rights and Freedoms*.

48   (2001) 205 CLR 507.

had twice (somewhat inexplicably) set aside a decision under s 501 of the Act to refuse Mr Jia a visa. The Minister's response, after publicly stating on radio that Mr Jia, a convicted rapist, was not a person of good character, was to grant the visa and then cancel it under s 501. Mr Jia argued in the High Court that the Minister could not lawfully circumvent the decision of the AAT in this way, and that the Minister's decision was affected by both actual and apprehended bias. The High Court unanimously rejected the first two arguments, and Gleeson CJ and Gummow J noted as follows:[49]

> The position of the Minister is substantially different from that of a judge, or quasi-judicial officer, adjudicating in adversarial litigation. It would be wrong to apply to his conduct the standards of detachment which apply to judicial officers or jurors. There is no reason to conclude that the legislature intended to impose such standards upon the Minister, and every reason to conclude otherwise.

If the Minister had attempted to circumvent the decision of a *court* the outcome may have been different, but the review tribunals are creatures of the executive, and there was therefore no breach of the principle of the separation of powers on the part of the Minister.[50]

Finally, the institutional bias argument has been run, generally unsuccessfully, overseas. In *Sethi v Canada (Minister of Employment and Immigration)*[51] the applicant ran the argument that because, at the time, members of the Refugee Protection Division were employed on fixed-term contracts, similar to members of the RRT in Australia, any decision made by that body was affected by institutional bias. Mr Sethi was successful at first instance, but the Federal Court of Appeal allowed the Minister's appeal.[52] The Federal Court of Appeal decision has since been upheld in *Law Society of Upper Canada v Canada (Minister of Citizenship and Immigration)*[53] and *Ahumada v Canada (Minister of Citizenship and Immigration)*,[54] the latter case noting that 'the allegation of bias in *Sethi* would, if successful, have disqualified all the members of the Board and would have had a highly disruptive effect on the administration of the Act'.[55] This may be the real reason behind both the Australian and Canadian decisions. It is, however, notable that since the first instance decision in *Sethi*, members of

---

49   Ibid at paragraph 102.
50   The High Court in *Jia* also found by a 4-1 margin that the Minister's decision was not affected by apprehended bias, Kirby J dissenting.
51   (1988) 2 FC 552 (CA).
52   *Minister of Employment and Immigration v Sethi* (1988) 52 DLR (4th) 681.
53   (2009) 2 FCR 243.
54   (2001) 3 FCR 605.
55   Ibid at paragraph 52.

the RPD have been appointed under the *Public Service Employment Act*[56] and not on individual short-term contracts, thus giving them a greater degree of independence than is currently enjoyed by members of the RRT.

The 'duty to inquire'

The MRT and RRT have been described by Australian courts on numerous occasions as operating in an 'inquisitorial' fashion, as opposed to the 'adversarial' approach of the courts. For example, in *Minister for Immigration and Citizenship v SZIAI* the High Court stated as follows:[57]

> It has been said in this Court on more than one occasion that proceedings before the Tribunal are inquisitorial, rather than adversarial in their general character. There is no joinder of issues as understood between parties to adversarial litigation. The word 'inquisitorial' has been used to indicate that the Tribunal, which can exercise all the powers and discretions of the primary decision maker, is not itself a contradictor to the cause of the applicant for review. Nor does the primary decision maker appear before the Tribunal as a contradictor. The relevant ordinary meaning of 'inquisitorial' is 'having or exercising the function of an inquisitor', that is to say 'one whose official duty it is to inquire, examine or investigate'. As applied to the Tribunal 'inquisitorial' does not carry that full ordinary meaning. It merely delimits the nature of the Tribunal's functions. They are to be found in the provisions of the Migration Act. The core function, in the words of s 414 of the Act, is to 'review the decision', which is the subject of a valid application made to the Tribunal under s 412 of the Act.

While it is true that the words 'inquire' or 'inquisitorial' do not appear in the *Migration Act*, it is nevertheless peculiar that the High Court has been firm, at least in the 21st century, that the tribunals have no stand-alone duty to inquire into an applicant's claims. While it is certainly not the role of an administrative tribunal to make an applicant's case for him or her, one would expect the RRT in particular to take an active role in examining whether an applicant's claims before it are true or at least plausible. This is in fact what the RRT does – the tribunal historically included a large 'Country Information Section' which was staffed by employees whose job it was to examine applicants' claims against known facts about the country, or at least known facts as reported by government (such as the Australian Department of Foreign Affairs and Trade and the US State Department) and non-government (such as the UNHCR and

---

56   SC 2003, c 22.
57   (2009) HCA 39 at paragraph 18.

Amnesty International) agencies.[58] However, the courts have been very reluctant to impose a legal *obligation* on the tribunals to have recourse to these kinds of resources (although it could be said that Direction 56 under s 499 imposes a legal obligation on the Tribunal to have regard to DFAT advice).

In 1994, Wilcox J in the Federal Court found that a duty to inquire does arise in limited circumstances. In *Prasad v Minister for Immigration and Ethnic Affairs* his Honour stated as follows:[59]

> Where it is obvious that material is readily available which is centrally relevant to the decision to be made ... to proceed to a decision without making any attempt to obtain that information may properly be described as an exercise of the decision-making power in a manner so unreasonable that no reasonable person would have so exercised it.

The kinds of situations in which applicants have argued for a duty to inquire to be imposed on the tribunals have varied greatly. In *Cabal v Minister for Immigration and Multicultural Affairs*[60] the applicant provided a large amount of untranslated material, including entire textbooks, to the RRT without explaining its relevance, and argued that the RRT had a positive duty to translate all the material and consider it in deciding the applicant's case. The Full Federal Court had little difficulty in determining that the RRT had no such duty. On the other hand, in *Sun v Minister for Immigration and Ethnic Affairs*[61] the applicant claimed that he had entered Australia after boarding a flight at Port Moresby, where an immigration officer had permitted him to board without a visa. A country research officer was informed by the Department that it could provide an 88-page printout of the passenger lists for Port Moresby airport around the claimed date, but the presiding member, Ms Smidt, then cancelled the request. Ms Smidt's refusal to obtain the document was found by the Full Federal Court to be evidence of apprehended bias on her part against Mr Sun, and the decision of the RRT was set aside.

The High Court, however, has generally shown very little enthusiasm for creating *any* kind of duty to inquire. The key decision is probably still *Re Minister for Immigration and Multicultural and Indigenous Affairs, Ex parte S134/2002*, a case involving the somewhat famous, and certainly very media-savvy, Bakhtiyari family. The full exploits of the family will not be considered

---

58   The RRT's country information section was transferred to the Department with effect from 1 July 2013 – see Part 3 of the MRT and RRT's Annual Report for 2012–13 (http://www.mrt-rrt.gov.au/ Annual Reports/ar1213/part-3.html, extracted 20 October 2014). The report states that 'Country of origin information services will be provided to the tribunals by the department via a service level agreement that will govern the provision of products and services'.

59   (1985) 6 FCR 155 at 170.

60   (2001) FCA 546.

61   (1997) FCA 1488.

here, but the father, Ali Reza Bakhtiyari, came to Australia by boat in 2000 and was found to be a refugee from Afghanistan. Mr Bakhtiyari's wife and five children followed him on a later boat, and were found not to be Afghans, but Pakistanis, and refused protection visas. It is not clear whether the Department was immediately aware of all the familial links, it seems that at least by the time of the RRT hearing both the Department and the RRT knew that Mr and Mrs Bakhtiyari were husband and wife. Despite this, a majority of the High Court found that the RRT committed no error of law by not obtaining and considering Mr Bakhtiyari's successful application in coming to the adverse decision against the other family members. This is an extraordinary decision, as quite apart from any duty to inquire, this seems like a classic failure to take a relevant consideration into account.

Similarly, in *Minister for Immigration and Multicultural and Indigenous Affairs v SGLB*,[62] the RRT applicant, a long-term detainee, stated repeatedly at the hearing that he wished to proceed, but nevertheless showed clear signs of severe psychiatric disturbance. The RRT affirmed the Departmental decision, primarily on the basis of inconsistencies in the applicant's own evidence. Despite his signs of distress, the High Court found that the RRT had no duty to inquire into the applicant's psychiatric state before making a decision.

However, in *SZIAI*, the High Court may have shown a willingness to return to the *Prasad* approach. While the High Court's comments on the duty to inquire were strictly obiter, as the court expressly stated that it did not need to resolve the issue to decide the case[63], the majority stated as follows:[64]

> Although decisions in the Federal Court concerned with a failure to make obvious inquiries have led to references to a 'duty to inquire', that term is apt to direct consideration away from the question whether the decision which is under review is vitiated by jurisdictional error. The duty imposed upon the Tribunal by the *Migration Act* is a duty to review. It may be that a failure to make an obvious inquiry about a critical fact, the existence of which is easily ascertained, could, in some circumstances, supply a sufficient link to the outcome to constitute a failure to review. If so, such a failure could give rise to jurisdictional error by constructive failure to exercise jurisdiction. It may be that failure to make such an inquiry results in a decision being affected in some other way that manifests itself as jurisdictional error.

Commentators have been split on the effect of *SZIAI*. On one hand, Crock and Berg state that 'the case underscores once again that the High Court has shown

---

62   (2004) 207 ALR 12.
63   Supra n57 at paragraph 25.
64   Ibid.

no enthusiasm to develop even the smallest requirement that the tribunals should be duty-bound to institute their own inquiries'.[65] However, Mark Smyth[66] opines that since *SZIAI* was decided, the Federal Court has effectively reverted to the *Prasad* approach, citing a number of Federal Court judgements in support.[67] It would seem that further High Court authority will be required to shed further light on this matter.

Part 3 – Tribunal processes

As previously noted, the MRT and RRT have very detailed 'codes of procedures' that must be followed in making their decisions. These codes are very similar but not identical.

The main difference between Parts 5 and 7 of the Act, so far as procedures are concerned, is that ss 366A–366D expressly limit the right of a MRT applicant to be represented at a hearing, but no such limitations exist for RRT hearings. Also there is no equivalent of s 363A in Part 7, which again appears to be intended to limit a person's right of representation before the MRT. The difference appears to be a recognition that claims for refugee status are extremely complex, as well as emotional, and that an applicant seeking review of a protection visa decision is more likely to *need* assistance at the hearing than a MRT applicant. This is not to say that hearings related to, say, a refusal of a partner visa are not also complex and potentially emotionally draining, but they do not have the potential life-and-death consequences of a RRT hearing.[68]

It is simply impossible in this chapter to examine in detail all of the procedural. It is sufficient to note two things – the reason for the 'exhaustive statement' provisions in ss 357A and 422B of the Act, and the vast volume of law surrounding the 'disclosure of adverse information' provisions in ss 359A and 424A.

---

65   Crock and Berg, supra n4 at paragraph 18.130.
66   Mark Smyth, 'Inquisitorial Adjudication: The Duty to Inquire in Merits Review Tribunals', (2010) 34(1) *Melbourne University Law Review* 230.
67   *Brown v Minister for Immigration and Citizenship* (2009) FCA 1098; (2009) 112 ALD 67; *Lohse v Arthur [No. 3]* (2009) FCA 1118; (2009) 180 FCR 334; *Minister for Immigration and Citizenship v Dhanoa* (2009) FCAFC 153; (2009) 180 FCR 510; *SZNHU v Minister for Immigration and Citizenship* (2009) FCA 1243 (4 November 2009); *Khant v Minister for Immigration and Citizenship* (2009) FCA 1247; *SZNLQ v Minister for Immigration and Citizenship* (2009) FCA 1312 (13 November 2009); *SZNBX v Minister for Immigration and Citizenship* (2009) FCA 1403; (2009) 112 ALD 475; *SZLGP v Minister for Immigration and Citizenship* (2009) FCA 1470; *SZMXS v Minister for Immigration and Citizenship* (2009) FCA 1542 (22 December 2009); *SZNOA v Minister for Immigration and Citizenship* (2010) FCA 60 (12 February 2010); *SZNPS v Minister for Immigration and Citizenship* (2010) FCA 101 (15 February 2010); *SZNSJ v Minister for Immigration and Citizenship* (2010) FCA 100 (16 February 2010); *SZNNU v Minister for Immigration and Citizenship* (2010) FCA 175 (17 February 2010); *SZGUR v Minister for Immigration and Citizenship* (2010) FCA 171 (4 March 2010).
68   There are some interesting comments on who is allowed to be present at an RRT hearing, given the requirement in s 429 that the hearing be in private, in *SZAYW* (2006) HCA 49, especially at [21]–[29].

The *Migration Legislation Amendment (Procedural Fairness) Act 2002*

The *Migration Legislation Amendment (Procedural Fairness) Act 2002* ('the MLAPF Act') was an attempt to ensure that the various 'codes of procedure' set out in the Act for dealing with visa or review applications were in fact an exhaustive statement of natural justice requirements under the Act. The MLAPF Act was a response to the High Court's decision in *Re Minister for Immigration and Multicultural Affairs; Ex parte Miah*,[69] which had found that Subdivision AB of the Act, despite setting out a 'Code of Procedure' for dealing with visa applications, did not exclude the common law rules of procedural fairness. Gleeson CJ and Hayne J noted as follows:[70]

> [95] The only indication of the matters which are to inform the decision of the Minister whether or not to seek submissions or further information from the applicant is to be found in the heading to subdiv AB, namely 'dealing fairly, efficiently and quickly with visa applications'. That being so, those powers are to be exercised to ensure procedural fairness, albeit in a manner that is quick and efficient. Accordingly, the obligation to accord procedural fairness is not excluded by subdiv AB.

> [96] Once it is accepted that the Minister's power to invite submissions or further information is to be exercised to ensure procedural fairness, the fact that the Act confers a right of review by the Refugee Review Tribunal becomes irrelevant. The existence of a right of review cannot deprive the provisions of subdiv AB of the meaning and effect which the heading to that subdivision directs.

Most relevantly, the MLAPF Act inserted new sections 359A and 422B into the Act, which deal with reviews by the MRT and RRT respectively. Subsections 359A(1) and 422B(1) are identical, and provide that '[t]his Division is taken to be an exhaustive statement of the requirements of the natural justice hearing rule in relation to the matters it deals with'. As will be seen, ss 359A and 422B have not been particularly effective. The EM to the Bill expressly referred to the *Miah* decision as follows:

> [3] In *Re MIMA; Ex parte Miah* [2001] HCA 22 the High Court held, by a narrow majority, that the 'code of procedure' for dealing fairly, efficiently and quickly with visa applications in Subdivision AB of Division 3 of Part 2 of the Act did not exclude common law natural

---

69   (2001) 206 CLR 57.

70   Ibid at paragraphs 95 and 96.

justice requirements. The majority considered that such exclusion would require a clear legislative intention and that there was no such clear intention in the Act.

[4] The purpose of this Bill is to provide a clear legislative statement that the 'codes of procedure' identified in the Bill are an exhaustive statement of the requirements of the natural justice hearing rule in relation to the matters they deal with.

The MLAPF Bill received Royal Assent on 3 July 2002 and came into effect on the following day.[71]

If the purpose of the MLAPF Act was to ensure that the MRT's and RRT's procedural obligations would be met by mechanically complying with Parts 5 and 7 respectively, this has not proven to be the case. The courts have continued to imply a duty to exercise those procedural powers fairly. For example, in *SZFDE v Minister for Immigration and Citizenship*[72] the RRT, as required by s 425, invited the applicant to a hearing, which the applicant declined. The RRT affirmed the Departmental decision. It transpired that the applicant was acting with the 'assistance' of one Mr Hussain, who no longer held a lawyer's practising certificate or registration as a migration agent, despite claiming to be both. Mr Hussain had advised the applicant not to attend the RRT hearing, it seems partly to avoid the RRT discovering his (unlawful) involvement with the application, and stated that he would seek Ministerial intervention under s 417 instead. Mr Hussain's actions were found to represent a fraud on the RRT, and that despite it acting in good faith at all times, the RRT had been prevented from exercising its role to review the Departmental decision. The RRT's decision was therefore set aside, and the applicant presumably engaged a properly registered migration agent for the new RRT hearing.[73]

Further, in light of the unanimous High Court decision of *SZBEL v Minister for Immigration and Multicultural Affairs*[74] it is now settled that ss 360 and 425 incorporate common law natural justice requirements in addition to dealing with the right to a hearing. The High Court held in that case that s 425 requires the RRT to provide an applicant with the opportunity to give evidence and present arguments in relation to issues arising in relation to the decision under review, and the failure to notify applicant of issues that the tribunal considers determinative but were not considered dispositive by the delegate constitutes jurisdictional error. This interpretation effectively provides a separate common

---

71   Section 2 of the MLAPF Act; http://www.comlaw.gov.au/Details/C2004A01001/Download, extracted 21 October 2014.
72   (2007) 237 ALR 64.
73   For a thorough examination of this case, see Zac Chami, 'Fraud In Administrative Law and The Right To A Fair Hearing', (2010) 61 *Australian Institute of Administrative Law Forum* 5.
74   (2006) 231 ALR 592.

law obligation for the tribunals in addition to those under ss 359A and 424A, and also allows common law obligations to remain alive, regardless of the MLAPF Act.

Perhaps even more significantly, the Full Federal Court found in *Minister for Immigration and Citizenship v Li*[75] that a refusal to adjourn a MRT hearing amounted to a jurisdictional error, despite the existence of s 359A. The Court stated as follows at paragraph 29:

> Consideration of the statutory context in which s 353 and s 357A(3) appear does not negate the proposition that an unreasonable refusal of an adjournment can constitute jurisdictional error on the part of the MRT. The MRT's 'core function' is to review an MRT reviewable decision such as that made in respect of, the respondent, Ms Li: s 348. In so doing, it must invite her to appear: s 360. The appearance afforded by the MRT to an applicant by that invitation must be meaningful, not perfunctory, or it will be no appearance at all. The MRT is given power to adjourn proceedings from time to time: s 363(1)(b) of the Act. An *unreasonable refusal* of an adjournment of the proceeding will not just deny a *meaningful appearance* to an applicant. It will mean that the MRT has not discharged its core statutory function of reviewing the decision. This failure constitutes jurisdictional error for the purposes of s 75(v) of the Constitution.

The decision of the Full Federal Court was upheld on appeal by the High Court.[76] The High Court had nothing at all to say about s 359A, and affirmed the decision primarily on the basis of a breach of s 363 by the MRT. The High Court also made some interesting comments on the ground of 'unreasonableness', and seems to have moved Australian law forward from the '*Wednesbury* unreasonableness'[77] which had hitherto dominated.

The notion that, by failing to comply with the requirements of natural justice, the MRT or RRT would not in fact offer a hearing and would fail to fulfill their core function, resurfaced in *SZJSS v Minister for Immigration and Citizenship*.[78] The Full Federal Court in this case simply ignored s 422B, and found that apprehended bias on behalf the decision maker had the effect that the RRT had constructively failed to exercise its jurisdiction and effectively failed to

---

75   (2012) FCAFC 74.
76   *Minister for Immigration and Citizenship v Li* (2013) HCA 18.
77   Referring to *Associated Provisional Picture Houses Limited v Wednesbury Corporation* (1948) 1 KB 223.
78   (2009) FCA 1577 at paragraph 64.

provide the applicant with a hearing.[79] On appeal, the High Court also did not address s 422B – instead, it assumed that apprehended bias would amount to a jurisdictional error but found none existed in the case at hand.[80]

Sections 359A and 424A

The High Court has generally struck down attempts by lower courts, at least prior to *S157 v Commonwealth*[81] (the 'privative clause case') to restore the common law rules of procedural fairness to tribunal decision-making by the 'back door'. For example, in *Minister for Immigration and Multicultural Affairs v Eshetu*[82] the High Court found that ss 353 and 420 of the Act were exhortatory provisions, and did not import a common law duty of procedural fairness, overruling a number of Federal Court decisions. A similar attempt to imply a common law duty of procedural fairness into ss 368 and 430 was also struck down by the High Court in *Minister for Immigration and Multicultural Affairs v Yusuf*.[83]

Post-*Yusuf* cases have concentrated primarily on the wording of Parts 5 and 7 themselves, and found that any deviation from the strict wording of those provisions amounts to a jurisdictional error. This has been particularly the case in the interpretation of ss 359A and 424A of the Act, although recent decisions such as *Minister for Immigration and Citizenship v SZIZO*[84] may indicate that the High Court is now prepared to take a more purposive approach to the construction of Parts 5 and 7. Judges themselves have recognised the lack of flexibility in Parts 5 and 7 of the Act, including Weinberg J in *SZEEU v Minister for Immigration and Multicultural Affairs*:[85]

> With great respect, I doubt that the legislature ever contemplated that s 424A would give rise to the difficulties that it has, or lead to the results that it does. The problems that have arisen stem directly from the attempt to codify, and prescribe exhaustively, the requirements of natural justice, without having given adequate attention to the need to maintain some flexibility in this area. This desire to set out by way of a highly prescriptive code those requirements was no doubt well-intentioned, and perhaps motivated by a concern to promote consistency. However, the achievement of consistency (assuming that this goal can be attained) comes at a price. As is demonstrated by the outcome of at least some

---

79   Ibid at paragraph 64.
80   *Minister for Immigration and Citizenship v SZJSS* (2010) HCA 48.
81   (2003) 211 CLR 476.
82   (1999) 197 CLR 611.
83   (2001) 206 CLR 323.
84   (2009) 238 CLR 627.
85   (2006) 150 FCR 214 at paragraph 183.

of these appeals, codification in this area can lead to complexity, and a degree of confusion, resulting in unnecessary and unwarranted delay and expense. To put the matter colloquially, and to paraphrase, 'the cake may not be worth the candle'.

Breach of ss 359A or 424A is a Jurisdictional Error

Unsurprisingly, a breach of ss 359A or 424A of the Act has been found by the courts to be a jurisdictional error[86], meaning that a breach of those provisions leaves the decision liable to be set aside by a court despite the existence of the privative clause in s 474 of the Act.[87] In SAAP, the Hayne J stated that 'whether [that process] would be judged to be necessary or even desirable in the circumstances of a particular case, to give procedural fairness to that applicant, is not to the point … [t]he Act prescribes what is to be done in every case'.[88] But what obligations do ss 359A and 424A place on the respective tribunals?

Sections 359A and 424A apply to information taken into account in the decision

Sections 359A and 424A apply only to information that is at least a reason for affirming the decision under review. For example, in *VEAL v Minister for Immigration and Multicultural and Indigenous Affairs*[89] the RRT had received a classic 'dob-in' letter claiming that the applicant had committed human rights abuses in his home country. The RRT stated in its reasons that it had been unable to test the claims made in the letter and therefore gave it 'no weight'.[90] The High Court found that this reasoning meant that s 424A did not apply:[91]

> As for s 424A, it is enough to notice that that provision is directed to 'information that the Tribunal considers would be the reason, or a part of the reason, for affirming the decision that is under review'. The Tribunal said, in its reasons, that it did not act on the letter or the information it contained. That is reason enough to conclude that s 424A was not engaged.

The same reasoning was applied to s 359A in *Minister for Immigration and Citizenship v Kumar*,[92] although in that case the MRT *had* considered the dob-in

---

86   *SAAP v Minister for Immigration and Multicultural and Indigenous Affairs* (2005) 215 ALR 162.
87   *S157 v Commonwealth*, supra n77.
88   Supra n86 at paragraph 208.
89   (2005) 225 CLR 88.
90   Ibid at paragraph 5.
91   Ibid at paragraph 12.
92   (2010) 238 CLR 448.

letter. The decision under review in *VEAL* was set aside in this pre-s 422B case because the RRT, at common law, should nevertheless have provided the applicant with the substance of the allegations.

Sections 359A and 424A do not apply to information provided by the applicant

Paragraphs 359A(4)(b) and 424A(4)(b) each provide that the respective section does not apply to information 'that the applicant gave for the purpose of the application for review'. The obvious intention of this provision is to prevent the tribunal from having regurgitate information it received from the applicant back to the applicant and ask for the applicant's comments on it. The courts have taken a fairly strict line on these provisions. For example, information provided by one family member cannot be used to decide an application lodged by another family member without seeking the second family member's comment, even when the cases were heard together.[93] Further, until ss 359A(4)(ba) and 424A(4)(ba) were inserted by means of the *Migration Amendment (Review Processes) Act 2007*, which came into effect on 29 June 2007,[94] information provided to the Department in the primary decision-making process that could result in an adverse decision also had to be provided to the applicant by the tribunals.[95]

Sections 359A and 424A do not apply to every step in the Tribunals' reasoning

It is clear on the face of ss 359A and 424A that the Tribunals are not required to disclose every single step of their reasoning process, but only information that could lead to a decision adverse to the applicant. For example, in *NAOX v Minister for Immigration and Citizenship*[96] the RRT had received information from another 'dob-in' letter that the applicants were not a same-sex couple as they claimed, but actually cousins. The RRT member had conducted Google searches relating to a claim by the applicants that there was a fatwa against homosexuals in Bangladesh, and also the meaning of the words 'cousins' and 'second cousins'. The results of the first search but not the second were put to the applicants under s 424A. Ormiston FM found that the RRT was not required to disclose the Google search terms and results in relation to the second search to the applicants, because the information sought and obtained was not personal to them.

---

93   *SZGSI v Minister for Immigration and Citizenship* (2007) 160 FCR 506.
94   Section 2 of the *Migration Amendment (Review Processes) Act 2007*; http://www.comlaw.gov.au/Details/C2007A00100, extracted 21 October 2014.
95   *SZBYR v Minister for Immigration and Citizenship* (2007) 235 ALR 609.
96   (2008) FMCA 1467.

On the other hand, in *SZEEU*[97] one of the main reasons for the RRT's decision to affirm the Departmental decision was that the applicant claimed to be an active member of the Awami League in Bangladesh, but had not had any involvement with the Australian branch of the League. This was despite the fact that the applicant's migration agent, a Mr Haque, was himself a prominent member of the Australian Awami League and could easily have put his client in contact with them. The RRT found as follows:[98]

> The claims of political association and involvement are vague and unconvincing. Whilst he knows of political party members and people who stood for election and who won I do not accept that his level of explanation of what he did for the party displayed an actual involvement. Apart from this he states that he has made no contact with the Awami League in Australia though had heard about them. This is somewhat strange in itself as it is known to the Tribunal that the applicant's adviser – Mr. Sirajul Haque – plays a prominent role in the Awami League association in Australia. I consider it reasonable to assume that if the applicant had wanted to make contact with his claimed political party he could easily have done so. The fact that he has not further indicates that he was not involved.

The Minister argued that the reasons for the RRT's decision were that SZEEU's evidence was 'vague and unconvincing', and that he had not joined in any Awami League activities in Australia. The fact that Mr Haque had contacts in the League was a 'side comment' and not a reason for the decision. However, Moore J found that:[99]

> What the Tribunal was saying was that not only did the appellant not engage in activities associated with AL in Australia, but also that he had an immediate and direct opportunity of doing so because of his association with Mr Haque. The Tribunal said that had the appellant wanted to make contact with the AL it could easily have done so. The reason why it spoke of the ease with which the appellant could have made contact, was its knowledge about Mr Haque. In my opinion, that was information that the Tribunal should have provided particulars of under s 424A.

---

97   Supra n85.
98   Ibid at paragraph 84.
99   Ibid at paragraph 88.

Sections 359A and 424A do not apply to matters such as the overall credibility of the applicant (as opposed to specific third-party information that contradicts one or more claims). In *Minister for Immigration and Citizenship v SZGUR* the High Court found as follows:[100]

> [8] The 'information' upon which the Tribunal invited comment, was the existence of 'contradictions and inconsistencies' between what SZGUR had stated orally and in writing to the Tribunal, variously constituted, during the iterations of the review process. The contradictions and inconsistencies, which were elaborated at some length in the letter, related to SZGUR's claimed involvement with the Communist Party of Nepal, whether he and his family had gone into hiding in Nepal, whether he had been helped to leave the country and his claim that two colleagues had been executed by the Nepalese Army.
>
> [9] Despite the language of the Tribunal's letter, the existence of 'inconsistencies' and 'contradictions' in an applicant's testimony and written submissions to the Tribunal is not 'information' of the kind to which s 424A is directed. As was explained by the plurality in *SZBYR v Minister for Immigration and Citizenship*, the term 'information' in s 424A does not extend to the Tribunal's 'subjective appraisals, thought processes or determinations'.[101] Their Honours said:
>
>> However broadly 'information' be defined its meaning in this context is related to the existence of evidentiary material or documentation, not the existence of doubts, inconsistencies or the absence of evidence.
>
> The exclusion of this class of information from the obligation imposed by s 424A is consistent with limits on the procedural fairness hearing rule at common law. Procedural fairness requires a decision maker to identify for the person affected any critical issue not apparent from the nature of the decision or the terms of the statutory power. The decision maker must also advise of any adverse conclusion which would not obviously be open on the known material. However, a decision maker is not otherwise required to expose his or her thought processes or provisional views for comment before making the decision.[102]

In other words, if the MRT or RRT notes contradictions or internal inconsistencies in an applicant's evidence, ss 359A and 424A do not oblige the tribunal to inform the applicant of such prior to a decision being made. Sections 359A and 424A

---

100 Supra n67 at paragraphs 8 and 9.
101 (2007) 81 ALJR 1190 at 1196.
102 *Commissioner for Australian Capital Territory Revenue v Alphaone Pty Ltd* (1994) 49 FCR 576 at 591–92.

relate to specific information that contradicts or casts doubt on an applicant's case, not the applicant's own consistency and demeanour. Nor does it require the tribunal to disclose every step in its reasoning in determining that a piece of information is in fact adverse to the applicant. These sections require only the disclosure of adverse and objective evidence.

Relaxation of the strict compliance approach?

Although the courts have generally imposed a very strict obligation on the MRT and RRT to conform precisely to the codes of procedure, the High Court's decision in *SZIZO*[103] indicates a possible relaxation to this approach. In *SZIZO*, the appellants – husband, wife and four children – had been refused protection visas. When applying for review to the RRT, the husband nominated his eldest daughter (one of the applicants) to be his authorised recipient. Section 441G the *Migration Act* provides that 'the Tribunal must give the authorised recipient, instead of the applicant, any document that it would otherwise have given to the applicant'. However, despite the requirement in that provision, the Tribunal corresponded only with the applicant father about the hearing. The husband, wife and four children appeared before the Tribunal and the husband, wife and eldest daughter (who was also the authorised recipient) gave evidence.

The Full Federal Court had held that the breach of the requirement in s 441G constituted a jurisdictional error. The Court considered that the provisions in the Act purporting to exhaustively set out the RRT's procedural requirements, including s 422B, suggested 'that Parliament intended that there be strict adherence to each of the procedural steps leading up to the hearing'.[104] This result was reached despite the fact that there had been no unfairness or prejudice to the appellants and there would not have been a contravention of common law procedural fairness requirements. As in *SAAP*,[105] there was a breach here of a statutory requirement and that breach resulted in the decision being affected by jurisdictional error.

However, the High Court rejected that conclusion. *SAAP*, it was said, was decided before the introduction of s 422B into the Act, and the scope of s 424A would now have to be interpreted in light of s 422B. The Court then drew a distinction between, on the one hand, core procedural fairness provisions and, on the other hand, provisions which are merely facilitative of a fair hearing. Section 441G fell into the second category, as it is a procedural step that goes to the 'manner' of giving notice. By contrast, s 424A(1) sets out the obligation

---

103 Supra n84.
104 *SZIZO v Minister for Immigration and Citizenship* [2008] FCAFC 122 at paragraph 87.
105 Supra n86.

to give particulars of adverse information and s 425 sets out the obligation to invite the applicant to give evidence and present arguments. These are both core procedural fairness provisions.

For the High Court, as far as s 441G was concerned, while compliance with the statutory requirements might have been intended by Parliament to discharge the Tribunal's obligations, a failure to comply need not result in jurisdictional error. Instead, such a determination requires a consideration of the 'extent and consequences of the departure'.[106] The consequences here were not sufficient to give rise to invalidity, as there was no injustice and the applicants received timely and effective notice of the hearing. It remains to be seen whether the High Court will continue on the path of finding 'core' and 'non-core' procedural requirements in the Act.

Part 4 – Ministerial intervention

The Minister has the power in some situations to exercise a non-compellable discretion, such as to permit an 'unauthorised maritime arrival' to make an application for a visa under s 46A of the Act.[107] The Minister also has particular power to substitute a 'more favourable' decision for that of the MRT or RRT.[108]

Sections 351 and 417 of the Act are substantially identical, and provide these intervention powers.

A number of important features can be seen from these provisions:

• The intervention power applies only when an applicant has made an unsuccessful application for review to the MRT or RRT.

• The power to substitute a decision may only be exercised by the Minister personally. The Act says nothing about the means by which cases may be brought to the Minister's attention.

• Ministerial intervention is clearly meant to be exceptional – it may only be done in the 'public interest' (ss 351(1) and 417(1)), and details of its exercise are to be provided to Parliament (ss 351(4)–(6) and 417(4)–(6)).

• The Minister has no duty to consider the exercise of his or her power in any particular case. That is, the Minister is not obliged to make a decision on each and every request for intervention – he or she may simply ignore any or all requests.

---

106   Supra n84 at paragraph 35.
107   See Chapter 2 for more examples.
108   Note that there is also an intervention power in 501J in respect of AAT decisions in protection visa cases.

History of intervention powers

A limited form of Ministerial intervention was provided for in the *Migration Legislation Amendment Act (No. 2) 1989*, one of a number of Acts that made substantial amendments to the Act in 1989. Originally, the then Minister, Senator Ray, had wanted to exclude almost all elements of Ministerial discretion,[109] but the Opposition parties combined to block a version of the Bill that removed all elements of discretion. The Bill was eventually passed giving the Minister limited powers to intervene on humanitarian grounds. However, Senator Ray continued to have reservations about the exercise of discretion, noting as follows in his Second Reading Speech to the Bill:[110]

> I have only one objection to ministerial discretion. It is a remaining objection and one I will probably always have. What I do not like about it is access. Who has access to a Minister? Can a Minister personally decide every immigration case? The answer is always no. Those who tend to get access to a Minister are members of parliament and other prominent people around the country. I worry for those who do not have access and whether they are being treated equally by not having access to a Minister.

This has continued to be a common ground of objection to Ministerial intervention powers.

The Ministerial intervention powers have remained basically the same since the *Migration Reform Act 1992* came into effect on 1 September 1994, except to amend section references from the IRT to the MRT. The Explanatory Memorandum for the Migration Reform Bill 1992[111] stated as follows at paragraph 302 in relation to new s 121 (which became s 351 after the renumbering of the Act):

> This section provides the Minister with an extraordinary power to substitute a new decision for a decision of the IRT, whether or not the IRT could have made the new decision, when the Minister considers it in the public interest to do so. The new decision must be more favourable to the applicant than the decision of the IRT which is being substituted.

Note the use of the word 'extraordinary'. However, the use of the intervention powers seems to have become less extraordinary over time. Consolidated

---

109   Report of the Senate Select Committee on Ministerial Discretion in Migration Matters, March 2004. http://www.aph.gov.au/Parliamentary_Business/Committees/Senate/Former_Committees/minmig/index, extracted 21 October 2014, at paragraph 2.5.
110   Senator Robert Ray, Senate Hansard, 30 May 1989 at 3012.
111   https://www.aph.gov.au/binaries/library/pubs/explanmem/docs/1992migrationreformbillem.pdf, extracted 21 October 2014.

statistics on the use of the Ministerial intervention power are hard to come by, but the Senate Select Committee on Ministerial Discretion in Migration Matters published the following statistics in March 2004:[112]

> The increasing numbers are obvious, and the large jump from 1997–98 to 1998–99 is of particular interest. In this table, 'humanitarian' intervention includes Ministerial intervention under ss 417, 454 (referrals from the RRT to AAT) and 501J. These increased from 309 in 1996–97 to 4,489 in 2002–03. Whilst 'non-humanitarian' intervention covers ss 345 (the old MIRO intervention power), 351 and 391 (referrals from the MRT to AAT). The humanitarian powers in relation to referrals have never been used.

Compare this to the most recent publicly available statistics, those for the second half of 2012[113] where total requests for intervention have dropped to 2,869 in 2012–13. This statistics identify the Minister's public interest powers, s 417, s 351 ,s 48B and 'other powers'. Between 2011–12 the 'other powers' figure dropped from 2,852 requests to 76. The large change in the 'other powers' figure is explained by the Department as follows:[114]

> 'Other powers' includes 195A, s 345, s 391, s 454 and s 501J. The 2011–12 figures include the Minister's use of the s 195A power to grant a Bridging Visa E (BVE) to allow IMAs to live in the community while their claims for protection are being considered. At 30 June 2012, 2741 BVEs had been granted to eligible IMAs[115] under s 195A. This type of visa grant is no longer included in this publication.

When one notes that exercises of power under ss 345, 391, 454 and 501J will be few and far between, it appears that has been a significant fall in s 417 requests since 2003, and a smaller though still noticeable fall in s 351 requests. Even on 2012 figures, however, Ministerial intervention does not appear to be an 'extraordinary' event.

Ministerial intervention in practice

The Minister does not in practice examine every request for ss 351 and 417 intervention that is sent to him or her. Instead, the Minister has published guidelines on the exercise of these powers, which are set out at the end of this

---

112   Supra n109 at paragraph 3.9.
113   Ministerial Intervention Statistics Australia, 2012–13 July to December at 1. http://www.immi.gov.au/media/publications/statistics/ministerial-intervention/min-stats-australia-2012-13.pdf, extracted 21 October 2014.
114   Ibid.
115   Illegal Maritime Arrivals.

chapter. A dedicated unit within the Minister's office examines all requests, and then those staff members forward for the Minister's attention those that they regard as falling within the guidelines.

This, unsurprisingly, has led to litigation. In *Ozmanian v Minister for Immigration and Ethnic Affairs*[116] the applicant argued that this process effectively resulted in Ministerial staff members exercising the Minister's powers, or at least the power to refuse to intervene, under ss 351 and 417. As the decision-making power in those sections is reserved for the Minister personally, any decision made by a staff member not to refer a matter to the Minister was made unlawfully. The process in dealing with the request was set out in some detail as follows:[117]

> [39] The application under s 417 was immediately referred by the Minister's office to the Department. Ms Donna Fraser, as case officer, was given the task of assessing the application.

> [40] Ms Fraser considered the written application, the annexures to it, Ms Carlson's file note concerning the failure of the applicant's case before the RRT to fall within the guidelines[118] and the applicant's DORS file …

> [42] After considering all of the foregoing matters Ms Fraser concluded that the matter did not warrant referral to the Minister personally …

> [44] Ms Fraser proceeded to draft a response to the applicant's s 417 application for signature by the Minister's Senior Adviser. The draft Minute and draft response were then sent by her to her departmental supervisor, Mr Noel Barnsley, who in turn signed the Minute and approved the draft response. I infer from the evidence that the relevant departmental officers expected that, in the usual course, the ministerial officers would act on the departmental recommendation without making their own independent enquiries.

> [45] The relevant material was then sent to the Minister's office for consideration by Mr John Richardson, a ministerial adviser. After considering the matter he had no disagreement with the conclusion reached within the Department that the matter did not fall within the Minister's guidelines. His evidence was that, had he considered the matter a borderline one or otherwise had a different view to that of the Department, he would have either required further information or raised the matter with the Minister personally.

---

116   (1996) FCA 1467.
117   Ibid at paragraphs 39 to 49.
118   Ms Carlson was a Departmental Officer who was a member of the Determination of Refugee Status (DORS) unit. The Department at that time reviewed all unsuccessful RRT applications to determine whether the applicant fell within the s 417 guidelines.

[46] Mr Richardson then passed the material on to Ms Bronwyn McNaughton, the second respondent, who was then the Minister's Senior Adviser. In accordance with the established general procedures, she signed the letter which had been drafted for her by Ms Fraser. She appeared to do so on the basis that its contents had been considered to be appropriate by the Department and Mr Richardson.

[47] The letter dated 29 November 1994 was signed by Ms McNaughton as 'Senior Adviser' and was sent to the solicitor for the applicant on that date.

[48] The document's letterhead stated it was from the 'Office of the Minister'. It read as follows:

> Thank you for your letter of 4 October 1994 to the Minister for Immigration and Ethnic Affairs, Senator the Hon Nick Bolkus, on behalf of Mr Tosn Ozmanian. Senator Bolkus has asked me to reply on his behalf.
>
> You have asked that the Minister exercise his discretion under section 417 of the Migration Act 1958 and grant Mr Ozmanian a visa on humanitarian grounds. Under section 417 of the Act, the Minister may substitute for a decision of the Refugee Review Tribunal (RRT) a decision more favourable to the applicant where he considers it is in the public interest to do so. However, this power is discretionary and the Minister is under no obligation to consider a case. When documents relating to a decided review are returned to the Department from the RRT, the applicant's claims are examined against the Ministerial Guidelines for Stay in Australia on Humanitarian Grounds as to whether the case is one which the Minister may wish to consider under subsection 417(1) of the Act. As Mr Ozmanian's case does not fall within the scope of these guidelines, it has not been referred to the Minister for his consideration ... Thank you for raising the matter with us.

[49] Although the letter was stated to have been sent at the request of the Minister, it was an agreed fact before me that the Minister had at no stage seen the letter.

Merkel J at first instance found that the decision not to intervene in Mr Ozmanian's case had been made by Ms McNaughton and not the Minister, and was therefore unlawful.[119] However, this ruling was reversed on appeal to the

---

119   Supra n116 at paragraph 116.

Full Federal Court by the Minister,[120] although it could be argued that the Full Court sidestepped the real issue. Sackville J, who wrote the leading judgement, came to the conclusion that s 485 of the Act as it then stood precluded judicial review, at least by the Federal Court, of any exercise of power under s 417, and that therefore the decision, whether it was made by the Minister or Ms McNaughton, was unreviewable.[121]

This is a strange decision, for two reasons. Firstly, as s 417 clearly stated that the decision could only be made by the Minister, if the decision was in fact made by Ms McNaughton it was simply not a decision under s 417. Whether an s 417 was reviewable under s 485 or not was irrelevant. Secondly, why did the Full Federal Court not *address* the issue of who made the decision? Mr Ozmanian's application for special leave to the High Court was refused,[122] despite the fact that even if the Full Federal Court was correct and an exercise of s 417 was unreviewable in that court, the High Court *could* review it in its original jurisdiction under s 75 of the Constitution. The special leave decision could be explained by the fact that it was leave to *appeal*, and not an original application under s 75, but one is still left with the impression that the substantive issues raised by Merkel J were never really addressed on appeal.

The matter was resolved, however, in *Bedlington v Chong*,[123] a case involving the Minister's power in s 48B to waive the s 48A bar. In that case, the Full Federal Court came to the conclusion that the Minister had the power to set out guidelines as to which circumstances he or she wished to intervene, and as long as staff followed those guidelines in making a decision whether to personally refer a matter to the Minster or not, this amounted to a valid exercise of the s 48B power. The same reasoning would apply to ss 351 and 417.

Criticism of the ministerial intervention powers

The main criticism levelled at the intervention powers are very much the same as those identified by Senator Ray in 1989 – who gets access to the Minister? Is it possible that some undeserving cases are granted visas because of 'favours' done in the past? A number of allegations of this kind were made by the 2004 Senate Select Committee on Ministerial Discretion in Migration Matters, which basically accused Minister Ruddock of allowing his intervention powers to be

---

120   *Minister for Immigration and Multicultural Affairs v Ozmanian* (1996) 141 ALR 322.
121   Ibid at 347.
122   *Ozmanian v Minister for Immigration M89/1996* (1997) HCATrans 75.
123   (1998) FCA 1139.

bought in some circumstances.[124] The circumstances in which one Francesco Madafferi, an alleged Mafia member, was granted a visa after intervention from Minister Vanstone have also attracted comment.[125]

Many academics have argued that successive governments have attempted to use the Ministerial intervention powers as a substitute for 'complementary protection', or allowing an application for a visa on the basis that the applicant faces severe difficulties in their home country, but fall outside the Refugees Convention. Jane McAdam for example writes as follows:[126]

> There has been no mechanism for having claims based on a fear of return to torture, a threat to life, or a risk of cruel, inhuman or degrading treatment or punishment, assessed, except via the 'public interest' power of the Minister for Immigration and Citizenship under s 417 of the *Migration Act 1958* (Cth) (known as ministerial intervention). The s 417 process is lengthy and inefficient, accessible only once an unsuccessful appeal has been made to the Refugee Review Tribunal. Furthermore, whether or not a claim is considered, and whether or not a visa to remain in Australia is granted, is wholly discretionary and non-reviewable. The s 417 mechanism is appropriate for purely humanitarian and compassionate cases, but not for those engaging Australia's *non-refoulement* obligations under international law.

One reason for the downturn seen in s 417 requests in 2012 may be the passage of the *Migration Amendment (Complementary Protection) Act 2011*, which inserted 'complementary protection' provisions into s 36 of the Act. However, the current government has introduced the *Migration Amendment (Regaining Control Over Australia's Protection Obligations) Bill 2013*, which would once again remove all complementary protection provisions from the Act. It seems that Ministerial intervention powers are not going to be substantially amended any time soon.

Part 5 – Other review bodies

A number of other Commonwealth bodies may have an interest in immigration decision-making. Bodies such as the Australian Customs Service (ACS), the Australian Quarantine and Inspection Service (AQIS), and the Australian Fisheries Management Authority (AFMA) all have an interest in immigration

---

124   Supra n105, in particular at paragraphs 6.50–6.53.
125   See for example 'Anti-Mafia Police Slam Vanstone', *The Age*, 28 September 2008. http://www.theage.com.au/national/antimafia-police-slam-vanstone-20080927-4pde.html, extracted 25 October 2008.
126   Jane McAdam, 'Australian Complementary Protection: A Step-by-Step Approach', (2011) 33 *Sydney Law Review* 687 at 698.

legislation and policy. The Attorney-General's Department, primarily the legislative drafting branches of the Office of Parliamentary Counsel (Acts) and Office of Legislative Drafting and Policy (regulations) also frequently work with the Department. However, this section will deal with two Commonwealth bodies that have a clear interest in *reviewing* immigration decisions – the Ombudsman and the Australian Human Rights Commission (AHRC).

Ombudsman

Powers and functions generally

The office of the Commonwealth Ombudsman was created by the *Ombudsman Act 1976*. The functions of the Ombudsman are set out in s 5(1) of that Act, which provides as follows:

> Subject to this Act, the Ombudsman:
>
> (a) shall investigate action, being action that relates to a matter of administration, taken either before or after the commencement of this Act by a Department, or by a prescribed authority, and in respect of which a complaint has been made to the Ombudsman; and
>
> (b) may, of his or her own motion, investigate any action, being action that relates to a matter of administration, taken either before or after the commencement of this Act by a Department or by a prescribed authority; and
>
> (c) with the consent of the Minister, may enter into an arrangement under which the Ombudsman will perform functions of an ombudsman under an ombudsman scheme established in accordance with the conditions of licences or authorities granted under an enactment.

The term 'administration' is not defined in the *Ombudsman Act*, and is therefore given a wide interpretation. There is no dispute that the Department of Immigration and Border Protection (as it is currently known) is a 'Department' for the purposes of the *Ombudsman Act*. It is clear from s 5(1) that the Ombudsman can investigate a matter either because a complaint has been lodged, or on his or her own motion.

Subsection 5(2) places limits on the Ombudsman's powers as follows. Most of the restrictions on the Ombudsman's powers relate to courts or judicial officers, but s 5(2)(a) provides that the Ombudsman may not investigate 'action taken by a Minister'. This would appear at first glance to prevent the Ombudsman from investigating, for example, a personal decision of the Minister under s 501(3) to cancel or refuse a visa, or the exercise of the Minister's intervention powers (discussed in the previous section of this chapter). It appears that the scope of this paragraph has never been judicially tested. Subsection 5(3A) also provides as follows:

> For the purposes of the application of this Act to or in relation to the Ombudsman, action taken by a Department or by a prescribed authority shall not be regarded as having been taken by a Minister by reason only that the action was taken by the Department or authority in relation to action that has been, is proposed to be, or may be, taken by a Minister personally.

This appears to mean that the Ombudsman *can* investigate decisions made personally by a Minister, at least where the action *could* have been taken by the Department. For example, a s 501 cancellation need not be the subject of a personal decision by the Minister, but a decision under ss 351 or 417 must be. In its submission to the Senate Select Committee on Ministerial Discretion in Migration Matters, the Ombudsman described its power in relation to ss 351 and 417 intervention as follows:[127]

> The exercise of that discretion by the Minister cannot be the subject of investigation by the Commonwealth Ombudsman, consistently with s 5(2)(a) of the *Ombudsman Act 1976* (Cth) which provides that '*the Ombudsman is not authorised to investigate ... action taken by a Minister*'. Section 5(2)(a) does not, however, preclude the Ombudsman from investigating action taken by a Department in relation to a Ministerial decision: see s 5(3A), providing that '*action taken by a Department ....* *shall not be regarded as having been taken by a Minister by reason only that* *the action was taken by the Department ... in relation to action that has* *been ... taken by a Minister personally*'. Thus, for example, in relation to decisions made by the Minister under ss 351 and 417, the Ombudsman is able to investigate:
>
> • action taken by the Department in identifying cases where the Minister's powers might be exercised, and in providing a briefing and advice to the Minister;
>
> • (probably) action taken by Ministerial staff related to Ministerial functions; and
>
> • action taken by the Department.

---

127 Commonwealth Ombudsman, 'Senate Select Committee on Ministerial Discretion in Migration Matters – Submission by the Office of the Commonwealth Ombudsman', August 2003 at paragraph 2.3.2. http://www.ombudsman.gov.au/files/Commonwealth_Ombudsman_to_Senate_Select_Committee_Inquiry_into_Ministerial_discretion_in_migration_matters.pdf, extracted 30 October 2014.

It is important to note that the Ombudsman has no power to set aside a Departmental decision. Instead, the Ombudsman is to give the relevant Department a report, in the circumstances set out in s 15 of the *Ombudsman Act*, and may make recommendations. If the Department fails to act on the report, the Ombudsman may inform the Prime Minister of such (s 16), and may send copies to the Speaker of the House of Representatives and the President of the Senate for tabling (s 17). A report tabled in Parliament is protected by Parliamentary privilege.

The best known Ombudsman inquiry in the immigration field was the own motion inquiry into Immigration Detention Centres (IDCs) in 2001,[128] but a similar own motion inquiry into the use of State correctional facilities as places of detention, also in 2001, is a close second.[129]

The 'Immigration Ombudsman'

Since 2005, the Ombudsman has held the title of 'Immigration Ombudsman' (amongst others). This change was brought about by the *Migration and Ombudsman Legislation Amendment Act 2005*, and came about as a result of the inquiries into the unlawful detention of Cornelia Rau and Vivienne Alvarez, and the unlawful removal from Australia of the latter. Another 2005 Act, the *Migration Amendment (Detention Arrangements) Act 2005*[130] ('the MADAA Act'), inserted Part 8C of the *Migration Act*, which requires the Ombudsman to regularly inquire into the circumstances of persons held in immigration detention for two years or more. The position of Immigration Ombudsman has been described as follows:[131]

- The Ombudsman can investigate action taken by the Department of Immigration and Citizenship (DIAC) in relation to visa, citizenship, immigration and detention issues. This includes DIAC's processing of visa and citizenship applications, and visa refusal or cancellation decisions.

- The Ombudsman has a compliance role and undertakes file inspections, site visits and observations of DIAC's field operations. The Ombudsman monitors

---

128   Commonwealth Ombudsman, 'Report of an Own Motion Investigation into DIMA's Detention Centres', Report no. 5 of 2001, http://www.ombudsman.com.au/files/investigation_2001_05.pdf, extracted 30 October 2014.
129   Commonwealth Ombudsman, 'Report of an Own Motion Investigation into Immigration Detainees Held in State Correctional Facilities', Report no. 6 of 2001, http://www.ombudsman.com.au/files/investigation_2001_06.pdf, extracted 30 October 2014.
130   The drafting and passage of the MADAA Act was quite extraordinary. The author of the text, Alan Freckelton, was employed in the Detention Services Division of the Department at the time, and the MADAA Bill was introduced into Parliament without, to the author's awareness, any apparent knowledge of the Department, or the Office of Parliamentary Counsel. It has never been established where the Bill came from, but it seems likely that it was drafted by an external law firm directly for the Minister's office.
131   http://www.lawhandbook.org.au/handbook/ch21s04s01.php, extracted 30 October 2014.

DIAC's functions concerning the location, identification, detention and removal of unlawful non-citizens.

- The Ombudsman regularly visits immigration detention centres and other facilities that are used to accommodate detainees, such as residential housing and alternative places of detention. Immigration detention centres are currently operated by an outsourced service provider engaged by DIAC.

- In the Ombudsman's complaint role, detention-related complaints generally concern internal complaint handling procedures, access to health services, access to internal and external activities and property related matters. The Ombudsman also regularly visits offshore immigration detention centres (e.g. Christmas Island). One of the Ombudsman's roles is to ensure that the refugee assessment process for unlawful non-citizens is conducted in a timely and reasonable manner.

- Under Part 8C of the *Migration Act 1958* (Cth), the Ombudsman assesses, reports on and makes recommendations in relation to persons held in immigration detention for more than two years.

Part 8C of the *Migration Act*

Under s 486N of the Act, the Secretary must provide the Ombudsman with a report on each immigration detainee, within 21 days of that detainee's 'detention reporting time'. Read together, ss 486L and 486M have the effect that the 'detention reporting time' is the date on which the detainee has been detained for a total of two years, and each six months thereafter. Under s 486O(1), the Ombudsman must 'give the Minister an assessment of the appropriateness of the arrangements for the person's detention' as soon as possible after receiving the relevant s 486N report, and may make recommendations as to the detainee's future detention under ss 486O(2) and (3). Under s 486O(5), the 'assessment must also include a statement, for the purpose of tabling in Parliament, that sets out or paraphrases so much of the content of the assessment as the Commonwealth Ombudsman considers can be tabled without adversely affecting the privacy of any person', and s 486P requires the s 486O(5) summary to be tabled in Parliament. The Ombudsman publishes annual analyses of s 486O reports given in that year.[132]

A common criticism of Part 8C is that the Ombudsman lacks the power to take any substantive action, and that the Minister can simply ignore its recommendations, even when specific recommendations are made. The 'Right Now' organisation comments as follows:[133]

---

132   The 2013 analysis can be found at: http://www.ombudsman.gov.au/docs/Analysis_of_reports_under_section_486O_in_2013.pdf, extracted 30 October 2014.

133   http://rightnow.org.au/topics/asylum-seekers/the-erosion-of-health-in-detention-and-the-erosion-of-oversight/, extracted 30 October 2014.

Where the Ombudsman does make a substantive recommendation, the Minister responds with comments so laden with misdirection they would fit better in a Kafka novel than they do in a Parliamentary Tabling Statement:

> I note the Ombudsman's recommendation in regard to each of these persons. The Government's policy is currently being implemented in regard to the detention placement of detainees. Once implemented, and if appropriate, my Department will prepare advice to me, in relation to these persons' detention placement. (The Hon. Scott Morrison MP, 4 December 2013)

In a similar vein, Civil Liberties Australia has called for the Ombudsman's s 486O recommendations to be made binding on the Minister.[134]

Finally on this point, the increasing Part 8C workload on the Ombudsman has not gone unnoticed either. Right Now comments as follows:[135]

> The Ombudsman is so overstretched that more than a third of reviews were presented in a simplified format. The reason is clear: the number of people in long-term immigration detention has been growing too rapidly to manage. In 2013 there were 686 section 486O reviews, while in 2012 only 297, in 2011 there were 52 reviews, and in 2010 there were a mere 28.

The Australian Human Rights Commission

General powers and responsibilities

The AHRC has been known by a number of titles, including the Human Rights and Equal Opportunity Commission (HREOC), and was established by the *Australian Human Rights Commission Act 1986* (Cth) ('the AHRC Act'). A lengthy list of functions of the AHRC is set out in s 11 of the AHRC Act, but the most relevant provision is probably s 11(1)(f), which provides that the AHRC may:

> inquire into any act or practice that may be inconsistent with or contrary to any human right, and:

> where the Commission considers it appropriate to do so – to endeavour, by conciliation, to effect a settlement of the matters that gave rise to the inquiry; and

---

134   https://www.cla.asn.au/Article/2013/Review%20HRP%20s486O.pdf, extracted 30 October 2014.
135   Supra n133.

where the Commission is of the opinion that the act or practice is inconsistent with or contrary to any human right, and the Commission has not considered it appropriate to endeavour to effect a settlement of the matters that gave rise to the inquiry or has endeavoured without success to effect such a settlement – to report to the Minister in relation to the inquiry.

The term 'human right' is defined in s 3 of the AHRC Act as 'the rights and freedoms recognised in the Covenant, declared by the Declarations or recognised or declared by any relevant international instrument'. The terms 'Covenant', 'Declarations' and 'relevant international instrument' are in turn defined in s 3 as follows:

'Covenant' means the International Covenant on Civil and Political Rights, a copy of the English text of which is set out in Schedule 2, as that International Covenant applies in relation to Australia.

'Declarations' means:

the Declaration of the Rights of the Child proclaimed by the General Assembly of the United Nations on 20 November 1959, a copy of the English text of which is set out in Schedule 3;

the Declaration on the Rights of Mentally Retarded Persons proclaimed by the General Assembly of the United Nations on 20 December 1971, a copy of the English text of which is set out in Schedule 4; and

the Declaration on the Rights of Disabled Persons proclaimed by the General Assembly of the United Nations on 9 December 1975, a copy of the English text of which is set out in Schedule 5.

'relevant international instrument' means an international instrument in respect of which a declaration under section 47 is in force.

The 'relevant international instruments' at present are the Convention on the Rights of Persons with Disabilities, the Convention on the Rights of the Child and the Declaration on the Elimination of All Forms of Intolerance and Discrimination Based on Religion or Belief.[136]

Like the Ombudsman, the AHRC has no power to set a government decision or policy aside. Despite the broad wording of s 13 of the AHRC Act, which states that 'the Commission has power to do all things that are necessary or convenient to be done for or in connection with the performance of its functions', those

---

136 https://www.humanrights.gov.au/human-rights-explained-fact-sheet-1-defining-human-rights, extracted 30 October 2014.

functions are limited by s 11 to inquiring into and reporting on alleged breaches of human rights. The AHRC may act on a complaint made by a Minister or on the basis of a written complaint by an 'aggrieved person' (ss 20(1)(a) and 20(1)(b) of the AHRC Act), or on its own motion (s 20(1)(c) of the AHRC Act). AHRC reports are to be tabled in Parliament (s 46).

AHRC reports into immigration detention

The AHRC has released two substantial reports into Australia's immigration detention system. A 1998 report entitled 'Those Who've Come Across the Seas: Detention of Unauthorised Arrivals',[137] cleverly using a line from the national anthem, was held to be 'damning' of the conditions in Australian IDCs, although follow-up reports were slightly more complimentary to the Department.[138] An even more comprehensive report into the treatment of children in IDCs was tabled in 2004.[139] The Department devoted an entire 'task force'[140] to drafting the government's response to the draft of this report, The task force spent most of its time criticising errors in the draft HREOC report, such as a misquote of Article 37(b) of the Convention on the Rights of the Child,[141] without addressing any of the substantive issues.

The AHRC is currently conducting another inquiry into the situation of children in immigration detention. The current inquiry is described on the AHRC website as follows:[142]

> On 3 February 2014 the President of the Commission, Professor Gillian Triggs, launched an inquiry into children in closed immigration detention. The purpose of this inquiry is to investigate the ways in which life in immigration detention affects the health, well-being and development of children. The inquiry will assess the impact on children by seeking the views of people who were previously detained as children in closed immigration detention and by assessing the current circumstances and responses of children to immigration detention.

---

137   HREOC, 'Those Who've Come Across the Seas: Detention of Unauthorised Arrivals', Commonwealth of Australia, 1998. https://www.humanrights.gov.au/sites/default/files/document/publication/h5_2_2.pdf, extracted 30 October 2014.

138   Peter Mares, *Borderline*, Reportage 2002 at 87.

139   HREOC, 'A Last Resort? National Inquiry into Children in Immigration Detention', Commonwealth of Australia, 2004. https://www.humanrights.gov.au/sites/default/files/document/publication/alr_complete.pdf, extracted 30 October 2014.

140   The author was a member of this task force.

141   One page of the draft quoted Article 37(b) as referring to detention lasting for the shortest *possible* period of time, instead of the shortest *appropriate* period of time. This error was rectified in the final version.

142   https://www.humanrights.gov.au/our-work/asylum-seekers-and-refugees/national-inquiry-children-immigration-detention-2014, extracted 30 October 2014.

The inquiry will investigate what has changed in the ten years since the Commission released *A last resort? The report of the National Inquiry into Children in Immigration Detention* in 2004.

The inquiry received 230 submissions[143] and handed down its report on 11 February 2015.[144] The AHRC was scathingly critical of the continuing detention of children in IDCs and similar environments, although the AHRC President, Gillian Triggs did note that '[s]ince the Inquiry began in February 2014, most of the 1138 children detained at that time are now in the community or in community detention'.[145] Despite this, around 330 children remained in immigration detention, and Professor Triggs noted that '34 per cent of children detained in Australia and Christmas Island have a mental health disorder of such severity that they require psychiatric support,[146] and that 'successive governments have failed children by locking them up in immigration detention'.[147]

The Federal government's reaction to the report was predictably vituperative, with PM Abbott describing the report as a 'blatantly partisan politicised exercise',[148] and questioned why the AHRC did not start its inquiry when the number of children in detention reached its peak of around 2000 under the previous government.[149] In response, Professor Triggs denied any bias, and stated that she 'made the decision to hold the inquiry last February because the release of children had slowed down over the first six months of the new Coalition Government.[150] It seems that once again no real action will be taken.

The AHRC also regularly receives complaints from individuals in immigration detention. The best known individual report is probably the report on the circumstances of the Shayan Badriae, a child who suffered severe psychiatric harm in immigration detention.[151] The experiences of the Badriae family were explained in depth in the book *The Bitter Shore*.[152]

---

143 https://www.humanrights.gov.au/our-work/asylum-seekers-and-refugees/national-inquiry-children-immigration-detention-2014, extracted 30 October 2014.
144 https://www.humanrights.gov.au/news/stories/locking-children-taints-us-all-says-commission-president, retrieved 20 February 2015.
145 Ibid.
146 Ibid.
147 Ibid.
148 http://www.abc.net.au/news/2015-02-12/human-rights-immigration-report-blatantly-partisan-abbott/6087148, retrieved 20 February 2015.
149 Ibid.
150 Ibid.
151 HREOC Report no 25, Report of an inquiry into a complaint by Mr Mohammed Badraie on behalf of his son Shayan regarding acts or practices of the Commonwealth of Australia (the Department of Immigration, Multicultural and Indigenous Affairs), https://www.humanrights.gov.au/publications/hreoc-report-no-25, extracted 30 October 2014.
152 Jacquie Everett, *The Bitter Shore*, Pan MacMillan Australia, 2008.

Chapter 5. Judicial Review of Administrative Decisions – General Principles

Part 1 – The meaning of 'Judicial Review'

Judicial Review has been defined by WJ Waluchow as follows:[1]

> A practice whereby courts are sometimes called upon to review a law or some other official act of government (e.g. the decision of an administrative agency such as a state or provincial labour relations board) to determine its constitutionality, or perhaps its reasonableness, rationality, or its compatibility with fundamental principles of justice.

It is important to note that judicial review is not *new*. Judicial review has existed at least since the time of the English prerogative writs, and in the former British colonies of Australia, Canada and New Zealand, amongst others, since the time those States came into existence.[2] It has always been a part of the common law of those countries, whether this has been acknowledged or not. The *ultra vires* principle operates, in the case of federal states, to invalidate state or provincial laws that are inconsistent with federal laws,[3] or actions of municipal governments that are inconsistent with their enabling legislation, as well as those of administrative decision makers.

Bastarache J of the Supreme Court of Canada, writing extrajudicially, has defined the term 'judicial review', in terms of review of administrative decisions, as 'the means by which the courts supervise those who exercise statutory powers, to ensure that they do not overstep their legal authority',[4] quoting paragraph 28 of the judgement in *Dunsmuir v New Brunswick*.[5] That paragraph went on to say that 'the function of judicial review is therefore to ensure the legality, the reasonableness and the fairness of the administrative process and its outcomes'.

From these definitions, we can see that judicial review in administrative law involves the review by one branch of government, the judiciary, of a decision

---

1   WJ Waluchow, 'Judicial Review', (2007) 2 *Philosophy Compass* 258 at 258.
2   For an early case involving judicial review of administrative decisions, see *Potter v Minahan* (1908) 7 CLR 277.
3   See for example s 109 of the Constitution.
4   Justice Michel Bastarache, 'Modernizing Judicial Review', (2009) 22 *Canadian Journal of Administrative Law and Practice* 227 at 228.
5   (2008) 1 SCR 190.

made by another branch of government, the executive. It can therefore be distinguished from an appeal from a lower court. The *purpose* of judicial review is for the court to examine whether the decision maker had the power to make the decision or grant the remedies in question (or even embark on the decision-making process in the first place), the process by which the decision was reached (for example, failure to afford procedural fairness), or the substance of the decision itself (review on the basis of 'reasonableness', however this term is defined).

De Smith notes two essential principles of true judicial review, as follows. Firstly, the issue of a prerogative writ (a term that will be defined shortly) is never given as of right – instead, the applicant must demonstrate why the writ should be granted.[6] Secondly, the remedies on judicial review are discretionary, meaning that a remedy will not be granted if, for example, there has been delay on the part of the applicant, or the applicant has been guilty of misconduct of some kind.[7]

The courts themselves have weighed in on the purpose of judicial review. In *Council for Civil Service Unions v Minister for the Civil Service* (popularly known as the 'GCHQ Case'), Diplock LJ stated that the role of the courts in judicial review was to:[8]

(i) Oversee the application of the law by ensuring that all and only relevant matters are taken into account in making a decision;

(ii) Ensure that fair procedures are followed; and

(iii) Ensure that the decision made is rational and reasonable in all the circumstances.

Judicial review can be contrasted with a statutory appeal. In some cases, an Act itself will provide for an appeal against an administrative decision to a court. For example, s 476 of the *Migration Act 1958* gives the Federal Circuit Court jurisdiction to review decisions of the Migration Review Tribunal and Refugee Review Tribunal for jurisdictional error. In Australia, the two terms are generally used interchangeably by lower courts. However, the distinction may prove to be of more significance in the High Court, because s 75 of the Australian Constitution guarantees some form of judicial review of administrative decisions, at least in that court.

One matter that is omitted from these definitions is what the courts can do if they find that a decision fails to meet any one of the criteria specified above.

6 SA De Smith, 'The Prerogative Writs', (1951–53) 11 *Cambridge Law Journal* 40 at 42.
7 Ibid at 44.
8 (1985) 1 AC 374 at 407.

In general, a court will have the power to set aside ('quash') a decision made without jurisdiction, or in breach of requirements of procedural or substantive fairness, and remit that decision to the individual or body concerned for reconsideration. A court cannot, in most cases, simply substitute its decision for that of an administrative decision maker. However, if a court is unable to actually *do* anything about a decision that falls foul of these principles, one wonders whether it is a true 'judicial review'.[9]

Why does Judicial Review exist at all?

The next question is 'why does judicial review of the decisions of administrators exist in the first place'? Why does a court have the authority to overturn a decision of the executive? There are three reasons – the historical prerogative writs and the background of the common law, decisions of the courts themselves, and constitutional entrenchment.

The shared common law

Modern administrative law in common law countries is based on the old English 'prerogative writs'. The writs were really a form of remedy for inappropriate administrative action or inaction as the case may be. The most important of these writs were mandamus, or an order to compel a decision maker to exercise their jurisdiction; prohibition, which was effectively a form of injunction preventing a decision maker from hearing a case; certiorari, which was originally 'essentially a royal demand for information',[10] but became a means by which a court could quash the decision of an administrator and order that the decision be made again, and *habeas corpus*, literally 'produce the body', which was usually an inquiry as to the legality of the detention of an individual. As can be seen from the name 'prerogative writs', the writs are discretionary in nature, and courts today retain the ability to refuse relief in situations such as the applicant not coming to the court with 'clean hands'.[11]

The usefulness of the old writs varies from jurisdiction to jurisdiction. At one extreme, they have been abolished in the Canadian province of British Columbia, and replaced by the general application for judicial review, through which a

---

9   This was an argument raised by Hill J (sitting at first instance) in *Eshetu v Minister for Immigration and Ethnic Affairs* (1997) FCA 19, and by the applicants in *Abebe v The Commonwealth; Re Minister for Immigration and Multicultural Affairs, Ex parte Abebe* (1999) 162 ALR 1.

10   De Smith, supra n6 at 45.

11   See for example *SAAP v Minister for Immigration and Multicultural and Indigenous Affairs* (2005) 215 ALR 162 at paragraph 80; *MZYSU v Minister for Immigration & Citizenship* (2012) FCA 1073; *Homex Realty Pty Ltd v Wyoming (Village)* (1980) 2 SCR 1011.

reviewing court may grant relief 'in the nature of' the old remedy.[12] On the other hand, the writs still have significant currency in Australia, at least at the High Court level, because they are specifically provided for the in the Constitution.

The constitutional baseline set by *Marbury v Madison*

The US case of *Marbury v Madison* has been relied on in Australia as a basis for the existence of judicial review. In that case, Marshall CJ stated as follows:[13]

> It is emphatically the province and duty of the Judicial Department to say what the law is. Those who apply the rule to particular cases must, of necessity, expound and interpret that rule. If two laws conflict with each other, the Courts must decide on the operation of each ... If, then, the Courts are to regard the Constitution, and the Constitution is superior to any ordinary act of the Legislature, the Constitution, and not such ordinary act, must govern the case to which they both apply.

That is, if a law is contrary to the constitution, it can and indeed must be overturned by the courts. The same principle can be applied to administrative decisions – if the decision is in some way contrary to the law, whether that be the constitution or the enabling legislation granting powers to the administrative decision maker, it can be set aside and a new decision ordered.

Marshall CJ identified a number of justifications for judicial review in his judgement. These include the written text of the constitution, which Marshall saw as ordinary law, although 'supreme' over all other ordinary laws,[14] the constitutional role of judges, which entails an ability to enforce their interpretations of the constitution against other branches of government; the grant of jurisdiction to the court for 'all cases arising under the Constitution',[15] the fact that judges and the President were required to swear an oath which, in part, required them to uphold the Constitution,[16] and the views of the framers.

Marbury v Madison, despite being a decision based on the construction of the US constitution, has been enthusiastically supported in Australia. In *Attorney-General (Western Australia) v Marquet* the High Court stated as follows:[17]

> Unlike Britain in the nineteenth century, the constitutional norms which apply in this country are more complex than an unadorned Diceyan

---

12   Subsections 2(1) and (2) of the *Judicial Review Procedure Act (BC)*, RSBC 1996 c 241.
13   (1803) 5 US (1 Cranch) 137 at 177.
14   Article VI, Clause 2 of the US Constitution. See also Mark Tushnet, '*Marbury v Madison* Around the World', (2003–04) 71 *Tennessee Law Journal* 251 at 258.
15   Article III, Section 2 of the US Constitution.
16   Supra n12 at 180.
17   (2003) 217 CLR 545 at paragraph 66.

precept of parliamentary sovereignty. Those constitutional norms accord an essential place to the obligation of the judicial branch to assess the validity of legislative and executive acts against relevant constitutional requirements. As Fullagar J said, in *Australian Communist Party v The Commonwealth*,[18] 'in our system the principle of *Marbury v Madison* is accepted as axiomatic'. It is the courts, rather than the legislature itself, which have the function of finally deciding whether an Act is or is not within power.

A consequence of constitutional entrenchment

This brings us neatly to the final reason for judicial review, which is that it is enshrined in some jurisdictions' constitutions. The best example of this is s 75 of the *Constitution Act 1900* (Australia), which provides as follows:

In all matters:

(i)   arising under any treaty;

(ii) affecting consuls or other representatives of other countries;

(iii) in which the Commonwealth, or a person suing or being sued on behalf of the Commonwealth, is a party;

(iv) between States, or between residents of different States, or between a State and a resident of another State;

(v)   in which a writ of Mandamus or prohibition or an injunction is sought against an officer of the Commonwealth;

the High Court shall have original jurisdiction.

The writ of certiorari was omitted from s 75(v) of the Constitution. However, the High Court has found on multiple occasions that it has the power to make an order of certiorari that is ancillary to an order for mandamus or prohibition.[19] Also, ss 30 and 32 of the Australian *Judiciary Act 1901* give the High Court the power to make such orders in specified circumstances.

---

18   (1953) 83 CLR 1 at 262.
19   See for example *Re Refugee Review Tribunal; Ex parte Aala* (2000) 204 CLR 82.

Part 2 – Constitutional entrenchment in Australia

The judicial power of the Commonwealth

Chapter III of the Australian Constitution is entitled 'The Judicature', and s 71, the first section in Chapter III, provides as follows:

> The judicial power of the Commonwealth shall be vested in a Federal Supreme Court, to be called the High Court of Australia, and in such other federal courts as the Parliament creates, and in such other courts as it invests with federal jurisdiction. The High Court shall consist of a Chief Justice, and so many other Justices, not less than two, as the Parliament prescribes.

A striking feature of Chapter III is that the term 'judicial power' is nowhere defined. It must therefore have been intended to be left to the High Court itself to determine what 'judicial power' actually is. There is, however, a marked lack of authority on this point. Stephen Gageler SC, then the Solicitor-General of Australia and now a High Court judge, has commented that '[t]he largest and most emphatic words in the Constitution – take "judicial power" and "absolutely free" as well-worn examples – have no fixed or intrinsic meaning and it would be in vain to attempt to search for one'.[20] Tony Blackshield and George Williams QC have stated as follows:[21]

> The characteristics and content of 'judicial power' have not proved susceptible to precise definition. In *Tasmanian Breweries*, Windeyer J observed that 'the concept seems ... to defy, perhaps it were better to say, transcend, purely abstract conceptual analysis'.[22] In *Chu Kheng Lim v Minister for Immigration, Local Government and Ethnic Affairs* (1992) 176 CLR 1, McHugh J noted that 'the line between judicial power and executive power in particular is very blurred',[23] and that the classification of a power 'frequently depends upon a value judgement ... having regard to the circumstances which call for its exercise ... The application of analytical tests and descriptions does not always determine the correct classification. Historical practice plays an

---

20   Stephen Gageler SC, 'Beyond the Text: A Vision for the Structure and Function of the Constitution', (2009) 32 *Australian Bar Review* 138 at 141.
21   Tony Blackshield and George Williams QC, *Australian Constitutional Law and Theory: Cases and Materials*, Federation Press, 2006 at 664.
22   *R v Trade Practices Commission, Ex parte Tasmanian Breweries Ltd* (1970) 123 CLR 361 at 394.
23   (1992) 176 CLR 1 at 67.

important, and sometimes decisive, part'.[24] And in *R v Quinn, Ex parte Consolidated Foods Corporation* (1977) 138 CLR 1, Aicken J concluded that 'in substance, all that the courts have been able to say towards a definition has been the formulation of negative propositions by which it has been said that no one list of factors is itself conclusive and perhaps the presence of all is not conclusive'.[25]

Despite this unpromising background, Blackshield and Williams state[26] that the 'classic' definition of judicial power is still that given by Griffith CJ in *Huddart, Parker and Co Ltd v Moorehead*, in which his Honour stated as follows:[27]

> I am of the opinion that the words 'judicial power' as used in sec 71 of the *Constitution* mean the power which every sovereign authority must of necessity have to decide controversies between its subjects, or between itself and its subjects, whether the rights relate to life, liberty or property. The exercise of this power does not begin until some tribunal which has power to give a binding and authoritative decision (whether subject to appeal or not) is called upon to take action.

That is, unless there is a final determination of existing rights to be made, there is no exercise of 'judicial power'. The High Court has also made clear a number of particular propositions in relation to what is or is not judicial review. For example, the High Court has found that giving an advisory opinion is not an exercise of judicial power,[28] but making of control orders applied to terrorism suspects[29] and persons convicted of sexual offences after their release from prison[30] is.

Australian courts have also made it clear that judicial power may not be exercised by a body other than a Chapter III court, and a judicial body may not exercise executive power. This principle has been enunciated many times by the High Court, most notably in *R v Kirby; Ex parte Boilermakers' Society of Australia*,[31] which found that the Court of Conciliation and Arbitration could not exercise both the power to impose an award on the parties to an industrial dispute, and provide a final and binding legal interpretation of that award. The *Boilermakers* decision also makes clear that Chapter III is an *exhaustive* statement of the judicial power of the Commonwealth. The majority judges, Dixon CJ and McTiernan,

---

24   Ibid.

25   (1977) 138 CLR 1 at 15.

26   Blackshield and Williams QC, supra n21 at 662.

27   (1909) 8 CLR 330 at 357.

28   *Re Judiciary Act 1903–1920 and Re Navigation Act 1912–1920* (1921) 29 CLR 257 (popularly known as the 'Advisory Opinions Case').

29   *Thomas v Mowbray* (2007) HCA 33.

30   *Fardon v Attorney-General (Queensland)* (2004) 223 CLR 575.

31   (1956) 94 CLR 254.

Fullagar and Kitto JJ, stated that Chapter III is 'an exhaustive statement of the manner in which the judicial power of the Commonwealth is or may be vested … No part of the judicial power can be conferred in virtue of any other authority or otherwise than in accordance with the provisions of Chap III'.[32]

An interesting illustration of this principle can be seen in *Lim v Minister for Immigration, Local Government and Ethnic Affairs*.[33] In that case, the applicant argued that a number of provisions of the *Migration Act 1958* which provided for the mandatory detention of 'designated persons' (persons who arrived in Australia by boat without a visa or entry permit, and given a 'designation' by the Department) were unconstitutional on a number of grounds, including that orders for detention were inherently punitive in nature, and therefore amounted to an exercise of the judicial power of the Commonwealth. The High Court found that s 54L, which provided that a designated person must not be released from detention unless granted a visa or removed from Australia, and s 54N, which required an 'officer' to detain a person reasonably suspected of being a designated person, without a warrant, were valid, as they were powers exercised incidentally to s 51(xix) of the Constitution, and were not an exercise of judicial power. They could therefore be exercised by administrative decision makers.

'Judicial power' and 'merits review'

For the purposes of this topic, the crucial issue is the distinction drawn by Australian courts between 'merits review' and 'judicial review'. There have been more cases than can possibly be referred to in which courts have stated that they are not to interfere in the merits of a decision, but the reasons *why* this is the case, even leaving aside the pejorative use of the word 'interfere', are rather obscure.

Australian courts have generally taken the view that a court must stay out of consideration of the 'merits' of a decision altogether. A frequently cited statement of the rule against merits review by courts can be found in *Attorney-General (NSW) v Quin*, in which Brennan J (as he then was) stated as follows:[34]

> The duty and jurisdiction of the court to review administrative action do not go beyond the declaration and enforcing of the law which determines the limits and governs the exercise of the repository's power. If, in so doing, the court avoids administrative injustice or error, so be it; but the court has no jurisdiction simply to cure administrative injustice

---

32   Ibid at 270.
33   (1992) 176 CLR 1.
34   (1990) 170 CLR 1 at 36.

or error. The merits of administrative action, to the extent that they can be distinguished from legality, are for the repository of the relevant power and, subject to political control, for the repository alone.

The key phrase is, of course, 'to the extent that they [the merits] can be distinguished from legality'. Margaret Allars makes the following points on that issue:[35]

> Three principles of judicial review qualify the operation of the legality/merits distinction. First, review for abuse of power where a decision is *Wednesbury* unreasonable is in practical terms review of the factual basis of the decision. The *Wednesbury* test of abuse of power permits the court to strike down a decision which is so unreasonable that no reasonable decision maker could have reached it. This ground effectively sanctions as review for legality what is review of the merits in extreme cases of disproportionate decisions. Second, according to the 'no evidence' principle, an agency makes an error of law in the course of making a finding of fact if there is a complete absence of evidence to support the factual inference. The third qualification to the legality/merits distinction is the jurisdictional fact doctrine.

'Merits review' and 'review of the merits' distinguished

Much of the difficulty in this area can be resolved by carefully distinguishing the terms 'merits review' and 'review of the merits'. David Bennett has defined the terms 'merits review' and 'judicial review' as follows:[36]

> A merits review body will 'stand in the shoes' of the primary decision maker, and will make a fresh decision based upon all the evidence available to it. The object of merits review is to ensure that the 'correct or preferable'[37] decision is made on the material before the review body. The object of judicial review, on the other hand, is to ensure that the decision made by the primary decision maker was properly made within the legal limits of the relevant power.

That is, it is the role of a primary decision maker, or review tribunal, to make a new decision on the evidence before it. This is the same principle that the House of Lords enunciated in *Huang v Secretary of State for the Home Department*,[38]

---

35   Margaret Allars, '*Chevron* in Australia: A Duplicitous Rejection?', (2002) 54 *Administrative Law Review* 569 at 583–84.

36   Ibid at 7.

37   *Drake v Minister for Immigration and Ethnic Affairs* (1979) 2 ALD 60 at 68.

38   (2007) 2 AC 167.

where it found that the administrative adjudicator reviewing a primary decision had not fulfilled their function when they focused on whether there was an error in that primary decision. Instead, the adjudicator's role was to make a new decision on the basis of all the evidence, including evidence that may not have been available to the Home Department, before them.

It does not, however, follow that there is therefore no role in examining the merits of a case for a court. The court's role is judicial *review* – it is not the role of a court to simply reopen a case and make any order it sees fit. Its role is to *review* the administrative decision before it.[39] If the court stays out of substantive decision-making and limits itself to a review of the decision and, if the decision is to be set aside, remits it to the appropriate decision maker for reconsideration, this is an exercise of judicial and not executive power, even if the 'substance' or the 'merits' of the decision are in question. It does not offend the *Boilermakers* principle that judicial power cannot be exercised by any other body than a Chapter III court, and nor may an administrative body exercise anything other than executive power.

Sun v Minister for Immigration and Ethnic Affairs

A consideration of two Australian cases illustrates this point. In *Sun v Minister for Immigration and Ethnic Affairs.*[40] The applicant in *Sun* had been before the Refugee Review Tribunal (RRT) three times. The first decision, made by Member Fordham, accepted the truth of most (although not all) of the applicant's claims, but found that he was not a refugee. As the Department prepared to remove Mr Sun from Australia, the Chinese consulate refused to issue him with a passport, claiming they could not identify him. Mr Sun took this as further evidence of persecution, and applied again for refugee status.[41] This second application was also refused by the Department, and then by a different member of the RRT, Ms Ransome. Ms Ransome's decision was ultimately set aside by consent, on the fairly technical basis that she had referred to an incorrect provision of the *Migration Act 1958* in her decision.

The matter then went back for a third time to the RRT, this time before Member Smidt. Ms Smidt undertook a *de novo* review, in the face of Mr Sun's objection that she should accept Mr Fordham's finding that he was telling the truth about most of his claims, and that the only issue was whether he was a refugee on the basis of those facts. The full Federal Court found no error in Ms Smidt's

---

39 See for example *SZBEL v MIMIA* (2006) HCA 63, at paragraphs 34 and 40.
40 (1997) 81 FCR 71.
41 This course of action would now be prohibited by s 48A of the *Migration Act 1958*. Section 48A did not exist at the time of Mr Sun's second application.

approach to the matter in that sense.[42] Ms Smidt, unlike Mr Fordham, found that Mr Sun had fabricated most of his claims and again refused his application for review.

The full Federal Court, however, set Ms Smidt's decision aside on procedural fairness grounds. The question that remained was what to do with Mr Sun. There was uncontradicted evidence before the court (and Ms Smidt) that Mr Sun was suffering from post-traumatic stress disorder,[43] and the court was clearly concerned about putting him through another RRT hearing. The leading judgement was given by Wilcox and Burchett JJ, but North J, who concurred in the result, added as follows on the disposal of the case in the final paragraph of the judgement:[44]

> Finally, I wish to refer to the observation by Wilcox J that the Minister should consider exercising his power under s 417 in favour of the appellant. As the comprehensive analysis made by Wilcox J in his judgment reveals, the Court has had the opportunity to examine the entire history of the appellant's involvement in the review system. The circumstances of this case are exceptional and call for a quick and humane conclusion in favour of the appellant. No doubt, in many approaches to the Minister, cases are urged as 'special cases' which are special only in the eyes of their proponents. The history of this case does make it special. It is special because the appellant has special problems of depression and post-traumatic stress disorder arising out of the circumstances of the case. It is special because there have been a number of errors in the review system. A number of these errors make it oppressive to require the appellant to have to face another hearing.

North J seemed sorely tempted to make some kind of declaration that Mr Sun was a refugee, but declined to do so. Making an order to this effect would go beyond judicial review of an administrative decision, and would be an exercise of executive power.

The *Guo* litigation

Sun should be compared to the *Guo* cases in the full Federal Court and then the High Court. In the Full Federal Court, Einfeld J, having first ruled that an asylum seeker should be found to be a refugee unless the contrary could be

---

proved beyond reasonable doubt,[45] then made orders to the effect that Mr Guo and his wife Ms Pan were refugees and 'entitled to the appropriate entry visas'.[46] Foster J agreed with the orders proposed by Einfeld J.[47]

In a rare 7-0 judgement, the High Court[48] overturned both the 'beyond reasonable doubt' approach to refugee decision-making proposed by Einfeld J, and the orders his Honour proposed. The majority judges (Brennan CJ and Dawson, Toohey, Gaudron, McHugh and Gummow JJ) found on the first point that '[i]ngenious as his Honour's approach may be, it is not supported by the terms of the Convention or the proper approach to administrative decision making in this context'.[49] On the power to make orders, the majority stated as follows:[50]

> The orders of the Full Court included a declaration 'that both appellants are refugees and are entitled to the appropriate entry visas'. A declaration in these terms lacked utility because it did not specify with reference to the legislation the 'appropriate entry visas' nor did it indicate any ready means of identification thereof. A declaration so loosely framed is objectionable in form.
>
> Moreover, a declaration, even if drawn in specific terms, should not have been made. The Tribunal was empowered by s 166BC(1) of the Act to exercise all the powers and discretions conferred upon the primary decision maker. The Act provided (s 22AA) for determination by the Minister that a person was a refugee, but this power was exercisable upon the Minister being satisfied that a person had that status or character. The rights of the appellants to the issue of visas, which the Full Court purported to declare with present effect, would only arise upon satisfaction of statutory conditions including the determination by the Minister under s 22AA or by the Tribunal under s 166BC. In those circumstances, the appropriate course would have been for the Full Court to set aside the orders of Sackville J and to return the matter to the Tribunal for determination in accordance with law.

Kirby J concurred as follows:[51]

---

45 *Guo v Minister for Immigration and Ethnic Affairs* (1996) 135 ALR 421, paragraph 25 of the judgment of Einfeld J.

46 Ibid at paragraphs 63 and 68. Incidentally, there is no such a thing as an 'entry visa' in the current legislation – Einfeld J apparently conflated the terms 'visa' and 'entry permit'. The latter kind of document was abolished with the passage of the *Migration Reform Act 1992*, which came into effect on 1 September 1994, and the visa has been the sole authority for entry to Australia by a non-citizen since that date.

47 Ibid at paragraph 54 of the judgment of Foster J.

48 *Minister for Immigration and Ethnic Affairs v Guo* (1997) 191 CLR 559.

49 Ibid at 574.

50 Ibid at 579.

51 Ibid at 600.

[I]t is sufficient in my view to say that it was not appropriate for the Federal Court to adopt the course which the majority did. The proper course, legal error having been found, was to return the matter to the Tribunal. In that way, each of the relevant organs of government performs the functions proper to it. The Judicial Branch authoritatively clarifies and declares the law as it applies to the facts found. The Executive Branch, by power vested in it by the Legislature, performs its functions according to the law as so clarified and declared. Neither branch usurps or intrudes upon the functions proper to the other.

It is no part of the judicial function to make a decision of an administrative nature such as the grant of a visa. This is indeed a breach of the principle of separation of powers. This does not mean, however, that a court has no place in *reviewing* the merits of a decision, and leaving the substantive decision to the duly designated administrative decision maker. This kind of reasoning complies with the admonition of Mason J in *Minister for Aboriginal Affairs v Peko-Wallsend Ltd* that '[i]t is not the function of the court to substitute its own decision for that of the administrator by exercising a discretion which the legislature has vested in the administrator'[52] while still ensuring that the courts can truly *review* the merits of the decision.

Kirby J also noted in *Guo* as follows:[53]

[C]are must be exercised in applying decisions about the available and appropriate remedy apt to an appeal when the process before the Court is that of judicial review. Whereas on appeal a court will often enjoy the power and responsibility of substituting its decision for that under appeal, judicial review is designed, fundamentally, to uphold the lawfulness, fairness and reasonableness (rationality) of the process under review. It is thus ordinarily an adjunct to, and not a substitution for, the decision of the relevant administrator.

S297/2013

A recent case in which the High Court *did* effectively order the grant of a visa is *S297/2013 v Minister for Immigration and Border Protection*,[54] a case that involved a complex and probably unique set of facts. S297 had arrived in Australia at Christmas Island by boat in May 2012. At the time, he was an 'offshore entry person', by means of his arrival at an 'excised offshore place', and therefore could not make a valid visa application (s 46A of the Act). However, in September 2012 the Minister decided, under s 46A(2), to lift the s 46A bar

---

52   *Minister for Aboriginal Affairs v Peko-Wallsend Ltd* (1986) 162 CLR 24 at 42.
53   Supra n44 at 600.
54   (2015) HCA 3.

and allow S297 to make an application for a Protection Visa. In February 2013 a delegate refused S297's application, a decision which was set aside by the RRT and remitted to the decision maker in May 2013 with a direction that that S297 met the requirements of s 36(2)(a) of the Act.

The Minister and Department simply failed to make a decision on the remitted application, a situation which was complicated by the election of a new government on 7 September 2013. In 2014 the Minister purported to impose caps on the granting of protection visas, an approach that was struck down by the High Court in June 2014.[55] In the end, French CJ made a consent order on 1 July 2014, issuing a writ of mandamus directing the Minister to decide S297's application according to law. What happened next can best be explained by quoting the judgement in the 2015 decision:[56]

> On 17 July 2014, the Minister decided to refuse to grant the plaintiff a Protection (Class XA) visa. The parties agree that the only reason the Minister refused to grant the plaintiff a protection visa was that the Minister was not satisfied that the cl 866.226 criterion was met. (It will be recalled that this criterion required the Minister to be satisfied that the grant of the visa 'is in the national interest'.) The Minister's decision record shows that he saw 'the national interest' as requiring refusal of a Protection (Class XA) visa to any and every unauthorised maritime arrival. That is, even though the Act provided, at all times relevant to these proceedings, that the Minister could decide that it is 'in the public interest' to permit an unauthorised maritime arrival to make a valid application for a permanent protection visa, the Minister's decision in this case was that the national interest required that no such application should be granted.

The High Court found that this reasoning was unlawful, essentially on the following basis:

- Section 46A prohibited an offshore entry person from making a valid visa application unless the bar was lifted under s 46A(2).
- The Minister did lift that bar in 2012. (The fact that this was a different Minister to the Minister who made the ultimate refusal decision was irrelevant.)
- The Minister could not therefore refuse the visa on the basis that the applicant had arrived in Australia unlawfully, as that issue had already been decided in the applicant's favour by lifting the bar in the first place.

---

55   *Plaintiff S297/2013 v Minister for Immigration and Border Protection* (2014) 88 ALJR 722.
56   Supra n54 at paragraph 13.

The remaining issue was what to do with the decision. The High Court found that the sole basis for the Minister's refusal decision was that grant of the visa was not in the national interest, a ground that had just been set aside by the court. The Court stated as follows:[57]

> No other basis for the decision having been identified, the Minister cannot, and should not, now be given any further opportunity to consider the matter afresh. It is not suggested that, in the time between the issue of the writ of mandamus and this Court's determination of the present dispute about the sufficiency of the Minister's return to that writ, there has been any relevant change in any circumstances affecting the disposition of the plaintiff's application … [I]t is enough to observe that only one reason was given by the Minister for refusing the plaintiff's application. That reason was legally insufficient. And in his return to the writ, the Minister had the opportunity to identify any other reason for refusing the application. None was identified. The Minister should not now be given any further opportunity to identify a reason for refusing the plaintiff's application.

That is, because the RRT had already found S297 to be a person to whom Australia owed protection obligations, and the Minister's sole reason for refusing the remitted application was found to be unlawful, there was nothing left for the Minister to decide and the court could issue a peremptory writ of mandamus,[58] which is a very unusual remedy and not necessary to discuss in detail here, directing the grant of a permanent protection visa. *Guo* was not cited in the judgement. It therefore seems that a court *can* order the grant of a visa, but only in the very limited circumstances where there are no factual questions to be resolved and every ground for the refusal decision has been set aside by the court. It remains to be seen whether and how lower courts take advantage of this precedent and whether they see it (probably incorrectly) as overruling *Guo*.

Part 3 – Common law grounds of judicial review

The grounds on which an administrative decision can, at common law, be reviewed by a court is a topic for a textbook by itself. However, errors of law can be grouped into two broad categories – procedural and substantive. The substantive ground of 'unreasonableness' can be regarded as a synthesis of all other substantive errors, and will be considered separately as a result.

---

57   Ibid at paragraph 41.
58   Ibid at paragraphs 37–47.

Procedural errors

Procedural errors are errors of law that relate to the procedure by which the decision was made, and not the substance of the decision. This is also known as a breach of 'natural justice' or 'procedural fairness'. Failures of natural justice can be further classified as follows:

Failure to hear the 'other side'

In the case of a migration application, the issue is usually whether the Minister has permitted an applicant to make his or her case, and in particular whether the applicant has been made aware of the substance of any information held by the decision maker that could result in the application being refused. The following points should be made:

1. It is not always necessary that the decision maker provide the applicant with the opportunity for an oral hearing. Written submissions can be sufficient.[59]

2. The officer who hears the matter must decide it. In the recent Full Federal Court decision of *WZARH v Minister for Immigration and Border Protection*[60] an independent merits reviewer, appointed for the purpose of advising the Minister whether to permit a visa application under s 46A of the Act, became unavailable part-way through an application, after interviewing the applicant. The matter was handed to another reviewer who, without personally hearing from the applicant, recommended against an s 46A decision. The Full Federal Court found that the second decision maker should have heard from the applicant, and for that reason (amongst others) set the decision aside.

3. As previously discussed, the substance of any information held by the decision maker that is adverse to the applicant must be disclosed to that applicant for comment.[61]

4. The common law rules of natural justice can be displaced by clear statutory to the contrary.[62]

---

59   See for example *Seiffert v Prisoners Review Board* (2011) WASCA 148 at paragraph 72. See, however, the decision of the Supreme Court of Canada in *Singh (Harbhajan) v Minister of Employment and Immigration* (1985) 1 SCR 177, which found that applicants for refugee status *did* always require an oral hearing.
60   (2014) FCAFC 137.
61   *Kioa v West* (1985) 159 CLR 550.
62   See for example *Plaintiff S10-2011 v Minister for Immigration and Citizenship* (2012) HCA 31. Compare this situation to Canada, which has enshrined natural justice as a constitutional right under s 7 of the Charter – see for example *Charkaoui v Canada (Minister of Citizenship and Immigration)* (2007) 1 SCR 350.

Bias

The decision must not be affected by bias (whether actual or apprehended) on the part of the decision maker.[63] The difference between the two tests is that the former looks at the *subjective* thought processes of the decision maker, and relies on a finding that the particular decision maker cannot in fact be persuaded by the evidence from his or her existing mindset, while the latter is a claim that a *reasonable person* would be likely to apprehend that a decision maker cannot be swayed by any evidence from an existing position, and is therefore an *objective* test.[64] It is important to note that the mere existence of a pre-existing opinion on the part of the decision maker is not sufficient to set aside a decision on the grounds of actual or apprehended bias. Instead, 'what must be firmly established is a reasonable fear that the decision maker's mind is so prejudiced in favour of a conclusion already formed that he or she *will not alter that conclusion* irrespective of the evidence or arguments presented to him or her'.[65]

Bias, although regarded as a procedural error, can often only be established once the decision is made and its reasons examined. For that reason, it is not uncommon for applicants to argue that a decision maker was biased, or in the alternative, that the decision was unreasonable.[66]

There is a variety of ways in which the impartiality of a court or a tribunal may be or may appear to be compromised. Deane J in *Webb v The Queen*[67] identified four of them as 'distinct, though sometimes overlapping, main categories of case'. They were:

a) Interest – where the judge has an interest in the proceedings, whether pecuniary or otherwise, giving rise to a reasonable apprehension of prejudice, partiality or prejudgment;

b) Conduct – where the judge has engaged in conduct in the course of, or outside, the proceedings (the evidence of which can sometimes be seen in the decision itself), giving rise to such an apprehension of bias;

c) Association – where the judge has a direct or indirect relationship, experience or contact with a person or persons interested in, or otherwise involved in, the proceedings; and

d) Extraneous information – where the judge has knowledge of some prejudicial but inadmissible fact or circumstance giving rise to the apprehension of bias.

---

63   For a detailed history of the law of apprehended bias in Australia, see *Ebner v Official Trustee in Bankruptcy* (2000) 75 ALJR 277.
64   *Minister for Immigration and Multicultural Affairs v Jia* (2001) 205 CLR 507.
65   *Bond v Australian Broadcasting Tribunal* (1991) 173 CLR 78 at 86.
66   *Sun*, supra n38, is just one example.
67   (1994) 181 CLR 41 at 74.

Procedural legitimate expectations[68]

Where an applicant has been led to believe that an administrative decision maker will follow a particular procedure, the decision maker cannot then depart from that procedure without first permitting the applicant to comment.

The best way to explain this principle is by example. In *Ng Yuen Shiu v Attorney-General (Hong Kong)*[69] the Attorney-General, who was responsible for immigration in Hong Kong, issued a policy document stating that illegal entrants who came forward within a particular timeframe would be permitted to apply for permanent residence. Mr Ng came forward, and was promptly detained and scheduled for deportation. The Privy Council, hearing the appeal from a Hong Kong court, found that the Attorney-General must either allow Mr Ng to apply for permanent residence, or allow him to argue that the stated policy should be applied.

Ng was followed in Australia in *Haoucher v Minister for Immigration and Ethnic Affairs,*[70] in which the Department informed Mr Haoucher, who had been convicted of an offence, that it did not propose to deport him on the basis of that offence. When Mr Haoucher was later convicted of another, less serious offence, the Department changed its mind and started deportation proceedings on the basis of the first offence. The same result as in *Ng* ensued – the Minister either had to abide by his word or allow Mr Haoucher to make submissions as to why the earlier representation should be followed. More recently, the Federal Court has found, in *Misiura v Minister for Immigration and Multicultural Affairs*[71] and *WASB v Minister for Immigration and Citizenship*[72] that while the Minister, acting personally, is not bound by a s 499 direction, departure from a relevant direction without prior notification to an applicant could amount to a failure to afford procedural fairness on the legitimate expectations ground.

Even more controversially, the High Court found in *Minister for Immigration and Ethnic Affairs v Teoh*[73] that ratification of an international instrument acted as a 'representation' for the purposes of procedural legitimate expectations. The result was that any decision to deport Mr Teoh had to take the best interests of his seven Australian citizen children into account, because of Australia's ratification of the Convention on the Rights of the Child. *Teoh* never created the legal revolution that it could have, for a number of reasons not necessary to

---

68   In the UK, it is possible to argue for an error of law on the basis of *substantive* legitimate expectations, that is, that the applicant had been led to expect a certain *result* of an application, not merely a certain *process* – *R v North and East Devon Health Authority, Ex parte Coughlan* (2001) QB 213. This argument has never been accepted in Australia.

69   (1983) 2 AC 629.

70   (1990) 169 CLR 648.

71   (2001) FCA 133.

72   (2013) FCA 1016 at paragraph 48.

73   (1995) 183 CLR 273.

discuss here, but it did create a fertile field for academics.[74] The legal effectiveness of *Teoh* now appears to have been questioned by *Re Minister for Immigration and Multicultural Affairs; Ex parte Lam*[75] in any event.

The concept of procedural legitimate expectations is somewhat similar to the concept of promissory estoppel. In *Waltons (Interstate) Stores v Maher*[76] Waltons told Mr Maher that it would like to purchase certain vacant land owned by him on the condition that it was first cleared and remediated. Mr Maher did so, expending a considerable amount of his own money, but Waltons then reneged on the deal. The High Court found that Waltons had made a representation and that Mr Maher had relied on it to his detriment (in the form of land clearing costs), and that Waltons was therefore prevented ('estopped') from going back on its word. This concept is not exactly the same as procedural legitimate expectations because it can be difficult to show that the subject of an administrative decision 'relied' on any particular advice to his or her detriment. For example, did Mr Haoucher decide to reoffend on the basis of the deportation advice given to him by the Department?

Finally, neither estoppel nor legitimate expectations can prevent the application of *legislation* to an individual. In *Minister for Immigration and Ethnic Affairs v Polat*[77], Mr Polat attempted to lodge an application for an entry permit at a counter, only to be wrongly told that the application could not be lodged without a marriage certificate. By the time Mr Polat received a certified copy of his marriage certificate the entry permit class had closed and his application could not be accepted. Mr Polat argued that the incorrect information provided to him meant that the Department was estopped from denying that the application was valid when it was finally made after the nominal closing date. The Full Federal Court rejected this argument, finding that the Regulations made it clear that the application could not be made after a certain date, and not even incorrect advice from the Department itself could change the situation. Mr Polat's only redress was to sue the Commonwealth for negligence.

---

74   As just a few examples – Leslie Katz, 'A Teoh FAQ', (1998) 16 *Australian Institute of Administrative Law Forum* 1; Anne Twomey, '*Minister for Immigration and Ethnic Affairs v Teoh*' (1995) 23 *Federal Law Review* 348; Margaret Allars, 'One Small Step for Legal Doctrine, One Giant Leap Towards Integrity in Government: Teoh's Case and the Internationalisation of Administrative Law' (1995) 17 *Sydney Law Review* 202; S Sheridan, 'Legitimate Expectations: Where Does the Law Now Lie?' (1998) 87 *Canberra Bulletin of Public Administration* 125–33; Kristen Walker, 'Who's The Boss? The Judiciary, the Executive, the Parliament and the Protection of Human Rights' (1995) 25 *Western Australian Law Review* 238; Ryszard Piotrowicz, 'Unincorporated Treaties in Australian Law: The Official Response to the Teoh Decision' (1997) 71 *Australian Law Journal* 503; Ryszard Piotrowicz, 'Unincorporated Treaties in Australian Law' (1996) *Public Law* 190; PW Perry, 'At the Intersection: Australian Law and International Law' (1997) 71 *Australian Law Journal* 841; Wendy Lacey, 'In the Wake of *Teoh*: Finding an Appropriate Government Response', (2001) 29 *Federal Law Review* 219.
75   (2003) 195 ALR 502.
76   (1988) 164 CLR 387.
77   (1995) 37 ALD 394.

Substantive errors

The second kind of error of law is known as a *substantive* error, that is, one that goes to the substance of the decision and not merely the process by which it was made. Some of the major substantive errors are as follows.

Failure to take a relevant consideration into account and taking irrelevant considerations into account

The 'relevant/irrelevant considerations' ground, as it is popularly known, has a long history in Australia. For example, Latham CJ stated as follows in *R v Connell; Ex parte Hetton Bellbird Collieries Ltd*:[78]

> It should be emphasised that the application of the principle now under discussion does not mean that the court substitutes its opinion for the opinion of the person or authority in question. What the court does do is to inquire whether the opinion required by the relevant legislative provision has really been formed. If the opinion which was in fact formed was reached by taking into account irrelevant considerations or by otherwise misconstruing the terms of the relevant legislation, then it must be held that the opinion required has not been formed.

The obvious question is then when a consideration is deemed to be relevant or irrelevant. The key issue is the decision maker's enabling legislation. For example, in *Minister for Immigration and Multicultural Affairs v Yusuf* McHugh, Gummow and Hayne JJ stated that '[t]he considerations that are, or are not, relevant to the Tribunal's task are to be identified primarily, perhaps even entirely, by reference to the Act rather than the particular facts of the case that the Tribunal is called on to consider',[79] and further that '[t]hey are not grounds that are centrally concerned with the process of making the particular findings of fact upon which the decision maker acts'.[80]

That is, in considering the grant or refusal of a visa, the relevant considerations are the relevant provisions of the Act and Regulations (in particular the Schedules 1 and 2 criteria) and applicable policy, at least where this is not inconsistent with the legislation. Obviously, when one gets to terms subject to interpretation, such as 'real chance of persecution' or 'genuine and continuing relationship', many sub-criteria open up. For example, in *Minister for Immigration and Citizenship v Li*[81]

---

78   (1944) 69 CLR 407 at 430; cited with approval in *NAAV v Minister for Immigration and Multicultural and Indigenous Affairs* (2002) FCAFC 228 at paragraph 26.
79   (2001) 206 CLR 323 at paragraph 73.
80   Ibid at paragraph 74.
81   (2013) HCA 18.

the High Court, amongst other findings, found that the MRT had taken certain prior conduct on Ms Li's part into account in deciding whether to adjourn a hearing, and stated as follows:[82]

[84] There remains the possibility that the previous conduct of Ms Li influenced the Tribunal. It had continued to question her about the false information associated with her application despite her repeated admissions and the advice that the case she wished to put forward did not depend upon that information. If her prior conduct was influential, the Tribunal took into account an irrelevant consideration for the reason that Ms Li's conduct per se was not relevant to the visa criteria. The concern of the criteria is with the information relied upon to satisfy them, a point Ms Li's migration agent attempted to make to the Tribunal.

[85] ... In the circumstances of this case, it could not have been decided that the review should be brought to an end if all relevant and no irrelevant considerations were taken into account and regard was had to the scope and purpose of the statute. Because error must be inferred, it follows that the Tribunal did not discharge its function (of deciding whether to adjourn the review) according to law. The Tribunal did not conduct the review in the manner required by the *Migration Act* and consequently acted beyond its jurisdiction.

No evidence

A ground of review that is obviously related to the 'relevant / irrelevant considerations' ground is the no evidence ground. In this case, the argument is that the decision maker had no evidence at all on which to base his or her decision. It appears that, in Australia, an administrative decision will only be set aside on the 'no evidence' ground where the decision maker had no evidence in relation to a finding on a jurisdictional fact.[83] A 'jurisdictional fact' is a complex concept, but essentially it is a fact that must exist before the decision maker can even consider the matter before them. For example, *M70/2011 and M106/2011 v Minister for Immigration and Citizenship*[84] was concerned with s 198A of the *Migration Act* 1958, and in particular with the government's so-called 'Malaysia solution', which involved processing of asylum-seekers who arrived illegally in Australia in Malaysia, in return for Australia accepting persons from Malaysia who had been determined by the United Nations High Commission for Refugees (UNHCR) as having refugee status. Subsection 198A(1) provided that 'an officer

---

82   Ibid at paragraphs 84 and 85.

83   *Television Capricornia Pty Ltd v Australian Broadcasting Tribunal* (1986) 13 FCR 511 at 514 at 519–20.

84   (2011) HCA 32.

may take an offshore entry person from Australia to a country in respect of which a declaration is in force under subsection (3)'. Subsection 198A(3) then provided as follows:

The Minister may:

(a)   declare in writing that a specified country:

   (i)   provides access, for persons seeking asylum, to effective procedures for assessing their need for protection; and

   (ii)   provides protection for persons seeking asylum, pending determination of their refugee status; and

   (iii)   provides protection to persons who are given refugee status, pending their voluntary repatriation to their country of origin or resettlement in another country; and

   (iv)   relevant human rights standards in providing that protection; and

(b)   in writing, revoke a declaration made under paragraph (a).

The High Court found that ss 198A(3)(a)(i)–(iv) were jurisdictional facts, and the Minister could not make a s 198A(1) determination unless he or she could be satisfied that all were met. The High Court went on to find that as Malaysia was not a signatory to the Convention on the Status of Refugees, the Minister had no evidence that any of ss 198A(3)(a)(i)–(iv) were met, and that the declaration of Malaysia as a 'specified country' was therefore invalid.[85]

Inflexible application of policy

While it is perfectly lawful for a decision maker to set out policy to assist him or her in making decisions, he or she must not act as if he or she is *bound* by that policy in the same way as legislation. That is, a 'refusal to entertain the possibility that a particular case might fall outside the policy, or require its reconsideration'[86] is an error of law.

As has been previously noted, policy is a crucial consideration in Departmental decision-making. The Full Federal Court has noted that it is open to the MRT and RRT 'in the interests of consistency, to apply the departmental policy unless

---

85   For more discussion of this case and jurisdictional facts generally, see Alan Freckelton, 'The Concept of Deference in Judicial Review of Administrative Decisions in Australia (Part 1)', (2013) 73 *Australian Institute of Administrative Law Forum* 52 at 62–64.

86   *Neat Domestic Trading Pty Ltd v AWB Ltd* (2003) 216 CLR 277 at paragraph 26; citing with approval *British Oxygen Co Ltd v Minister of Technology* (1971) AC 610 at 624–25.

there were cogent reasons for departing from it'.[87] However, there is a difference between deciding to follow a policy unless good reasons can be shown to depart from it, and following policy as if it was law. It is therefore somewhat curious that this ground has rarely been successfully argued in Australian courts in immigration cases.

One case where the inflexible application of policy argument *was* successfully run was *Jackson v Minister for Immigration and Multicultural and Indigenous Affairs*.[88] In this case the MRT found that an applicant was not a 'special need relative', based primarily on its application of the PAMs. In particular, the PAMs stated that '[i]t is policy that, in the absence of other extenuating circumstances, NONE OF THE FOLLOWING ON THEIR OWN CONSTITUTES A SERIOUS CIRCUMSTANCE, A PERMANENT OR LONG-TERM NEED OR REQUIRES SUBSTANTIAL AND CONTINUING ASSISTANCE' (emphasis in original), and then provided a list of such circumstances. The MRT found that 'at the time of the visa application, the further evidence is that the assistance rendered by the visa applicant was of the kind excluded by policy'.[89] Lee, Carr and Moore JJ, constituting the Full Federal Court, stated as follows:[90]

> [19] As is apparent from paras 35, 36 and 37 from the Tribunal's reasons it did not accept that the assistance actually being provided by the appellant to the nominator at the time of the application could be viewed as substantial for the purposes of the definition of 'special need relative' and therefore could not sustain a conclusion that the nominator had a permanent or long-term need for assistance.

> [20] In adopting this approach the Tribunal erred in one and possibly two respects. First it took the view that the terms in which the Procedures Advice Manual was expressed, excluded from consideration any assistance which might be provided by the appellant to his mother which took the form of the assistance described in para 3 of the Manual … [B]y adopting this approach, the Tribunal did not consider for itself whether the assistance being provided and which might continue to be provided, was substantial. It said the assistance relied on 'was of the kind excluded by the policy'. In effect, the Tribunal did not treat the Manual as a guide but rather treated it as actually determining in a prescriptive way the question the Tribunal was required to answer having regard to the definition of 'special need relative'.

---

87   *Braganza v Minister for Immigration and Multicultural and Indigenous Affairs* (2003) FCAFC 170 at paragraph 31.
88   (2003) FCAFC 203.
89   Ibid at paragraph 14, quoting paragraph 36 of the MRT's decision.
90   Ibid at paragraphs 19 and 20.

Their Honours went on to note that inflexible application of policy by a decision maker can be characterised as a jurisdictional error[91] and set the MRT's decision aside.

Improper exercise of power

The term 'improper exercise of power' means exactly what it says. Even when a discretion is entirely unconstrained by the terms of the legislation, an administrative decision maker will make an error of law if he or she uses that power for purposes other than those that were intended by the legislation.

The best known example of a case in which a decision was found to amount to an improper exercise of power is the decision of the Supreme Court of Canada in *Roncarelli v Duplessis*.[92] Mr Roncarelli was a restaurant owner in Montreal and a prominent Jehovah's Witness, and M Duplessis was the Premier of Quebec. At that time, many Jehovah's Witnesses were being arrested for distributing religious tracts in violation of provincial and municipal laws, and Mr Roncarelli regularly posted bail for them. Duplessis publicly warned Roncarelli to cease this practice, and when he did not, Mr Roncarelli's liquor licence was cancelled. This forced the closure of his restaurant, and Roncarelli went to the Supreme Court.

Duplessis argued that the relevant legislation, the *Loi Concernant les Spiritueux* (*'Act Respecting Alcoholic Liquor'*), gave the decision maker complete discretion as to the cancellation of a liquor licence. The Supreme Court nevertheless overturned the decision because it was incompatible with the purpose of the Act. Mr Roncarelli's licence had been cancelled not because he served alcohol irresponsibly, but because he was being punished for assisting Jehovah's Witnesses with posting bail.

Cases in which an improper exercise of power has been successfully argued in Australia are rare. On occasion, a court has found that the cumulative effect of numerous errors in a decision-making process can lead to a finding of an improper exercise of power,[93] but *Roncarelli*-type rulings are few and far between. One example of a finding of an improper exercise of power was in *Park v Minister for Immigration and Ethnic Affairs*. Holding the detained Korean workers in detention until they 'snitched' on the organisers of the perceived 'racket' was held to be an improper purpose of immigration detention.

---

91   *British Oxygen*, supra n84; *Rendell v Release on Licence Board* (1987) 10 NSWLR 449; *Bread Manufacturers of New South Wales v Evans* (1981) 180 CLR 404 at 418.
92   (1959) SCR 121.
93   See for example *Che Guang Xiang v Minister of Immigration Local Government and Ethnic Affairs* (1994) FCA 1037.

One case in which an improper exercise of power was prominently but unsuccessfully argued was *Minister for Immigration and Multicultural Affairs v Jia*,[94] in which the Minister, after the AAT set aside a decision to refuse Mr Jia's visa under s 501, granted the visa and then cancelled it. Jia argued that this was an abuse of power, and a decision aimed at punishing him rather than genuinely assessing his case. The High Court unanimously disagreed, finding that as the Act did not prevent the Minister from acting as he did, his actions were lawful. In particular, the AAT is part of the executive, and circumventing its decision did not breach the separation of powers principle.[95]

The sum of all substantive review: Unreasonableness

Unreasonableness is the most problematic of the substantive grounds of review, and strongly questions the insistence of Australian courts that they do not engage in 'merits review'. Unreasonableness requires an inquiry into the merits of the decision. Even if a court finds that it will only set that decision aside if the unreasonableness is extreme in some sense, it is still a review of the merits of the decision. In Canada, all substantive grounds of review have been collapsed into the general ground of unreasonableness, and Canadian administrative law is much simpler for it.

The ground of judicial review known as 'unreasonableness', sometimes known as 'Wednesbury unreasonableness',[96] has a long history in Australian administrative law. For most of its existence, a decision must have been found to be outrageous or completely devoid of merit – 'so unreasonable that no reasonable authority could ever come to it'[97] – to be struck down on this basis. For example, in *Australian Retailers Association v Reserve Bank of Australia*[98] Weinberg J stated that 'the current view, in this country, seems to be ... to regard this ground as representing a safety net, designed to catch the rare and totally absurd decision which has somehow managed to survive the application of all other grounds of review'.

---

94   Supra n64.
95   A case where an improper purpose argument was upheld is *Park Oh Ho v MIEA* (1988) 20 FCR 104.
96   Referring to *Associated Provisional Picture Houses Limited v Wednesbury Corporation* (1948) 1 KB 223.
97   Ibid at 230.
98   (2005) FCA 1707 at paragraph 555, citing M Aronson, B Dyer and M Groves, *Judicial Review of Administrative Action* (3rd ed, 2004).

History in the High Court prior to 2013

It appears that the first High Court decision based at least partly on a *Wednesbury* unreasonableness argument was *Election Importing Co Pty Ltd v Courtice*,[99] which was handed down on 1 July 1949. *Courtice* concerned a dispute over the imposition of import duties, and one of the grounds of the appeal was that Mr Courtice had exercised a discretionary power in an unreasonable manner. Williams J found that despite the fact that the discretion was unfettered on its face, 'the *Customs (Import Licensing) Regulations* do not in my opinion confer on the Minister or his delegate an arbitrary and uncontrolled power to revoke a licence'.[100]

The High Court did not decide another unreasonableness case until the 1972 decision of *Parramatta City Council v Pestell*,[101] which concerned the council's ability to impose a 'local rate' on specified land, under s 121 of the *Local Government Act 1919 (NSW)*. Gibbs JA, as he then was, summed up the issue as follows:[102]

> [T]he legislature has left it to the council to form its opinion as to whether a particular work is of special benefit to a portion of the area. A court has no power to override the council's opinion on such a matter simply because it considers it to be wrong. However, a court may interfere to ensure that the council acts within the powers confided to it by law ... Even if the council has not erred in this way an opinion will nevertheless not be valid if it is so unreasonable that no reasonable council could have formed it.

The High Court found that the Council had misconstrued its power under the Act. A particular concern was that 90 dwellings had been specifically excluded from the special rating provisions, and there was no clear reason why. Stephen J stated that 'the facts make it clear that that portion of the council area left after excising the ninety-odd lots is not such a portion as is reasonably capable of being considered as the portion specially benefited by the works here proposed'.[103] Fourteen years later, Mason J, as he then was, stated in *Minister for Aboriginal Affairs v Peko-Wallsend Ltd* that *Pestell* 'embraced' the *Wednesbury* test in Australia.[104]

---

99   (1949) 80 CLR 657.
100   Ibid at paragraph 12. This finding is similar to *Roncarelli v Duplessis*, supra n90, but unlike Mr Roncarelli, the applicants in *Courtice* failed to demonstrate unreasonableness on the part of the decision maker.
101   (1972) 128 CLR 305.
102   Ibid at paragraph 2 of the judgment of Gibbs JA.
103   Ibid at paragraph 13 of the judgment of Stephen J.
104   (1986) 162 CLR 24 at paragraph 15 of the judgment of Mason J.

Prior to the decision in *Minister for Immigration and Citizenship v Li,*[105] the High Court made the following important comments on the unreasonableness ground:

1. The basis of the unreasonableness ground was briefly discussed in *Kruger v Commonwealth* (the 'Stolen Generations Case'), where Brennan CJ stated that 'when a discretionary power is statutorily conferred on a repository, the power must be exercised reasonably, for the legislature is taken to intend that the discretion be so exercised'.[106] Brennan CJ also noted that '[r]easonableness can be determined only by reference to the community standards at the time of the exercise of the discretion'.[107]

2. In *Abebe v Commonwealth*[108] the High Court found that s 476 of the *Migration Act 1958*, which at that time excluded a claim of *Wednesbury* unreasonableness from the jurisdiction of the Federal Court, was constitutionally valid.

3. It was made clear in *Eshetu v Minister for Immigration and Multicultural Affairs*[109] that mere disagreement with an administrative decision is not sufficient for a finding of unreasonableness. Gleeson CJ and McHugh J stated as follows:[110]

    > Someone who disagrees strongly with someone else's process of reasoning on an issue of fact may express such disagreement by describing the reasoning as 'illogical' or 'unreasonable', or even 'so unreasonable that no reasonable person could adopt it'. If these are merely emphatic ways of saying that the reasoning is wrong, then they may have no particular legal consequence.

4. Along similar lines, the Mason CJ and Deane J of the High Court found in *Minister of State for Immigration and Ethnic Affairs v Teoh* that for a decision to be *Wednesbury* unreasonable, the decision maker must make his or her decision 'in a manner so devoid of plausible justification that no reasonable person could have taken that course'.[111]

---

105 Supra n81.
106 (1997) 146 ALR 126 at 135.
107 Ibid.
108 *Abebe*, supra n8.
109 *Eshetu*, supra n8.
110 Ibid at paragraph 40.
111 (1995) 183 CLR 273 at 290.

5.   The 'weight' given to certain considerations may, at least in extreme circumstances, render a decision unreasonable. Mason CJ stated as follows in *Minister for Aboriginal Affairs v Peko-Wallsend Ltd*:[112]

> [I]n some circumstances a court may set aside an administrative decision which has failed to give adequate weight to a relevant factor of great importance, or has given excessive weight to a relevant factor of no great importance. The preferred ground on which this is done, however, is not the failure to take into account relevant considerations or the taking into account of irrelevant considerations, but that the decision is 'manifestly unreasonable'.

SZMDS

The High Court gave detailed consideration to the unreasonableness ground in the 2010 decision of *SZMDS v Minister for Immigration and Citizenship*.[113] The case involved an applicant for a Protection Visa, who claimed a well-founded fear of persecution on the basis of his membership of a particular social group, namely homosexuals. The RRT rejected his claim, not accepting that he was even homosexual.

The RRT decision was set aside by the Federal Court, which found that the 'Tribunal's conclusion that the applicant was not a homosexual was based squarely on an illogical process of reasoning'.[114] On appeal to the High Court, the Minister argued that the RRT's findings were not illogical, and that even if they were, this did not amount to a 'jurisdictional error'. The leading judgement was given by Crennan and Bell JJ, with whom Heydon J agreed. Gummow ACJ and Kiefel J gave separate reasons, concurring on this point. Crennan and Bell JJ started by finding that the Minister's satisfaction, referred to in s 65, was a jurisdictional fact.[115] The key passage in the judgement is at paragraphs 119 and 120:

> [119] Whilst the first respondent accepted that not every instance of illogicality or irrationality in reasoning could give rise to jurisdictional error, it was contended that if illogicality or irrationality occurs at the point of satisfaction (... s 65 of the Act) then this is a jurisdictional fact and a jurisdictional error is established. This submission should be accepted ...

---

112   Supra n52.
113   (2010) HCA 16.
114   *SZMDS v Minister for Immigration and Citizenship* (2009) FCA 210 at paragraph 29.
115   Referring to *Minister for Immigration and Multicultural Affairs v SGLB* (2004) 207 ALR 12.

[120] An erroneously determined jurisdictional fact may give rise to jurisdictional error. The decision maker might, for example, have asked the wrong question or may have mistaken or exceeded the statutory specification or prescription in relation to the relevant jurisdictional fact. Equally, entertaining a matter in the absence of a jurisdictional fact will constitute jurisdictional error.

In other words, illogicality or irrationality in finding of jurisdictional facts is a jurisdictional error and will result in the decision under review being set aside. Crennan and Bell JJ further elaborated on this point as follows:[116]

> In the context of the Tribunal's decision here, 'illogicality' or 'irrationality' sufficient to give rise to jurisdictional error must mean the decision to which the Tribunal came, in relation to the state of satisfaction required under s 65, is one at which no rational or logical decision maker could arrive on the same evidence. In other words … it is an allegation of the same order as a complaint that a decision is 'clearly unjust' or 'arbitrary' or 'capricious' or 'unreasonable' in the sense that the state of satisfaction mandated by the statute imports a requirement that the opinion as to the state of satisfaction must be one that could be formed by a reasonable person. The same applies in the case of an opinion that a mandated state of satisfaction has not been reached.

However, Crennan and Bell JJ found that the RRT's findings were open to it on the evidence before it, and that 'a decision will not be illogical or irrational if there is room for a logical or rational person to reach the same decision on the material before the decision maker'.[117] The Federal Court decision was therefore set aside and the RRT decision restored.

Minister for Immigration and Citizenship v Li

The basic facts in *Li* are set out in paragraph 3 of the judgement, in which French CJ states as follows:[118]

> The first respondent applied for a Skilled – Independent Overseas Student (Residence) (Class DD) visa on 10 February 2007 which required satisfaction of a 'time of decision criterion' set out in cl 880.230(1) of sch 2 to the Migration Regulations 1994 (Cth) ('the Regulations'), namely that:
>
> > 'A relevant assessing authority has assessed the skills of the applicant as suitable for his or her nominated skilled occupation, and no

---

116   Supra n113 at paragraph 30.
117   Ibid at paragraph 135.
118   Supra n81 at paragraph 3.

evidence has become available that the information given or used as part of the assessment of the applicant's skills is false or misleading in a material particular.'

The application was supported by a skills assessment made on 8 January 2007 by TRA[119]... The assessment was found to be based on false information submitted to TRA by the first respondent's former migration agent and on 13 January 2009 the Minister's delegate refused the application for a visa. The first respondent, through a new migration agent, applied to the MRT for review of the delegate's decision on 30 January 2009. The migration agent submitted a fresh application to TRA for a new skills assessment on 4 November 2009.

The MRT convened a hearing for 18 December 2009 and on 21 December 2009 wrote to the first respondent inviting comment upon allegedly untruthful answers given to departmental officers in connection with her initial application. It required a response by 18 January 2010, but advised the first respondent that she could seek an extension of time.

On 18 January 2010, the first respondent's migration agent replied to the MRT's letter of 21 December 2009 and advised that the application for a second skills assessment had been unsuccessful. The migration agent pointed out 'two fundamental errors' in TRA's assessment and said that the first respondent had applied to TRA for review of its adverse decision. The migration agent requested the MRT to 'forbear from making any final decision regarding her review application until the outcome of her skills assessment application is finalised'...

On 25 January 2010, without waiting for advice of the outcome of the migration agent's representations to TRA, the MRT affirmed the delegate's decision ... It did not explain its decision to proceed to a determination beyond saying:

'The Tribunal considers that the applicant has been provided with enough opportunities to present her case and is not prepared to delay any further and in any event, considers that clause 880.230 necessarily covers each and every relevant assessing authority's assessment.'

---

119 Trades Recognition Australia.

Ms Li succeeded at the Full Federal Court in her argument that the MRT had acted unreasonably in making its decision prior to the new skills assessment being provided. The Full Federal Court found that a refusal to adjourn the MRT hearing amounted to a jurisdictional error, and stated as follows:[120]

> The appearance afforded by the MRT to an applicant by [an] invitation must be meaningful, not perfunctory, or it will be no appearance at all. The MRT is given power to adjourn proceedings from time to time: s 363(1)(b) of the Act. An *unreasonable refusal* of an adjournment of the proceeding will not just deny a *meaningful appearance* to an applicant. It will mean that the MRT has not discharged its core statutory function of reviewing the decision. This failure constitutes jurisdictional error for the purposes of s 75(v) of the Constitution.

In other words, the MRT's unreasonable refusal to adjourn the hearing led to a breach of its own enabling legislation, and therefore to a jurisdictional error.

High Court judgement

On the Minister's appeal to the High Court, French CJ found that the reasons of the MRT made 'no reference to the probability that [Ms Li] would be able, within a reasonable time, to secure the requisite skills assessment'.[121] The Chief Justice held that the concept of unreasonableness:[122]

> … reflects a limitation imputed to the legislature on the basis of which courts can say that parliament never intended to authorise that kind of decision. After all the requirements of administrative justice have been met in the process and reasoning leading to the point of decision in the exercise of a discretion, there is generally an area of decisional freedom. Within that area reasonable minds may reach different conclusion about the correct or preferable decision. However the freedom thus left by the statute cannot be construed as attracting a legislative sanction to be arbitrary or capricious or to abandon common sense.

As a result, French CJ found that the MRT decision to deny Ms Li the adjournment did not engage with the submission made on her behalf about the imminent decision by TRA. His Honour held that there was 'an arbitrariness about the decision, which rendered it unreasonable'.[123]

---

120   (2012) FCAFC 74 at paragraph 29.
121   Supra n81 at paragraph 21.
122   Ibid at paragraph 28.
123   Ibid at paragraph 31.

In a joint judgment, Justices Hayne, Kiefel and Bell developed further the idea that unreasonableness is linked to rationality and logicality. Their Honours held that '[u]nreasonableness is a conclusion which may be applied to a decision which lacks an evident and intelligible justification'.[124] While their judgment admitted that in some cases decision maker may decide that 'enough is enough', and certainly an administrative tribunal cannot be expected to adjourn a matter indefinitely,[125] they held that it was not clear how the MRT reached that conclusion in the particular circumstances of Ms Li's case. As the decision lacked an 'evident and intelligible justification', it was unreasonable.

Hayne, Keifel and Bell JJ also noted as follows:[126]

> The legal standard of unreasonableness should not be considered as limited to what is in effect an irrational, if not bizarre, decision – which is to say one that is so unreasonable that no reasonable person could have arrived at it – nor should Lord Greene MR be taken to have limited unreasonableness in this way in his judgment in *Wednesbury*. This aspect of his Lordship's judgment may more sensibly be taken to recognise that an inference of unreasonableness may in some cases be objectively drawn even where a particular error in reasoning cannot be identified.

Here we see a clear acknowledgement that 'reasonableness' has moved on from indefensible 'red-haired teachers' situations. Unreasonableness can be ascertained from looking at the decision as a whole, and asking whether there is an intelligible basis to that decision. In this case, it was found that there was no attempt by the MRT to explain why Ms Li's request for an adjournment should be refused, looking at all the circumstances of her individual case, and this failure rendered the decision unreasonable.

Finally, Gageler J held that decision-making authority 'conferred by statute must be exercised according to law and to reason within limits set by the subject-matter, scope and purpose of the statute'.[127] His Honour found that the MRT's decision lacked a true weighing-up of Ms Li's application for an adjournment, stating that '[t]he MRT identified no consideration weighing in favour of an immediate decision on the review and none is suggested by the Minister'.[128] This is the same kind of reasoning as the joint judgement, looking at the matter from the opposite perspective – Hayne, Keifel and Bell JJ emphasised that the MRT failed to properly consider a request for an adjournment, while Gageler J

---

124 Ibid at paragraph 76.
125 Ibid at paragraph 81.
126 Ibid at paragraph 68.
127 Ibid at paragraph 90.
128 Ibid at paragraph 122.

takes the view that the MRT made a decision to proceed to an immediate conclusion of Ms Li's application. Either way, the decision was unreasonable, as it did not consider all the circumstances of Ms Li's case.

Gageler J also made some significant comments on the scope of unreasonableness in his judgement, and indicated that it should move on from the classic *Wednesbury* formulation. His Honour stated that '[r]eview by a court of the reasonableness of a decision made by another repository of power 'is concerned mostly with the existence of justification, transparency and intelligibility within the decision-making process' but also with 'whether the decision falls within a range of possible, acceptable outcomes which are defensible in respect of the facts and law',[129] expressly applying the Canadian reasonableness formulation. The 'possible, acceptable outcomes' formula has been applied in a number of cases since, although not expressly by the High Court.

In summary, the High Court in *Li* has expanded the unreasonableness formulation from outrageous and indefensible decisions to those that lack an 'intelligible basis', or those that fall outside a range of 'possible, acceptable outcomes'. The High Court now appears to be focused on whether the reasons for an administrative decision allow it to ascertain a justification for that decision, a theme taken up in the pre-*Li* decision of *SZOOR v Minister for Immigration and Citizenship*[130] and a number of cases since. The reasonableness of a decision maker's *procedures* will also be important.

Post-*Li* Decisions

Li has been cited frequently by all levels of courts since it was handed down. The High Court has yet to revisit the reasonableness issue, except to briefly dismiss the plaintiff's unreasonableness argument in *S156-2013 v Minister for Immigration and Border Protection*.[131] *Li* has, however, been successfully invoked in a number of court decisions, including:

1. *Minister for Immigration and Border Protection v Singh (Vikram)*,[132] which involved a set of facts remarkably similar to *Li* itself, this time concerning an English test score instead of a skills assessment. The decision of the MRT to refuse an adjournment to allow Mr Singh to seek review of an International English Language Testing System (IELTS) result with the testing authority was held to fall squarely within the *Li* scope of unreasonableness.

---

129   Ibid at paragraph 105, citing *Dunsmuir v New Brunswick*, supra n5 at paragraph 47.
130   (2012) FCAFC 58 at paragraph 8.
131   (2014) HCA 22 at paragraph 44.
132   (2014) FCAFC 1.

2. In *SZSNW v Minister for Immigration and Border Protection*[133] an 'independent merits reviewer' had made findings adverse to the applicant's credibility, after he raised an allegation of 'sexual torture' that had not been disclosed to the primary decision maker. The Federal Circuit Court found that a decision is unreasonable 'when a decision maker makes a choice that is arbitrary, capricious or without common sense',[134] and was particularly critical of the way in which the reviewer appeared to ignore procedural instructions for dealing with applicants for refugee status who make claims of this kind.[135] The decision was therefore set aside.

3. In *SZRHL v Minister for Immigration and Citizenship* the Federal Court noted as follows:[136]

> [H]aving regard to [*Li*], it must now be accepted that the Tribunal is constrained to undertake its 'core function' of review reasonably, which includes exercising, reasonably, ancillary discretionary powers granted to the Tribunal for that purpose. A decision on review would only transgress this underlying requirement of reasonableness and thereby constitute jurisdictional error if the decision were so unreasonable that no reasonable Tribunal could have so decided the review application. That is a conclusion to be reached with restraint, having regard to the constitutional separation of powers and recognition that the task of determining eligibility for the grant of a protection visa is one consigned by Parliament to the Executive, not to the Judiciary.

This was another credibility case, in which the applicant made claims before the Refugee Review Tribunal (RRT) that the RRT considered had not been made to the primary decision maker. The issues in question *had* been mentioned in the applicant's original protection visa application form, although they had not been expanded on since. The adverse credibility finding made by the RRT was therefore based on an incorrect set of facts, and the court found that they could therefore have 'been deprived of the possibility of a successful outcome on the merits of their protection visa applications'.[137] The RRT decision was therefore unreasonable and was set aside.

It is also worth noting that *Li* has been applied by a number of State Supreme Courts, seemingly most frequently in Victoria. For example, *Topouzakis v Greater Geelong City Council*[138] involved a decision by the Council to exclude

---

133 (2014) FCCA 134.
134 Ibid at paragraph 52.
135 Ibid at paragraph 47.
136 (2013) FCA 1093 at paragraph 19.
137 Ibid at paragraph 37.
138 (2014) VSC 87.

an employee from leisure centres managed by it, which effectively terminated his employment. A number of patrons had campaigned to have the applicant dismissed after a previous criminal conviction incurred by him came to light, a conviction of which the Council was already aware. After quoting from *Li*, the Supreme Court of Victoria stated that the issue in the case at hand was 'whether the Council's decision to impose the ban is 'reasonable' in the sense that there is evident and intelligible justification for it and whether the ban is proportionate to the breaches of the Local Law identified by the Council'.[139] In the end, the Court found that the decision to ban the applicant from the premises contravened Council by-laws, as it was made on the basis of a perceived lack of remorse on the part of the applicant, rather than the safety of patrons of Council property.

---

139   Ibid at paragraph 71.

Chapter 6. Judicial Review Under the *Migration Act 1958*

Immigration lawyers in Australia will be thoroughly familiar with the attempt by successive governments, dating from the major restructuring of the *Migration Act 1958* (Cth) ('the Act') in December 1989, to limit or even remove the power of the courts to judicially review decisions made under that Act. At that time, the Act was expanded and the *Migration Regulations 1989* introduced, with the purpose of removing discretion from individual decision makers and basing these decisions instead on law. It was thought at the time that setting out the criteria for grant of a visa or entry permit in legislation would make the immigration process clearer, and that applications for judicial review would fall in number. As we know, this approach failed to reduce the recourse to the courts by failed migration applicants.

The next major move was to bring the judicial review of migration decisions 'in house', under the Act itself. Until 1 September 1994, immigration decisions were simply one more Commonwealth decision that could be reviewed under the ADJR Act. The *Migration Reform Act 1992*, which came into effect on that date, created Part 8 of the Act, which purported to limit the grounds on which the Federal Court could set aside a decision of the Migration Review Tribunal (MRT) or Refugee Review Tribunal (RRT). While the constitutionality of Part 8 was upheld in *Abebe v Commonwealth*,[1] again the amendment did not achieve its objective of reducing applications for judicial review.

The final step was the introduction of the privative clause, by means of the *Migration Legislation Amendment (Judicial Review) Act 2001*, in the wake of the famed *Tampa* incident. This Act substituted the former Part 8 with a new Part 8, the centerpiece of which was s 474. However, the decision of the High Court in *Plaintiff S157/2002 v Commonwealth of Australia*[2] has rendered s 474 of little, if any, effect. Given that Australian courts have studiously avoided clearly delineating the scope of 'jurisdictional errors', and that a decided case has yet to turn on the question of whether an error of law is 'jurisdictional' or not, the question must now be asked whether there is any point to a separate regime of judicial review for migration decisions.

---

[1]   *Abebe v the Commonwealth; Re Minister for Immigration and Multicultural Affairs, Ex parte Abebe* (1999) 162 ALR 1.

[2]   (2003) 211 CLR 476.

Part 1 – Structure of the Act and mechanisms for judicial review

Prior to 21 December 1989, the date on which the *Migration Legislation Amendment Act 1989* came into effect, the *Migration Act 1958* conferred a largely unfettered discretion on the Minister and his or her delegates to grant visas or entry permits to non-citizens, or order the deportation of non-citizens from Australia. Stephen Gageler, then the Solicitor-General and now Gageler J of the High Court, has summed up the pre-1989 position as follows:[3]

> As it existed from 1983[4] until 1989, the central elements of the *Migration Act* were that:
>
> A non-citizen who entered or remained in Australia without an entry permit became a prohibited non-citizen (ss 6(1), 7(3)).
>
> The grant or withholding of an entry permit was a matter within the unconstrained discretion of a Commonwealth officer or a State or Territory police officer, save that a non-citizen could not be granted an entry permit after entry into Australia, unless one or more specified conditions was fulfilled (ss 6(1), 6A), one of those conditions being the existence of a determination that the non-citizen had the status of 'refugee' within the meaning of the Refugees Convention (s 6A(1)(c)); and
>
> The deportation of prohibited non-citizens (s 18), together some other non-citizens who had been convicted of offences (s 12), was a matter within the unconfined discretion of the Minister.

Decision-making guidelines were largely set out in policy prior to 1989. One of the main purposes of the 1989 legislation was to reduce the discretion available to immigration decision makers, and provide greater 'certainty' for both decision makers and applicants. It was felt that this, along with the creation of the IRT, would reduce the recourse of unsuccessful applicants to the courts.

Migration Reform Act 1992

The first attempt to limit the jurisdiction of the courts in immigration-decision making came with the insertion of a new Part 8 into the Act by means of the

---

3   Stephen Gageler SC, 'Impact of Migration Law on the Development of Australian Administrative Law', (2010) 17 *Australian Journal of Administrative Law* 92 at 94.

4   This was the year in which the Act was amended to shift its constitutional basis from the 'immigration and emigration' power in s 51(xxvii) of the Constitution to the 'aliens and naturalisation' power in s 51(xix). This change was made by way of the *Migration Amendment Act 1983*, which came into effect on 2 April 1984.

Migration Reform Act 1992 ('the MRA'). The MRA, which did not come into effect until 1 September 1994, substantially renumbered and reordered the Act. The key provision of the new Part 8 was s 476, which provided in part as follows:

(1) Subject to subsection (2), application may be made for review by the Federal Court of a judicially reviewable decision on any one or more of the following grounds:

   (a) that procedures that were required by this Act or the regulations to be observed in connection with the making of the decision were not observed;

   (b) that the person who purported to make the decision did not have jurisdiction to make the decision;

   (c) that the decision was not authorised by this Act or the regulations;

   (d) that the decision was an improper exercise of the power conferred by this Act or the regulations;

   (e) that the decision involved an error of law, being an error involving an incorrect interpretation of the applicable law or an incorrect application of the law to the facts as found by the person who made the decision, whether or not the error appears on the record of the decision;

   (f) that the decision was induced or affected by fraud or by actual bias;

   (g) that there was no evidence or other material to justify the making of the decision.

(2) The following are not grounds upon which an application may be made under subsection (1):

   (a) that a breach of the rules of natural justice occurred in connection with the making of the decision;

   (b) that the decision involved an exercise of a power that is so unreasonable that no reasonable person could have so exercised the power.

The term 'judicially reviewable decision' was defined in s 475 of the Act, and included decisions made by the Immigration Review Tribunal (IRT), Refugee Review Tribunal (RRT) or Administrative Appeals Tribunal (AAT) relating to visas. Primary decisions made by the Department were expressly excluded from that definition under s 475(2). At the same time, new Parts 5 and 7 of the Act essentially provided for independent merits review of all onshore decisions relating to visas. The clear intention was that applicants would pursue merits review *rather than* judicial review, but the end result was that many applicants pursued both merits *and* judicial review.

The Explanatory Memorandum (EM) to the MRA elucidated on Part 8 as follows:

> [44] In acknowledgement of the special nature of immigration decisions and as a result of the widened availability of merits review, the Reform Bill amends the Act to set down reformulated grounds of judicial review. To ensure procedural fairness, procedures for decision-making which embody the principles of natural justice have been set out in the Reform Bill.

> [45] The specific codified procedures in the Reform Bill, and those to be set out in the *Migration Regulations*, replace the current uncertain rules with regard to natural justice and statutory criteria for decision-making will clarify the matters that must be considered in making a decision. An applicant will be able to appeal to the Federal Court if the codified procedures and criteria have not been followed by decision makers, but a court appeal will only be permitted where the applicant has first pursued all merits review rights.

The EM explained the removal of the 'unreasonableness' ground at paragraph 415:

> New subsection [sic – paragraph] 166LB(2)(b)[5] provides that an application for review of a decision may not be made on the grounds that a decision was so unreasonable that no reasonable person could have so exercised that power. This ground of review, commonly known as *Wednesbury* unreasonableness,[6] is currently available where the court assesses that a decision maker has made a decision that is so unreasonable that no reasonable person could have made the decision. It has long been recognised that this ground of review, if not interpreted with great care and precision, will come close to a review of the decision on the merits, especially where review of the merits is not available. The review procedures established in this Bill provide for comprehensive merits review of all visa-related decisions, and in recognition of this, this ground of review will no longer be available.

---

5   Renumbered as s 476 after the passage of the *Migration Reform Act*.
6   Referring to *Associated Picture Houses Ltd v Wednesbury Corporation* (1948) 1 KB 223.

It has been argued[7] that *Wednesbury* unreasonableness *is* a form of review of the merits of a decision, and the only difference between this ground of review of the forms of substantive review of administrative decisions found in Canada and the United Kingdom is the degree of deference given to the decision maker. The rather touching belief that an independent merits reviewer could not possibly make an unreasonable decision is also a distinctive feature of this paragraph, and one that is hardly borne out in reality.

The then Minister for Immigration and Ethnic Affairs, Mr Hand, stated as follows in his second reading speech:[8]

> The measures I have announced so far will lead to greater precision in our efforts to control the border. Under the reforms, decision-making procedures will be codified. This will provide a fair **and** certain process with which both applicant **and** decision maker can be confident. Decision makers will be able to focus on the merits of each case knowing precisely what procedural requirements are to be followed. These procedures will replace the somewhat open-ended doctrines of natural justice **and** unreasonableness.
>
> The Reform Bill proposes significant extensions to the current system for review of migration decisions. Credible independent merits review will ensure that the Government's clear intentions in relation to controlling entry to Australia, as set out in the Migration Act, are not eroded by narrow judicial interpretations. Under the Reform Bill, the following people who are adversely affected by a decision will be entitled to independent merits review: onshore refugee claimants; onshore cancelled visa holders, except those cancelled at the border; onshore applicants for a visa, except those detected at the border; **and** an Australian sponsor of an offshore applicant for a visa.

Again, there was a clear assumption that the provision of independent merits review would have the effect that refused visa applicants would not go a step further and take their case to judicial review after receiving merits review. It is unclear where this assumption could have come from, and it was certainly not proved correct.

Because of the Constitutional entrenchment of the jurisdiction of the High Court, Part 8 of the Act could only apply to courts created by statute, such as the Federal Court. This meant that there was a significant shift of cases from the

---

7   Alan Freckelton, 'The Concept of Deference in Judicial Review of Administrative Decisions in Australia Part 1', (2013) 73 *Australian Institute of Administrative Law Forum* 52; Part 2, (2013) 74 *Australian Institute of Administrative Law Forum* 45.

8   House of Representatives Hansard, Wednesday, 4 November 1992 at 2620.

Federal Court to the High Court after the implementation of Part 8, especially after the High Court's decision in *Abebe*,[9] which upheld the constitutional validity of s 476. McHugh J commented as follows in *Re Minister for Immigration and Multicultural Affairs; Ex parte Durairajasingham*:[10]

> [13] Given this history and the need for this Court to concentrate on constitutional and important appellate matters, I find it difficult to see the rationale for the amendments to the *Migration Act* (Cth) ('the Act') which now prevent this Court from remitting to the Federal Court *all* issues arising under that Act which fall within this Court's original jurisdiction. No other constitutional or ultimate appellate court of any nation of which I am aware is called on to perform trial work of the nature that these amendments to the Act have now forced upon the Court.

> [14] There is no ground whatever for thinking that the judges of the Federal Court are not capable of dealing with all issues arising under the Act which fall within this Court's jurisdiction. Although the refugee matters that cannot be remitted to the Federal Court do arise under this Court's constitutionally entrenched jurisdiction, most of them are not constitutional matters as that term is ordinarily understood. The great majority of the matters which cannot be remitted simply involve questions of administrative law with which the Federal Court has long been familiar and in respect of which it has great experience and expertise.

> [15] The reforms brought about by the amendments are plainly in need of reform themselves if this Court is to have adequate time for the research and reflection necessary to fulfil its role as 'the keystone of the federal arch' and the ultimate appellate court of the nation. I hope that in the near future the Parliament will reconsider the jurisdictional issues involved.

It should also be pointed out that the restrictions on the grounds of judicial review in Part 8 of the Act occasionally backfired on the Minister. In 1996, the AAT handed down its decision *Jia and Minister of Immigration and Multicultural Affairs*,[11] finding that Mr Jia, who had a conviction for rape, was nevertheless of good character, essentially by blaming his victim for her own rape. When the Minister initially challenged this decision in the Federal Court, he could not rely on the grounds of unreasonableness or taking irrelevant considerations into account, which are the grounds on which the decision should really have been

---

9   Supra n1.
10   (2000) 168 ALR 407.
11   (1996) AAT 236.

challenged. Instead, the Minister was reduced to effectively arguing that the AAT had no *evidence* that the victim deserved to be raped, thereby continuing the stereotypes egregiously relied on by the AAT.[12]

Migration Amendment (Judicial Review) Act 2001

The next major amendment to the judicial review provisions of the Act came with the *Migration Amendment (Judicial Review) Act 2001* ('the MAJR Act'), which was introduced in the wake of the *Tampa* incident in August 2001. The key amendment was the introduction of a new s 474, and subsections 474(1) and (2) provided as follows:

(1) A privative clause decision:

    (a) is final and conclusive; and

    (b) must not be challenged, appealed against, reviewed, quashed or called in question in any court; and

    (c) is not subject to prohibition, mandamus, injunction, declaration or certiorari in any court on any account.

(2) In this section: 'privative clause decision' means a decision of an administrative character made, proposed to be made, or required to be made, as the case may be, under this Act or under a regulation or other instrument made under this Act (whether in the exercise of a discretion or not), other than a decision referred to in subsection (4) or (5).

Subsection 474(3) made it clear that a decision to grant or refuse a visa was a 'privative clause decision'. Subsections 474(4) and (5) listed a number of decisions that were taken not to be privative clause decisions.

At its simplest, a privative clause is a 'clause in regulatory legislation prohibiting review of decisions by courts'.[13] In fact, there are two kinds of privative clause, and both frequently appear in the same legislative provision. These are the finality clause which protects an administrative decision from further *internal* review, and the ouster clause, which purports to protect the decision from *judicial* review. Other varieties of privative clause may remove the remedial powers of the court, while still others may determine the kind of evidence that is final and conclusive. Section 474 combines the finality and ouster clauses in one provision of the Act.

---

12   *Jia v Minister for Immigration and Multicultural Affairs* (1998) 52 ALD 20.

13   Peter Bowal and Carlee Campbell, 'Key Concepts: Administrative Law from A to Z', (2007) 31 *Law Now* 31.

Judicial approaches to privative clauses

There is an obvious conflict to be resolved by a court when it is confronted with a privative clause, given that it is 'ultimately the constitutional function of an independent judiciary to determine the rights of individuals according to law'.[14] This is also a problem for the rule of law, as it is an attempt by the legislature (and the executive) to exclude the judiciary from its role as the final arbiter of the law. Australian commentators have generally taken the view that *all* privative clauses, or at least those that protect errors of law made by administrative decision makers, are contrary to the rule of law.[15]

The High Court of Australia has found that a privative clause can never completely oust judicial review, primarily because s 75 of the Constitution explicitly provides for a right to at least some judicial review of Commonwealth decisions. Nevertheless, the famous (or infamous) decision of *R v Hickman, Ex parte Fox and Clinton*[16] was broadly sympathetic to privative clauses, but more recently *S157/2002*[17] upheld the constitutional validity of s 474 of the *Migration Act*, but then proceeded to render it of almost no effect.

Stated reasons for the section 474 privative clause

Subsection 474(1) appears on its face to contradict ss 75(iii) and (v) of the Constitution, which guarantees a right of judicial review of Commonwealth administrative action. The Explanatory Memorandum to the Bill provided as follows:

[14] New subsection 474(1) introduces a privative clause for decisions made under the *Migration Act*, regulations made under that Act or other instruments under that Act except for decisions made under the provisions set out in new subsection 474(4) or as prescribed under new subsection 474(5). A privative clause affects the extent of judicial review by both the Federal Court and the High Court of decisions covered by the clause.

[15] A privative clause is a provision which, although on its face purports to oust all judicial review, in operation, by altering the substantive law, limits review by the courts to certain grounds. Such a clause has

---

14   John Evans, Hudson Janisch, David Mullan and RCB Risk, *Administrative Law – Cases, Text and Materials*, Edmond Montgomery Publications, 2003 at 702–03.

15   To give just one example, the Honourable Duncan Kerr, the former Commonwealth Minister for Justice, authored an article entitled 'Privative Clauses and the Courts: Why and How Australian Courts have Resisted Attempts to Remove the Citizen's Right to Judicial Review of Unlawful Executive Action' (2005) 5 *Queensland University of Technology Law and Justice Journal* 195. Kerr entitled two of the chapters in that article 'Attempts to Thwart Judicial Review of Executive Action' and 'A Detour to Deference: The *Hickman* Myth'.

16   (1945) 70 CLR 598.

17   Supra n2.

been interpreted by the High Court, in a line of authority stemming from the judgment of Dixon J in *R v Hickman; Ex parte Fox and Clinton* (1945) 70 CLR 598, to mean that a court can still review matters but the available grounds are confined to exceeding constitutional limits, narrow jurisdictional error or *mala fides*.

[16] The intention of the provision is to provide decision makers with wider lawful operation for their decisions such that, provided the decision maker is acting in good faith, has been given the authority to make the decision concerned (for example, by delegation of the power from the Minister or by virtue of holding a particular office) and does not exceed constitutional limits, the decision will be lawful.

In his second reading speech to the House of Representatives on 26 September 2001, Minister Ruddock stated that the then current Part 8 of the Act had failed to achieve its objectives:[18]

That scheme has not reduced the volume of cases before the courts: just the opposite. Recourse to the Federal Court and the High Court is trending upwards, with nearly 400 applications in 1994–95; nearly 600 in 1995–96; 740 in 1996–97; nearly 800 in 1997–98; around 1,130 in 1998–99; nearly 1,300 in 1999–2000; and around 1,640 in 2000–01. Based on current litigation trends it is anticipated that applications made to the courts will reach at least 2,000 in the current financial year.

Minister Ruddock then described the purpose of the privative clause as follows:[19]

In the migration area, litigation can be an end in itself – it is an area where delaying the final determination is seen as beneficial by those pursuing the court action. Given the importance they attach to staying in Australia, there is a high incentive for refused applicants to delay removal from Australia for as long as possible.

Faced with the problem I have outlined, I asked the Department of Immigration and Multicultural Affairs in early 1996 to explore options for best achieving the government's policy objective of restricting access to judicial review ... The advice received from legal counsel was that the only workable option was a privative clause ...

Counsels' advice was that a privative clause would have the effect of narrowing the scope of judicial review by the High Court and of course the Federal Court. That advice was largely based on the High Court's

---

18   House of Representatives Hansard, 27 September 2001 at 31559.
19   Ibid at 31560.

own interpretation of such clauses in cases following the seminal High Court case of *Hickman* in 1945. The privative clause in the bill is based on a very similar clause in *Hickman*'s case.

The High Court has not since, despite opportunities to do so, repudiated the *Hickman* principle as formulated by Justice Dixon in *Hickman*'s case. Indeed, that principle was described as 'classical' in a later High Court case. Members may be aware that the effect of a privative clause such as that used in *Hickman*'s case is to expand the legal validity of the acts done and the decisions made by decision makers. The result is to give decision makers wider lawful operation for their decisions, and this means that the grounds on which those decisions can be challenged in the Federal and High Courts are narrower than currently. In practice, the decision is lawful, provided:

- the decision maker is acting in good faith;

- the decision is reasonably capable of reference to the power given to the decision maker – that is, the decision maker had been given the authority to make the decision concerned, for example, had the authority delegated to him or her by the Minister for Immigration and Multicultural Affairs, or had been properly appointed as a tribunal member;

- the decision relates to the subject matter of the legislation – it is highly unlikely that this ground would be transgressed when making decisions about visas since the major purpose of the *Migration Act* is dealing with visa decisions; and

- constitutional limits are not exceeded – given the clear constitutional basis for visa decision making in the *Migration Act*, this is highly unlikely to arise.

The options available to the government were very much shaped by the Constitution. While the government accepts that the precise limits of privative clauses may need examination by the High Court, there is no other practical option open to the government to achieve its policy objective.

Migration Legislation Amendment Act (No 1) 2001

The *Migration Legislation Amendment Act (No 1) 2001*, which came into effect on 27 September 2001, inserted s 486A into the Act, which purported to impose time limits on applications to the High Court in its original jurisdiction. Section 486A was then further amended by the MAJR Act, which came into effect on 2 October 2001. At the time that *S157* was decided, ss 486A(1) and (2) provided as follows:

(1) An application to the High Court for a writ of mandamus, prohibition or certiorari or an injunction or a declaration in respect of a privative clause decision must be made to the High Court within 35 days of the actual (as opposed to deemed) notification of the decision.

(2) The High Court must not make an order allowing, or which has the effect of allowing, an applicant to make an application mentioned in subsection (1) outside that 35 day period.

Migration Legislation Amendment (Procedural Fairness) Act 2002

The *Migration Legislation Amendment (Procedural Fairness) Act 2002* ('the MLAPF Act') was an attempt to ensure that the various 'codes of procedure' set out in the Act for dealing with visa or review applications were in fact an exhaustive statement of natural justice requirements under the Act. The MLAPF Act was a response to the High Court's decision in *Re Minister for Immigration and Multicultural Affairs; Ex parte Miah*,[20] which had found that Subdivision AB of the Act, despite setting out a 'Code of Procedure' for dealing with visa applications, did not exclude the common law rules of procedural fairness.[21]

The MLAPF Act inserted new sections 359A and 422B into the Act, which deal with reviews by the MRT and RRT respectively. Subsections 359A(1) and 422B(1) are identical, and provide that '[t]his Division is taken to be an exhaustive statement of the requirements of the natural justice hearing rule in relation to the matters it deals with'. As will be seen, ss 359A and 422B have not been particularly effective either. The EM to the Bill expressly referred to the *Miah* decision as follows:

[3] In *Re MIMA; Ex parte Miah* [2001] HCA 22 the High Court held, by a narrow majority, that the 'code of procedure' for dealing fairly, efficiently and quickly with visa applications in Subdivision AB of Division 3 of Part 2 of the Act did not exclude common law natural justice requirements. The majority considered that such exclusion would require a clear legislative intention and that there was no such clear intention in the Act.

---

20   (2001) 206 CLR 57.
21   Ibid at paragraphs 95 and 96.

[4] The purpose of this Bill is to provide a clear legislative statement that the 'codes of procedure' identified in the Bill are an exhaustive statement of the requirements of the natural justice hearing rule in relation to the matters they deal with.

The MLAPF Bill received Royal Assent on 3 July 2002 and came into effect the following day.[22]

The High Court's decision in *S157*

Plaintiff S157/2002 v Commonwealth of Australia[23] involved a constitutional challenge to the validity of s 474 of the *Migration Act 1958* and administrative challenges to a number of decisions that were defended on the basis of this section. At the time of the judgment, subsections 474(1) and (2) relevantly provided as follows:

(1) A privative clause decision:

    (a)   is final and conclusive; and

    (b)   must not be challenged, appealed against, reviewed, quashed or called in question in any court; and

    (c)   is not subject to prohibition, mandamus, injunction, declaration or certiorari in any court on any account.

(2) In this section, privative clause decision means a decision of an administrative character made, proposed to be made, or required to be made, as the case may be, under this Act or under a regulation or other instrument made under this Act (whether in the exercise of a discretion or not) ...

Subsection 474(3) made it clear that a decision to grant or refuse a visa was a 'privative clause decision'.

The applicants argued that s 474 conflicted with s 75 of the Constitution and was therefore invalid, or alternatively that s 474 did not protect 'jurisdictional errors', a term that will be explained shortly. The High Court rejected the first argument but accepted the second, which left s 474 'on the books', but rendered it of almost no effect. The leading judgment was given by Gaudron, McHugh, Gurnmow, Kirby and Hayne JJ. At paragraph 73, their Honours stated that:

A privative clause cannot operate so as to oust the jurisdiction which other paragraphs of s 75 confer on this Court, including that conferred

---

22   Section 2 of the MLAPF Act; http://www.comlaw.gov.au/Details/C2004A01001/Download.

23   Supra n2.

by s 75(iii) in matters 'in which the Commonwealth, or a person suing or being sued on behalf of the Commonwealth, is a party'. Further, a privative clause cannot operate so as to allow a non-judicial tribunal or other non-judicial decision-making authority to exercise the judicial power of the Commonwealth.[24] Thus, it cannot confer on a non-judicial body the power to determine conclusively the limits of its own jurisdiction.

Their Honours stated at paragraph 76 that an administrative decision affected by jurisdictional error is a legal nullity, referring to *Minister for Immigration and Multicultural Affairs v Bhardwaj*.[25] Therefore, a 'decision' affected by a privative clause is only a putative decision and cannot be a 'privative clause decision' for the purposes of s 474. When read in this way, there was no conflict between s 474 and s 75 of the Constitution, and the provision was therefore constitutionally valid. Indeed, s 75(v) was reaffirmed to amount to 'an entrenched minimum provision of judicial review'[26] 'assuring to all people affected that officers of the Commonwealth obey the law and neither exceed nor neglect any jurisdiction which the law confers on them'.[27]

The remaining issue was the definition of 'jurisdictional error'. Curiously, none of the judgments referred to the High Court's decision of just two years previously, *Minister for Immigration and Multicultural Affairs v Yusuf*.[28] In that case, McHugh, Gummow and Hayne JJ defined the term as follows at paragraph 82:

> It is necessary, however, to understand what is meant by 'jurisdictional error' under the general law and the consequences that follow from a decision maker making such an error. As was said in *Craig v South Australia*,[29] if an administrative tribunal (like the Tribunal) 'falls into an error of law which causes it to identify a wrong issue, to ask itself a wrong question, to ignore relevant material, to rely on irrelevant material or, at least in some circumstances, to make an erroneous finding or to reach a mistaken conclusion, and the tribunal's exercise or purported exercise of power is thereby affected, it exceeds its authority or powers'. Such an error of law is a jurisdictional error which will invalidate any order or decision of the tribunal which reflects it.

'Jurisdictional error' can thus be seen to embrace a number of different kinds of error, the list of which, in the passage cited from *Craig*, is not

---

24   Referring to *R v Kirby; Ex parte Boilermakers' Society* of *Australia* (1956) 94 CLR 254.
25   (2002) 76 ALJR 598 at paragraph 51.
26   Supra n2 at paragraph 104.
27   Ibid at paragraph 105.
28   (2001) 206 CLR 323.
29   (1995) 184 CLR 163 at 179.

exhaustive[30] ... if an error of those types is made, the decision maker did not have authority to make the decision that was made; he or she did not have jurisdiction to make it.

The kinds of 'jurisdictional error' identified by *Craig* and *Yusuf* are very wide, and endorse the *Anisminic*[31] approach as far as possible without expressly abolishing the distinction between jurisdictional and non-jurisdictional errors. The majority judges in *S157* came to the conclusion that a failure of procedural fairness was a 'jurisdictional error' and therefore s 474 did not protect the Tribunal decision from such a claim.' The *Hickman*[32] principle has therefore been overturned. The result is that when a decision is protected by a privative clause, deference will be shown to the decision maker on a point of law to the extent that no jurisdictional error is involved. Otherwise, the decision will be set aside.

It is important to note that the High Court decision in *S157* does not simply return the law to a pre-*Hickman* position. On the contrary, the approach in *R v Commonwealth Court of Conciliation and Arbitration* ('the Tramways Case')[33] was to strike down the privative clause altogether as constitutionally invalid. The High Court in *S157* gutted s 474 of the *Migration Act* rather than invalidating it, and has effectively found that non-jurisdictional errors will be protected while jurisdictional errors will not. This gives the courts the power to determine what a jurisdictional error is and what is not, and allows the courts great control over the executive, while still upholding those decisions that do not (in their opinion) display any error of law.

Finally, the time limits on applications to the High Court also came under scrutiny in *S157*. As the Federal Court and Federal Circuit Court are courts created entirely by statute, applications to these courts can be restricted by any time limits the Parliament wishes. However, the High Court, with its constitutionally mandated original jurisdiction, is in a different position. The Court in *S157* found that the time limit in s 486A, like the privative clause in s 474(1), operated, in terms, only in respect of 'privative clause decisions'. Hence, the time limit was effectively inoperative in respect of decisions involving jurisdictional error.[34] Only Callinan J addressed the more general question of validity raised by the imposition of an absolute time limit on proceedings in the High Court. In his view, legislation imposing time limits would be authorised by the exercise of the incidental power in s 51(xxxix) of the *Constitution*, providing that the legislation was

---

30   See also *Re Refugee Review Tribunal; Ex parte Aala* (2000) 204 CLR 82 at paragraph 163.
31   *Anisminic Pty Ltd v Foreign Compensation Commission* (1969) 2 AC 147.
32   Supra n16.
33   (1914) 18 CLR 54.
34   Supra n2 at paragraph 91.

regulatory in character.[35] Section 486A, according to Callinan J, was not of such a character. Rather it was 'in substance a prohibition' because, having regard to the difficulties faced by non-English speaking applicants detained in remote places, it rendered 'any constitutional right of recourse virtually illusory'.[36] This is a fascinating decision made by one of the more conservative members of the bench!

Government response to *S157*

The government was very quick to respond to the High Court's decision in *S157*. The first attempt to deal with the judgment came with the *Migration Amendment (Judicial Review) Bill 2004*, which was introduced to the House of Representatives on 25 March 2004, but lapsed with the calling of the 2004 Federal election.[37] The key amendment in the Bill was the insertion of a definition of 'purported privative clause decision', which had the effect that even those tribunal decisions later found to be affected by jurisdictional error would be affected by time limits for judicial review and so on.

The 2004 Bill was largely resurrected as the *Migration Litigation Reform Act 2005* ('the MLRA') after the election. The MLRA included three main amendments. The first was the insertion of a definition of 'purported privative clause decision' in s 5E of the Act. Subsection 5E(1) provides as follows:

> In this Act, **purported privative clause decision** means a decision purportedly made, proposed to be made, or required to be made, under this Act or under a regulation or other instrument made under this Act (whether in purported exercise of a discretion or not), that would be a privative clause decision if there were not:
>
> (a) a failure to exercise jurisdiction; or
>
> (b) an excess of jurisdiction;
>
> in the making of the decision.

Under s 5(1) of the Act, a 'migration decision' now includes a privative clause decision, a 'non-privative clause decision' and a 'purported privative clause decision'.

Secondly, s 476(1) of the Act now provides that '[s]ubject to this section, the Federal Magistrates Court has the same original jurisdiction in relation to migration decisions as the High Court has under paragraph 75(v) of the

---

35   Ibid at paragraph 176.

36   Ibid.

37   http://www.aph.gov.au/Parliamentary_Business/Bills_Legislation/Bills_Search_Results/Result?bId=r2012.

Constitution'. This ensures that there is no longer any incentive for applicants to take a case to the High Court in its original jurisdiction, rather than the Federal Circuit Court, as it is now titled.

Thirdly, while a *prima facie* time limit for making an application to the High Court in its original jurisdiction remained, the High Court was given the power to extend that time limit. Subsections 486A(1) and (2) of the Act now provide as follows:

(1) An application to the High Court for a remedy to be granted in exercise of the court's original jurisdiction in relation to a migration decision must be made to the court within 35 days of the date of the migration decision.

(2) The High Court may, by order, extend that 35 day period as the High Court considers appropriate if:

   (a) an application for that order has been made in writing to the High Court specifying why the applicant considers that it is necessary in the interests of the administration of justice to make the order; and

   (b) the High Court is satisfied that it is necessary in the interests of the administration of justice to make the order.

Similar powers to extend time limits are found in ss 477 and 477A of the Act, relating to the jurisdiction of the Federal Circuit Court and Federal Court respectively. This appeared to remove the problem with strict time limits identified by *S157*. Note, however, that even the amended version of s 486A was found to be unconstitutional by the High Court in *Bodruddaza v Minister for Immigration and Multicultural Affairs*, in which Gleeson CJ and Gummow, Kirby, Hayne, Heydon and Crennan JJ stated as follows:[38]

[55] Section 486A is cast in a form that fixes upon the time of the actual notification of the decision in question. This has the consequence that the section does not allow for the range of vitiating circumstances which may affect administrative decision-making. It is from the deficiency that there flows the invalidity of the section ...

[57] The fixing upon the time of the notification of the decision as the basis of the limitation structure provided by s 486A does not allow for supervening events which may physically incapacitate the applicant or otherwise, without any shortcoming on the part of the applicant, lead to a failure to move within the stipulated time limit.

---

38   (2007) HCA 14 at paragraphs 55 and 57.

The Parliament finally surrendered on the issue of time limits on applications to the High Court with the *Migration Legislation Amendment Act (No 1) 2009*. This Act amended s 486A to provide for a prima facie limitation period of 35 days from the date of the 'migration decision' (a term defined in s 477(3) of the Act), but gives the High Court the power to extend this indefinitely if an application for that order has been made in writing to the High Court specifying why the applicant considers that it is necessary in the interests of the administration of justice to make the order; and the High Court is satisfied that it is necessary in the interests of the administration of justice to make the order (s 486A(2) of the Act).

Part 2 – Reasons for the attack on the courts in the migration jurisdiction

Incentives for delay in litigation

It has been argued on behalf of the Minister and the Department that judicial review of immigration decisions is different to any other kind of judicial review, because it is one of very few – maybe the only – fields of law in which the *plaintiff or applicant* has an incentive to delay proceedings,[39] where it is more common in civil litigation for a defendant to have an incentive to delay. We have already seen how the then Minister, Mr Ruddock, defended the introduction of the privative clause in his second reading speech to the *Migration Amendment (Judicial Review) Bill 2001* on the basis that 'litigation can be an end in itself'.[40] Mr Ruddock also stated as follows in 1997:[41]

> Much of the growth in applications for judicial review has come from the refugee area; that is, appeals from the RRT to the Federal Court. I see this high level of litigation, particularly by onshore asylum seekers, as highly undesirable given the associated costs and delays, and for those in detention, significantly longer periods of detention. I am also concerned that, given around 49% of applicants in all migration cases withdraw before hearing, there are a substantial number using the legal process as a means to extend their stay in Australia.

---

39   It could also be the case that a plaintiff may have an incentive to delay proceedings in some defamation cases, where the objective of the lawsuit might be to frighten critics of the plaintiff into silence rather than recovering damages from the defendant.

40   See page 12.

41   Phillip Ruddock, 'Narrowing of Judicial Review in the Migration Context', (1997) 15 *Australian Institute of Administrative Law Forum* 13 at 17.

Mr Ruddock made similar comments in 2002, defending the then new privative clause:[42]

> Between one third to one half of applicants withdraw their applications prior to the court hearing. Of the cases that go on to substantive hearings, the merits-based decision is currently upheld in over 90 per cent of cases. It is hard not to conclude that there is a substantial number of applicants who are using the legal process primarily in order to extend their stay in Australia.

This view that migration litigants often resort to the courts purely for the purpose of delaying their removal is not restricted to the Minister. The then General Counsel to the Department, Robyn Bicket wrote as follows in 2010:[43]

> Another noteworthy figure which supports delay as the primary litigation driver is the Minister's overwhelming success in matters defended. Since 1993–94. the Minister has been successful in, on average, 93% of cases. This means that, putting aside cases from which we withdrew, in only 7% of cases did the affected person get a favourable decision, which may have included a rehearing by the tribunal. (Of course, whether the person actually achieved a favourable visa outcome in the end is another matter.) When the success rate is viewed together with the upward trend in applications, 1,045 total new applications in 1997–98, 1,590 applications in 1999–2000, 2,605 applications in 2001–2002 and peaking in 2002–2003 with 5,397 new applications,' it is clear that delay is a real factor driving litigation, and one for which there is no easy solution, let alone a legislative one.

The current government seems to have accepted that appeals to the High Court cannot be stopped, but Minister Morrison has been reported as stating as follows:[44]

> The Coalition also announced it would retrospectively apply its tough temporary protection visa scheme to more than 30,000 people already in Australia awaiting refugee assessment decisions.[45]

---

42   Phillip Ruddock, 'Immigration Policy and the Separation of Powers', address to the Samuel Griffiths Society, 2002. http://samuelgriffith.org.au/docs/vol14/v14chap6.pdf, extracted 14 November 2014. See also Phillip Ruddock, 'Refugee Claims and Australian Migration Law: A Ministerial Perspective', (2000) 23(3) *University of New South Wales Law Journal* 1 at 8.

43   Robyn Bicket, 'Controlling Immigration Litigation: The Commonwealth Perspective', (2010) 63 *Australian Institute of Administrative Law Forum* 40 at 46.

44   http://hazaraasylumseekers.wordpress.com/category/courts-and-legal-challenges/page/3/, extracted 14 November 2014.

45   This is a reference to the Migration and Maritime Powers Legislation Amendment (Resolving the Asylum Legacy Caseload) Bill 2014.

Opposition immigration spokesman Scott Morrison conceded asylum seekers would still have the right to appeal to the High Court, but said a Coalition government would move to cut their access to the Refugee Review Tribunal and the Federal Court. 'At the end of the day . . . appeals can always be made to the High Court about pretty much anything', Mr Morrison said. 'We're not changing the constitution.'

When an applicant challenges a decision of Comcare or superannuation bodies in the courts, it is in their interests to get a decision as quickly as possible. On the other hand, a migration applicant may be able to delay his or her removal from Australia simply by making an application for judicial review, regardless of whether such an application is legally merited. It is notable that the Act does permit the removal of an unlawful non-citizen who has a current matter before the courts[46] (although not an applicant who has a *merits review* matter in process), but Departmental policy is that unlawful non-citizens with current applications before a court will not be removed until that application is finalised.[47] In any event, if the Department attempted to remove a non-citizen who had an active case before the courts, it is likely that the court in question would issue an injunction preventing any such removal – see for example s 15 of the *Federal Circuit Court Act*.

Polycentricity in immigration policy

Another reason that has been given for seeking to curtail rights of judicial review in immigration cases is the polycentric nature of immigration law and policy. The term 'polycentric' means that more than two competing interests are in play – in the case of formulation of immigration policy, matters such as population policy, national security, health policy and labour market policy (amongst others) may all be relevant, aside from the rights of individuals seeking to enter Australia. Another classic example of polycentric decision-making is in applications for development,[48] where a government has to weigh the rights and interests of developers against a number of other factors. Phillip Ruddock took up the theme of polycentricity in 2000:[49]

> The refugee determination system comprises more than a mechanism for judicial review of administrative action. As Margaret Allars acknowledges, many disciplines, such as political and organisational

---

46   Section 153 of the *Migration Act 1958*.
47   PAM3 – MIGRATION ACT > PAM – Compliance and Case Resolution > Case resolution > Returns and removals > PAM – Removal from Australia, section 38.
48   See for example Jeffrey Jowell, 'The Legal Control of Administrative Discretion', (1973) *Public Law* 178.
49   Phillip Ruddock, 'Refugee Claims and Australian Migration Law: A Ministerial Perspective', (2000) 23 *University of New South Wales Law Journal* 1 at 7–8.

theory, and social psychology, impinge upon administrative law.[50] Associated with these disciplines are values other than legal norms such as the rule of law, including public accountability, fiscal responsibility, administrative efficiency and, in the migration area, international comity.

The courts, charged with responsibility for the rule of law, are clearly not in a position to weigh the relative influence of these values in the refugee determination system. In part this is because, as McMillan has observed, the judiciary believes that it has a special duty to protect individual rights - or at least, to protect individual rights as portrayed in the circumstances of the case before the court. It is also because, as Lee J acknowledged in *Minister for Immigration and Multicultural Affairs v Amani*,[51] the courts are ill-suited to consider the sensitive political issues that arise in some aspects of the refugee determination system. The final reason for the courts' inability to balance the forces at play in the refugee determination system is that they are constitutionally barred from doing so.

Lest it be thought that only LNP politicians attack the courts, consider the following report of remarks made by then PM Julia Gillard in relation to the High Court's decision in *M70/2011 v Minister for Immigration and Citizenship*,[52] popularly known as the 'Malaysia Solution Case':[53]

In Brisbane, Ms Gillard said the High Court had missed an opportunity to enhance the nation's response to 'the evil of people-smuggling' and to make a 'real and important contribution' to a regional approach to transnational crime. 'It is a missed opportunity ... to send a message to asylum-seekers not to risk their lives at sea and get into boats.'

Ms Gillard, a former lawyer, said the High Court's decision 'basically turns on its head the understanding of the law in this country prior to yesterday's decision'. She added that some commentators 'are saying that they find the decision incomprehensible, beyond understanding'.

---

50   Margaret Allars, *Introduction to Australian Administrative Law*, Butterworths (1990), Chapter 1.
51   (1999) FCA 1040 at paragraph 23.
52   (2011) HCA 32.
53   Matthew Franklin, 'Julia Gillard versus the High Court as the PM takes aim at Chief Justice Robert French', *The Australian*, 2 September 2011. http://www.theaustralian.com.au/national-affairs/julia-gillard-versus-the-high-court-as-the-pm-takes-aim-at-chief-justice-robert-french/story-fn59niix-1226127707674?nk=0d47906ef641ebc76107314ea80c9030, extracted 20 November 2014.

Referring to Chief Justice French, Ms Gillard said: 'His honour ... considered comparable legal questions when he was a judge of the Federal Court and made different decisions to the one that the High Court made yesterday'.[54]

[Treasurer] Wayne Swan backed the attack, saying the court had 'struck out in a completely different direction' in a judgment that surprised the government.

That is, a court's sole role is held to be the adjudication of the rights of an individual (or corporation) that comes before it, and it is simply not capable of thinking in terms of wider government policy and responsibilities, such as 'send[ing] a message to asylum-seekers not to risk their lives at sea and get into boats'. Mary Crock and Laurie Berg are critical of successive governments on this point, stating that 'the central problem is that Parliament and the executive have come to see the courts as political subversives which preference the rights of individuals over the policy objectives of those elected to govern'.[55] Could the clash between the government and the courts simply be a result of the different roles that these two arms of government play? One could point to the constantly changing laws in relation to development in NSW, and in particular the rise of Ministerial 'call-in' powers,[56] to support the proposition that all polycentric policy will eventually lead to a clash between the executive and the judiciary.

Similar arguments about the effects of judicial system on polycentric policy like immigration have been made in Canada about the Supreme Court's decision in *Singh (Harbhajan) v Minister of Employment and Immigration*, which found that applicants for refugee status always reacquire an oral hearing. Peter Hogg QC has argued that the Supreme Court simply had no idea of the administration and financial burden it was placing on the Federal government.[57] The financial implications of a decision are not something that a court should take into account, but this may be Hogg's point. Further, polycentricity in decision-making has always been a ground on which a Canadian court will show 'deference' to a decision maker, and impose a standard of review of reasonableness rather than correctness,[58] so Minister Ruddock may actually have had some overseas

---

54   This is a reference to *Patto v Minister for Immigration and Multicultural Affairs* (2000) FCA 1554, where French J found at paragraph 37 that a person could obtain effective protection in a third country even if that country was not a signatory to the Refugees Convention.

55   Mary Crock and Laurie Berg, *Immigration, Refugees and Forced Migration – Law, Practice and Policy in Australia*, Federation Press, 2011 at paragraph 19.04.

56   See Part 4, Division 4.1 of the *Environmental Planning and Assessment Act 2011 (NSW)*.

57   Peter Hogg, *Constitutional Law of Canada* (Student edition 2009), Carswell, 2009 Part 47.4(b), pp 1075–76.

58   See for example *Bell Canada v Bell Aliant Regional Communications* (2009) 2 SCR 764.

jurisprudence on his side in this argument. However, the Supreme Court of Canada has generally regarded immigration decision-making in individual cases as an example of simple polar and not polycentric adjudication.[59]

The moral panic over loss of sovereignty

While it is tempting to see the clash between the government and the courts on immigration matters as inevitable to all polycentric decision-making, this cannot be the sole explanation for the scope of the attack by governments on courts in the immigration field. While one does see government Ministers criticise court decisions in land development cases, for example, the real vituperation seems to be reserved for immigration.

It is instructive to look at Parliamentary speeches, made 16 years apart, in relation to Bills amending the character provisions of the *Migration Act*. The *Migration Legislation Amendment (Strengthening of Provisions Relating to Character and Conduct) Bill 1997* was introduced into Parliament in 1997, and amended s 501 to create the more objective 'character test' that we have previously examined. The Minister, Mr Ruddock stated in his second reading speech as follows:[60]

> The fact is that there has been a considerable weakening in recent years of the way in which our provisions operate ... [O]ne of the reasons that we have a concern is not the large numbers of cases in which ministerial decisions and departmental decisions have been overturned by the AAT. I recognise that the cases where the AAT have acted to effectively degrade the quality of decision making have occurred not because of the numbers but because essentially of their precedential character.

> Every decision that is made by an AAT member, every decision that have been made at that level, becomes a basis upon which officers of my department when they seek then to apply the law are bound to take into account. They have not been made by the parliament; they have not been made by a minister. Essentially the framework of law under which character decisions are reached are degraded because AAT members are substituting their own judgment at times for that of a minister elected by the people.

> It is the view of the government that in these matters the final responsibility rests with the government of the day, not with unelected officials, to determine who shall be able to come and remain here permanently or temporarily in Australia.

---

59 *Pushpanathan v Canada (Minister of Citizenship and Immigration)* (1998) 1 SCR 982.
60 House of Representatives Hansard, 18 November 1997 at 10692.

Compare this to the second reading speech by the current Minister, Mr Morrison, for the *Migration Amendment (Character and General Visa Cancellation) Bill 2014*:[61]

> Consistent with community views and expectations, the Australian government has a low tolerance for criminal, noncompliant or fraudulent behaviour by noncitizens. Entry and stay in Australia by noncitizens is a privilege, not a right, and the Australian community expects that the Australian government can and should refuse entry to noncitizens, or cancel their visas, if they do not abide by Australian laws. Those who choose to break the law, fail to uphold the standards of behaviour expected by the Australian community or try to intentionally mislead or defraud the Australian government should expect to have that privilege removed. To meet this expectation the government must not only have the ability to act decisively and effectively, wherever necessary, to deal with unlawful, fraudulent or criminal behaviour by noncitizens, but also have the legislative basis to effect a visa cancellation or refusal for those noncitizens.

While Mr Morrison's speech does not mention the courts or the AAT by name, the similarities are obvious – the government *must* be able to act 'quickly and decisively', presumably without any 'interference' by review bodies. A similar disdain for independent review of migration decisions can be found in the current Minister's second reading speech for the *Migration and Maritime Powers Legislation Amendment (Resolving the Asylum Legacy Caseload) Bill 2014*:[62]

> The government is of the view that a 'one size fits all' approach to responding to the spectrum of asylum claims made under Australia's protection framework is inconsistent with a robust protection system that promotes efficiency and integrity. It limits the government's capacity to address and remove those found to have unmeritorious claims quickly while diverting resources away from those individuals with more complex claims. The government has no truck with people who want to game the system. A new approach is warranted in the Australian context. The fast-track assessment process introduced by schedule 4 of this bill will efficiently and effectively respond to unmeritorious claims for asylum and will replace access to the Refugee Review Tribunal with access to a new model of review, the Immigration Assessment Authority – to be known as the IAA. These measures are specifically aimed at

---

61   House of Representatives Hansard, 24 September 2014 at 10325.
62   House of Representatives Hansard, 25 September 2014 at 10545.

addressing the backlog of IMAs[63] – some 30,000—and will ensure their cases progress towards timely immigration outcomes, either positive or negative.

All fast-track applicants will have their protection claims fully assessed by my department under the *Migration Act*. However, it is the government's policy that, if fast-tracked applicants present unmeritorious claims or have protection elsewhere, their cases will be channelled towards a direct immigration outcome rather than accessing the broader merits review process to prolong their stay in Australia. Such fast-track applicants will be known as 'excluded fast-track review applicants' and will not have access to those broader forms of merits review.

The IAA will be established as a separate office of the Refugee Review Tribunal. Eligible fast-track review applicants will have their refusal cases automatically referred to the IAA and will not have to apply for a review by it. The IAA's primary function will be to conduct a review 'on the papers', only considering the material which was before my department when it made its refusal decision under section 65 of the *Migration Act*[64] … [T]he Immigration Assessment Authority will not accept or consider any new information presented at review by a fast-track review applicant unless exceptional circumstances apply and the IAA is satisfied that the new information was not, and could not have been, provided to the department before the section 65 decision was made.

This new approach to review will discourage asylum seekers who attempt to exploit the current review process by presenting manufactured claims or evidence to bolster their original unsuccessful claims only after they learn why they were found not to be refugees by the department. This behaviour has on numerous occasions led to considerable delay while new claims are explored.

It might be noted that at the time of writing these amendments, although passed by both Houses of Parliament, have not yet been proclaimed and have therefore yet to come into effect. So much for urgency!

Many authors have commented on the perception on the part of many governments – not just Australia's – that absolute control over that country's immigration intake is a necessary element of a government's sovereignty. One reason for this may be that increasing globalisation has in many ways diminished the sovereignty of nation-states, and control over immigration is one of the

---

63   Illegal Maritime Arrivals.
64   This, of course, is not a true merits review – see *Huang v Secretary of State for the Home Department* (2007) 2 AC 167 and *Huruglica v Minister of Citizenship and Immigration* (2014) FC 799.

few clear controls that they have left. It is almost an example of *Yes Minister's* 'Politician's Syllogism' – 'something must be done, this is something, therefore we must do it'.[65] Catherine Dauvergne, for example, has written as follows:[66]

> Control over migration is interpreted, therefore, as being somehow intrinsic to what is it to be a nation, to 'stateness' and to the core of membership and national identity. Images which convey this run from the Statue of Liberty to crack SAS troops boarding the MV Tampa. In the law, the strong links between migration provisions and the notion of sovereignty have lead to courts showing remarkable deference to executives in areas of immigration rule making and to an international definition of a state which includes a defined population as an essential element.

The Prime Minister at the time of the *Tampa* incident, John Howard, drew an explicit link between the notion of sovereignty and control over immigration (including asylum seekers) when he stated in Parliament that '[w]e are not a soft touch and we are not a nation whose sovereign rights, in relation to who comes here, are going to be trampled on'.[67] The then Minister, Phillip Ruddock, said much the same thing when he also stated in Parliament that '[t]he protection of our sovereignty, including Australia's sovereign right to determine who shall enter Australia, is a matter for the Australian government and this Parliament',[68] presumably as opposed to those seeking to enter it. More recently, the *Sydney Morning Herald* reported the current Prime Minister as stating that 'the sign of a sovereign country is secure borders' – *the* sign, not *a* sign.[69] So much has been written on the tactic used by both major parties in Australia, but particularly the LNP coalition, to demonise unlawful arrivals to Australia as a vote-winning tactic that it is really not possible to add to it, other than to refer to the concept of the 'other' as it has been applied particularly to unlawful boat arrivals to Australia.[70]

---

65   *Yes, Prime Minister*, 'Power to the People', first broadcast on the BBC 7 January 1988.

66   Catherine Dauvergne, 'Challenges to Sovereignty: Migration Laws for the 21st Century', paper presented at the 13th Commonwealth Law Conference in Melbourne, Australia, April 2003.

67   *Commonwealth of Australia Parliamentary Debates*, House of Representatives, 29 August 2001 at 30235.

68   *Commonwealth of Australia Parliamentary Debates*, House of Representatives, 18 September 2001 at 30869. For further discussion of the 'national sovereignty' aspect of the *Tampa* incident see Katharine Gelber and Matt McDonald, 'Representations of Sovereignty in Australia's Approach to Asylum-Seekers', (2006) 32 *Review of International Studies* 269.

69   http://www.smh.com.au/federal-politics/political-news/abbott-here-to-rescue-country-20140713bua2. html#ixzz37TnPxmLg, retrieved 14 July 2014.

70   As just one example, see Rachael Jacobs, 'Echoes of the Past in Asylum-Seeker Policies', *Sydney Morning Herald*, 6 January 2011. http://www.smh.com.au/federal-politics/political-opinion/echoes-of-the-past-in-asylum-seeker-policies-20110106-19gwf.html, extracted 19 November 2014.

Part 3 – Major cases and legislative response

A frequent feature of Australian immigration law is the reaction of the Commonwealth Parliament to court decisions that are adverse to the government. Much has been written in other jurisdictions about a concept of 'dialogue' between the courts and the legislature,[71] but this does not seem to be a concept that has ever been significantly explored in Australia. Instead, Australian governments tend to simply react, and sometimes strongly, to adverse court decisions, rather than engage in anything approaching a dialogue.

It is notable that an adverse court decision – or even sometimes decisions such as *Lim*,[72] where the government was largely successful – frequently results in a quick amendment to the Act in order to 'rectify' the situation. Sometimes a court decision is not even necessary. For example, the *Migration Amendment (Detention Arrangements) Act 2005*, was introduced to head off a revolt by some backbench Coalition MPs in relation to the situation of children in immigration detention. Regardless, the frequency of amending legislation, and the swiftness with which it often follows adverse court decisions, shows the desire of successive governments for control of the immigration program.

Part 4 – Is a separate regime for judicial review of migration decisions necessary?

The purpose of successive amendments made to Part 8 of the Act since 1994 demonstrate an attempt by successive governments to reduce the scope for judicial review of migration decisions. However, the judgment in *S157*[73] made it clear that s 474 of the *Migration Act* will not protect a decision affected by a 'jurisdictional error'. The question now is what that term means.

It is well-known that the distinction between jurisdictional and non-jurisdictional errors of law has been abolished in the UK.[74] That is, all errors of law are regarded as going to the decision maker's jurisdiction. In Canada, the Supreme Court has not quite been able to bring itself to abolish the distinction altogether, but the possibility has been canvassed. In particular, in *Alberta (Information and*

---

71   See for example Rosalind Dixon, 'The Supreme Court of Canada, Charter Dialogue and Deference', (2009) 47 *Osgoode Hall Law Journal* 235; Eliza Kaczynska-Nay, 'The *Human Rights Act 1998*: The UK 'Dialogue' Model of Human Rights Protection', Australian National University National Europe Centre Briefing Paper Series, July 2009.
72   (1992) 176 CLR 1.
73   Supra n2.
74   *Anisminic Pty Ltd v Foreign Compensation Commission* (1969) 2 AC 147, *Pearlman v Governors of Harrow School* (1979) QB 56.

Privacy Commissioner) v Alberta Teachers' Association, Rothstein J, writing for the majority, stated 'it may be that the time has come to reconsider whether, for purposes of judicial review, the category of true questions of jurisdiction exists and is necessary to identifying the appropriate standard of review'.[75] Regardless, not one Supreme Court decision since the crucial case of *Dunsmuir v New Brunswick*[76] has turned on whether a decision maker has committed a jurisdictional error or has simply made an unreasonable decision.

The elusive distinction between jurisdictional and non-jurisdictional errors of law

Australian courts, however, maintain that there is still a difference between jurisdictional and non-jurisdictional errors, but that nearly all errors of law will be jurisdictional errors. Keifel J attempted to explain the difference between jurisdictional and non-jurisdictional errors in *Linett v Australian Education Union* as follows:[77]

> The distinction between jurisdictional error and a 'mere error of law' is maintained, the latter being one which has been arrived at on an issue that has been entrusted to the inferior court or tribunal to decide for itself, even if the decision is wrong.

Despite this reasoning, there does not seem to have been a case in Australia decided since *S157*, at any judicial level, that has turned on whether an identified error of law is jurisdictional or not. That is, there has not been a decision since *S157* that has found the existence of an error of law, but has found that it is not a jurisdictional error.[78] It is notable that *Yusuf*[79] gave only an expressly non-exhaustive list of jurisdictional errors, and more recently, in *Kirk v Industrial Relations Commission (NSW)* the High Court has stated that 'it is neither necessary, nor possible, to mark the metes and bounds of jurisdictional error'.[80] That is, a jurisdictional error is whatever a court says it is. Further, if s 474 of the *Migration Act 1958* does not demonstrate that a 'migration decision' is an 'issue that has been entrusted to the inferior court or tribunal to decide for itself', what on earth does?

---

75   *Alberta (Information and Privacy Commissioner) v Alberta Teachers' Association* (2011) SCR 61 at paragraph 42.

76   (2008) 1 SCR 190.

77   (2002) 191 ALR 597 at 605.

78   Interestingly, Robert French, now French CJ of the High Court, came to a similar conclusion as far back as 1993, when he wrote that '[w]hatever the proper interpretation of *Anisminic* it is clear that the High Court has maintained the distinction between jurisdictional error and error within jurisdiction. The distinction seems to have little work to do in the cases relating to the operation of privative clauses'. See Robert S French, 'The Rise and Rise of Judicial Review', (1993) 23 *Western Australian Law Review* 120 at 128.

79   Supra n28 at paragraph 82.

80   (2010) 239 CLR 531 at paragraph 71.

It appears that the closest that a court has come to making such a finding was in *Ratumaiwai v Minister for Immigration and Multicultural Affairs*.[81] This was a case involving judicial review of a decision to refuse to find that a visa applicant was a 'special needs relative', and Hill J found as follows:

> [27] It is clear from the transcript that the Tribunal considered, and rejected, the claim of the applicant that the giving of financial assistance qualified him as a 'special need relative' within the meaning of that expression. Even although the Tribunal Member did not deal with the issue of financial assistance in the reasons for decision, as he was obliged to do under s 430(1)(b) of the Act, it is clear that the Member did not fail to consider the question. He did consider it and rejected it. So, it cannot be said that the Tribunal Member failed to take into account financial assistance as a relevant consideration ...

> [28] The distinction between error of fact and error of law is a fine one. While it is true that the ordinary English meaning of a word is a question of fact, so that a Tribunal which defines the word wrongly does not make an error of law, what was involved in the present case was whether it was open to the Tribunal to find that a person who gave financial assistance to a nominator came within the expression 'special need relative' ...

> [29] In my view, once it is seen that the Tribunal has addressed the issue of financial assistance, however, even if in so doing it has made an error of law, that error is not, in my opinion, a jurisdictional error.

Even Hill J was equivocal in his conclusion, and did not explain why the error of law in question, assuming that one had been made, was not a jurisdictional error. A number of cases since this decision was handed down have stated that making an error of fact is not a jurisdictional error, but do not make it clear whether that error is a non-jurisdictional error of law.[82]

Another case that might have come *close* to making a distinction between a jurisdictional and non-jurisdictional error, but ultimately did not do so, was *Minister for Immigration and Citizenship v SZIZO*[83]. Where the court distinguished between 'mandatory' and 'facilitative' provisions of the RRT Code of Procedure, and found that the RRT had not committed a jurisdictional error despite an apparent breach of s 441G of the Act. If the High Court continues

---

81   (2002) FCA 311. This was one of the cases considered in *NAAV v MIMIA* (2002) FCAFC 228.

82   See for example *SZGOW v Minister for Immigration and Anor* (2006) FMCA 1689; *SZINP v Minister for Immigration and Citizenship* (2007) FCA 1747; *M33 of 2004 v Minister for Immigration and Anor* (2007) FMCA 684; *MZYFO v Minister for Immigration and Anor* (2009) FMCA 1148 and *Patel v Minister for Immigration and Anor* (2011) FMCA 773.

83   (2009) HCA 37.

to find 'core' and 'non-core' provisions in the Codes of Procedure, this may be a way to relax the strict compliance approach to the codes without actually distinguishing between jurisdictional and non-jurisdictional errors.

A recent attempt at an explanation – *Minister for Immigration and Citizenship v MZYZA*

In 2013 a brave attempt to distinguish between jurisdictional and non-jurisdictional errors was made by the Federal Court in *Minister for Immigration and Citizenship v MZYZA*.[84] In this case, a Department of Immigration and Citizenship (DIAC) decision to refuse a Protection Visa was upheld by the Refugee Review Tribunal (RRT), which had been concerned with the authenticity of certain documents. The RRT had put to the applicant that it was 'very easy to obtain false documents in India',[85] but made no explicit finding that the specific documents in question, which appeared to support the applicant's case, were fraudulent. As a result, the Federal Magistrates Court found that the RRT had made a jurisdictional error. The Minister had argued that the 'weight' to be given to the letter was a matter for the RRT, and that the RRT had implicitly decided to give it little or no weight. However, the Federal Magistrate found as follows:[86] do not accept the submission that the Tribunal implicitly decided to give the letter little or no weight. There is no indication in the Tribunal's reasons for decision of any cognisance of the letter in the part of the Tribunal's reasons that records its reasons for decision, as opposed to its summary of the background. It seems to me that the Tribunal overlooked the letter while weighing up the evidence and formulating its decision, as opposed to setting out the background to the case.

The Federal Magistrate went on to find that the letter was a crucial piece of evidence, and that the RRT may have reached a different conclusion had it turned its mind to the matter.[87] The RRT decision was therefore set aside.

Tracey J upheld the Minister's appeal in the Federal Court. His Honour did so primarily on the basis that a mere defect in the reasons for a decision is not a ground of jurisdictional error,[88] and that it was clear from the RRT's reasons that it rejected the applicant's claim to be a member of a certain political party.[89] Tracey J summed up as follows:[90]

---

84   (2013) FCA 572.

85   Ibid at paragraph 15.

86   *MZYZA v Minister for Immigration and Citizenship* (2013) FMCA 15 at paragraph 23.

87   Ibid at paragraph 32.

88   Supra n85 at paragraphs 31 and 32.

89   Ibid at paragraph 42.

90   Ibid at paragraph 68.

> Even if it is accepted that the Tribunal failed to have regard to the contents of the letter, I do not consider that such a failure constituted jurisdictional error. The Tribunal was bound to have regard to and assess the first respondent's claim to have been persecuted because of the political and religious beliefs attributed to him ... It did so. It was not suggested that the failure (if there was one) to refer to the contents of the letter occurred because the Tribunal had misdirected itself as to the proper scope of its deliberations or by failing to identify the relevant claims and integers of the claims raised by the first respondent. It was not bound to consider each and every piece of evidence which related to those claims.

His Honour added that the letter 'did not, in my view, amount to evidence of pivotal importance, or as being so fundamental to the first respondent's claim, that a failure to give consideration to its contents caused jurisdictional error'.[91]

The analysis given by Tracey J is very thorough, but he himself admits that 'value judgments are involved in determining whether material can be regarded as so 'fundamental' or so 'important' or so 'overwhelming' that a failure to have regard to it constitutes jurisdictional error'.[92] It still seems apparent that courts have a lot of discretion in determining whether something is a 'jurisdictional error' or not, and *MZYZA* still does not provide an example of a decision turning on a classification of something found to be an error of law as jurisdictional or not.

Has migration jurisprudence returned to the ADJR grounds of review?

As discussed previously, s 5(1) of the ADJR Act provides as follows:

> A person who is aggrieved by a decision to which this Act applies that is made after the commencement of this Act may apply to the Federal Court or the Federal Circuit Court for an order of review in respect of the decision on any one or more of the following grounds:
>
> (a) that a breach of the rules of natural justice occurred in connection with the making of the decision;
>
> (b) that procedures that were required by law to be observed in connection with the making of the decision were not observed;

---

91   Ibid.
92   Ibid at paragraph 60.

(c) that the person who purported to make the decision did not have jurisdiction to make the decision;

(d) that the decision was not authorised by the enactment in pursuance of which it was purported to be made;

(e) that the making of the decision was an improper exercise of the power conferred by the enactment in pursuance of which it was purported to be made;

(f) that the decision involved an error of law, whether or not the error appears on the record of the decision;

(g) that the decision was induced or affected by fraud;

(h) that there was no evidence or other material to justify the making of the decision;

(i) that the decision was otherwise contrary to law.

If we look at ss 5(1) and 5(2) of the ADJR Act, it would appear that most of the grounds of review specified in those sections have been found to be jurisdictional errors by the courts. Paragraphs 5(1)(b)–(e) are jurisdictional errors in even the *Hickman* sense, while in relation to s 5(1)(g) the High Court has found in *SZFDE v Minister for Immigration and Citizenship*[93] that a fraud committed *against* the tribunal by the applicant's migration agent, where the applicant and the tribunal itself were innocent of any fraud, can result in a jurisdictional error. Much of s 5(1)(h) appears to have been subsumed by the finding in *Minister for Immigration and Citizenship v SZMDS*[94] that 'irrationality' on the part of an administrative decision maker can result in a jurisdictional error (although no such error was found in that case). Errors of the kind described by s 5(1)(f) would appear not to apply to review of immigration decisions, although it of course depends on the classification by a court of an error as 'jurisdictional' or 'non-jurisdictional', an argument that the courts are loath to have.

Paragraph 5(1)(j) could be enlivened in a situation where the decision maker lacked the delegation to make the decision, which is also a jurisdictional error even on Hickman principles. There has been very little jurisprudence on the kinds of errors that could be encompassed by s 5(1)(j). In *Scott v Human Rights and Equal Opportunity Commission* the applicants argued that an alleged failure to make certain inquiries on the part of the Commission fell within s 5(1)(j), but North J in the Federal Court rejected this submission.[95] It could also be argued

---

93   (2007) 232 CLR 189.

94   (2010) HCA 16.

95   (2010) FCA 1323 at paragraphs 117 and 175–76.

that s 5(1)(j) could be relevant where a decision maker misinterprets relevant legislation, as was argued in *French v Gray, Special Minister of State*,[96] but again the court found that no such error had been made, without elaborating on the meaning of s 5(1)(j).

It could be argued that the errors described by s 5(1)(a) of the ADJR Act have been excluded from judicial review by means of a combination of s 474 and ss 359A and 422B of the Migration Act. However, Australian courts have been quite creative in incorporating common law requirements of procedural fairness into judicial review of immigration decisions. For example, in *Minister for Immigration and Citizenship v Li*,[97] the Full Federal Court found that a refusal to adjourn a Migration Review Tribunal 9MRT) hearing amounted to a jurisdictional error, despite the existence of s 359A. The decision of the Full Federal Court was upheld on appeal by the High Court,[98] which had nothing at all to say about s 359A, and affirmed the decision primarily on the basis of a breach of s 363 by the MRT.

The notion that, by failing to comply with the requirements of natural justice, the MRT or RRT would not in fact offer a hearing and would fail to fulfill their core function, resurfaced in *SZJSS v Minister for Immigration and Citizenship*.[99] The Full Federal Court in this case ignored s 422B, and found that apprehended bias on behalf the decision maker had the effect that the RRT had constructively failed to exercise its jurisdiction and effectively failed to provide the applicant with a hearing.[100] On appeal, the High Court also did not address s 422B — instead, it assumed that apprehended bias would amount to a jurisdictional error but found none existed in the case at hand.[101] It would appear, then, that Australian courts have decided that ss 359A and 422B have as much practical effect as s 474, and that if a tribunal breaches the common law rules of natural justice it will have failed to exercise its duty to undertake a review, and set the decision aside on that basis.[102]

The question must then be asked — what is the point of continuing to have a separate regime for judicial review of immigration decisions? By introducing s 474 and related provisions, the Parliament left itself open to the High Court overturning the *Hickman* approach to privative clauses, which it duly did. All that was achieved was the highly unintended result of returning judicial review of migration decisions, in effect, to the same basis as under the ADJR Act. The *de facto* return to ADJR Act review might as well be made *de jure*.

---

96   (2013) FCA 263.
97   (2012) FCAFC 74.
98   *Minister for Immigration and Citizenship·v Li* (2013) HCA 18.
99   (2009) FCA 1577 at paragraph 64.
100 Ibid at paragraph 64.
101 *Minister for Immigration and Citizenship v SZJSS* (2010) HCA 48.
102 See also *SZBEL v MIMIA* (2006) HCA 63 for a similar decision.

www.ingramcontent.com/pod-product-compliance
Lightning Source LLC
Chambersburg PA
CBHW061245270326
41928CB00041B/3419